PENNY CHRISTIAN KNIGHT

DEVELOPING RESILIENCE

BOOK ONE

Secrets, Sex Abuse, and the
Quest for Love and Inner Peace

DEVELOPING RESILIENCE

Secrets, Sex Abuse, and the Quest for Love and Inner Peace
An Autobiographical Memoir • Book One in a Trilogy

Some names have been changed or shortened
to protect the privacy of particular people.

Printed in the United States of America
FIRST EDITION

BookBaby
7905 N. Crescent Blvd.
Pennsauken, NJ 08110
Info@bookbaby.com

Editing & Design by BookBaby Publishing
Cover Painting by Penny Christian Knight

ISBN 978-1-66788-592-6 (Print)
ISBN 978-1-66788-593-3 (eBook)

A HEARTFELT COMMENT
by Marta Szabo

Regarding Book One of
DEVELOPING RESILIENCE
Secrets, Sex Abuse, and the
Quest for Love and Inner Peace

Dear Penny,

Congratulations! What a mammoth task you have accomplished – wrestling all these years of experience into words and sentences, communicating a person through what her life brings her and how she responds. Gradually we get to see this character becoming more worldly wise, though every bit of wisdom is hard-won.

You have been open and honest, and I think many people will deeply appreciate your story and the beautiful way it is told. Something that came as a really wonderful surprise to me was the backdrop of history — who was president, what war was taking place, how much things cost, and whether televisions had appeared yet. It really creates added atmosphere and reminds us that our main character is not acting in a vacuum. She is a creature not just of her family and her own sensitivities but also of her times. This informs us and wipes away any preconceptions we might have about the eras with which we are unfamiliar. Brava!

I loved the strength of the voice. Even as the main character is unprotected and defenseless, she never gives up. She is always trying to figure things out, even when shocked and wide-eyed at some things happening to her. You present the dilemma so very well. Where does a young girl turn when the crimes against her cannot be spoken of, when, in a twisted way, she can't help but feel that they make *her* look bad? It would have been so easy to give up, to despair, to try and lose oneself in something that would numb the horror, as so many have done.

Book One makes me definitely interested to see what happens next.

Thank you for this enormous contribution to the world discussion of what life is really like. It's a beautiful piece of art.

With much appreciation, love, and respect,

Marta Szabo
The Author of *The First Two, The Impostors,* and
The Guru Looked Good is the Co-Director of
The Authentic Writing Workshops (AuthenticWriting.com).
Please see the Dedication page.

DEDICATION

This book is dedicated to authentic authors Fred Poole and Marta Szabo, who introduced me to Authentic Writing in their workshop at Omega Institute for Holistic Studies in Rhinebeck, New York. I attended their Omega workshop over two different years.

At the second workshop in 2014, I produced three personal essays that I suddenly realized could be part of a memoir (this one), which I had no intention of writing before. And since then, I have struggled for the time to write this memoir in my meager spare time.

The Authentic Writing workshops continue to be offered in person in Woodstock, New York, on occasional weekends. Participants also enjoy additional, frequent, and exciting workshops during the week on ZOOM.

You can find more information at Fred and Marta's website:
www.authenticwriting.com

TABLE OF CONTENTS

INTRODUCTION

IMPORTANT: PLEASE READ THIS INTRODUCTION

Live your life from your heart. Share from your heart.
And your story will touch and heal people's souls.

—MELODY BEATTIE

In the beginning, or as the story goes, God created Heaven and Earth. But what was the source of all my poor choices or the situations and challenges I created for myself as a minor god?

My life has been a Heroine's Journey with many rugged mountains to climb and dragons to slay. Those acquainted with reincarnation will know we are here to learn in this dimension (Earth). Earth is a virtual school, and that is what it has been for me. We are also here to meet ourselves, the personalities we once were. That is karma. Indeed, we do reap what we sow, both negative and positive. My life also has been about that. I have been living an extremely active vibration this time around. Hopefully, I have cleared up a lot of karma without creating more.

I did not always know about or believe in reincarnation, but I discovered it in my early thirties, at a time in my life when it made sense. I write about that discovery in Book One. It was the beginning of my healing and spiritual growth, and it helped provide for the development of my wisdom.

Please reserve your opinion about reincarnation if you do not share my belief until my story of sex abuse, assaults, and harassment and their consequences is finished. Correspondingly, there is also a theme of rejection and abandonment, which initiated my constant pursuit of love and prompted my many unwise choices.

I did not get to pick when, where, and with whom I would have my first sexual experience. Every woman or girl's right is to decide when and with whom she will indulge in sex. Some women desire to remain virgins until they marry. Although I might have had that desire, I never experienced it because of the abuse. Other women hold off having sex until they are mature enough to decide with whom they desire to have it. But, nowadays, women indulge in sex with anyone with total abandon. Other women fall somewhere in between these various options. Many women only want to engage in sex when they are in love. But these choices were different when I was growing up from 1934 to the 1950s.

I saw a documentary in the 1980s called *What You Are Is Where You Were When*. Morris Massey, Ph.D., a sociologist, and professor from Colorado, produced it. The theme of his presentation stuck with me as I attempted to understand people and myself. As I recall, we are a product of the time and place in history we existed, especially near 10 to 12. That theory seems to inform how we behave or who we become. It makes sense when you consider the various events we pass through and how they impact our existence.

Speaking now about the many experiences I have had, as opposed to when they happened, is something I can do currently because I am in my eighties. I am more aware of their outcome and how those experiences shaped my life and the person I have become. I have been the subject of my own research project without knowing it. Sharing my stories and how I have lived through my experiences, survived, and healed might be helpful to those pondering how to do the same.

My autobiographical memoir is presented in a trilogy. The books contain remembrances, letters, personal diaries, and journals. All these mediums tell my story, starting with me as a young girl becoming a victim of rape or attempted rape by my older brother, plus the attempted seductions by my stepfather as I got older. My story includes my distorted views about sex and encounters with other men or predators who sexually assaulted me (verbally or physically). The narrative also covers my inability to protect myself against men's advances and decipher which men I could trust. This total memoir contains my poor decisions regarding my body as a result, along with many other factors. It also concerns my sexual life, recovery, and healing from these assaults and other issues resulting from my poor choices.

My story also encompasses my romantic relationships with men and my incapacity to select a suitable mate, likely because I lacked a father figure when I needed one while growing up or of my flawed male role models. These experiences occurred against a backdrop of jobs, careers, and husbands. As a result, I always seemed to be seeking love from men or for what I thought passed for love. Loving women then became a consideration.

I will endeavor to be as accurate as I can with my memories. Sometimes I have changed names to protect specific individuals or have forgotten them. But my story is the truth of what happened. Likewise, many dialogues are as faithfully accurate as possible, but some are not. In those cases, I imagined what we said or what probably occurred. And in writing this story, I made several discoveries that completed missing pieces of memory that answered questions held too long. I will clarify these throughout. In this memoir, I discovered I have been writing it my entire life from the retrieved diaries, journals, letters, and other memorabilia I saved over the years and are presented herein.

CAVEAT FOR SURVIVORS WHO HAVE NOT DONE ANY RECOVERY WORK

It is possible that reading my story of abuse may set off various triggers within you. If you have untreated PTSD and are exposed to my experiences herein, you may experience flashbacks, nightmares, depression, anxiety, or a sense of unease.

Perhaps on the brighter side, you also may see yourself in me and my experiences, which have the potential to normalize yours. You might think you are the only one who has had a traumatic experience or feels the way you do but identifying with me may help you not feel so isolated.

Also, I want you to know that I am fine. In the pages of Book One, I began receiving therapeutic help, but you will see more of my healing work in Books Two and Three. But in Book One, you will discover my varied experiences and encounters. Many survivors have used suppression and repression to forget what happened to them. In my case, these eventually led to my reoccurring depression (from light to profound). My history often led me to therapy for the side effects of my sexual abuse. I have engaged in various therapeutic endeavors and other healing experiences, including discovering the means for spiritual growth. My Guardian Angels have assisted in my healing after I opened to their guidance. I now invite you into the story of my life, imperfections and all.

FAMILY

JOHN D. FATE / Great Grandfather – Founder of **J. D. Fate Company** that later merged with the **Root-Heath Company** to become the **Fate-Root-Heath Company,** following the passing of his son, **HARLEY H. FATE.**

> **HARLEY H. FATE / Grandfather** – Continued in the family business but died young of a heart attack. He married **ANNA LAWTON, Grandmother** (Gramma).

> > **HARLEY** and **ANNA FATE** begat two daughters – **MARY JO** (Aunt) and **EMELINE GERTRUDE** (Ine) (Mother).

> **MARY JO** married **JOY A. HERBERT** and begat a son and a daughter – (First Cousins) **JAY** and **JOYANNE** (Azasha).

> **EMELINE FATE** married **FRED HARRIS SIMMONS** and begat a son and a daughter – **THEODORE LAWTON** (Toby) and **PENELOPE** (Penny).

> > **INE** and **FRED** divorced, and **INE** later married **MILES W. CHRISTIAN** (stepfather). They begat one son – **MILES FATE** (Fate).

> > > **FRED** remarried twice more. In his second marriage, they begat a daughter – **LESLIE ANN.** His third wife was **ROSEMARY.** They begat two sons and two daughters – **LOUISE, FRED JR., JOHN,** and **ANGELA** (All half-sibs).

> **TOBY** married **XENIA ARMANDO** from Cuba and begat a son and a daughter – **DEAN THEODORE** and **LISA SUSIE** (nephew and niece). They divorced.

> **PENNY** married **EDWARD H.** (Ed). They begat three sons – **WILLIAM** (deceased after birth), **MICHAEL DAVID** (Mike), and **GARY ALAN** (Gary). They divorced after eight years.

> > **PENNY** also married **HARVEY STIFFLER** (Harv). They divorced after ten months.

> > > **PENNY** also married **IRVINE NOEL KNIGHT** (Irvine) (British). They divorced after five years.

CHAPTER 1

GENESIS

"The time has come," the Walrus said,
"to talk of many things."

—LEWIS CARROL, *THROUGH THE LOOKING-GLASS*

My Story Begins

My heart pounded frantically. It felt like it would break free from my chest while I fled to the bathroom as fast as my 14-year-old legs could go for the umpteenth time in what seemed like years. I felt like the terrified, vulnerable woman in the scary movies I saw. She ran from the vampire, who knew she couldn't escape him or his bite on her neck. And it was the only door in our turn-of-the-century house that locked, providing me with a false sense of safety. I slammed and latched the door, screaming at my older brother, "Leave me alone! Go away! I don't want to do it!"

Once again, my mother had left me alone with Toby, two-and-a-half years older. My younger brother, by 10 years, Miles Fate (we called him Fate), was either with my mother or grandmother.

7

Toby pushed hard on the other side of the door and was likely to break the flimsy hook and eye latch that pretended to keep me safe from him. I struggled hard on my side, attempting to prevent the door from being broken or the lock from releasing. If either broke, I pondered what my mother might say. I knew she would demand, "Why is this door broken?" And I would shrug my shoulders and say, "I don't know." I couldn't tell her that Toby was trying to rape me. I didn't even know that was what he was doing. It was 1948, and I didn't even have a word for it. I lacked the sex-abuse vocabulary. I only knew what my peers called sex, "*fuck*," but I could never say THAT word. It was vulgar and dirty. And IT was not sex.

My fear and inability to communicate are why there was always a different version of my childhood challenge of sex abuse and the actual truth. My version was that Toby was physically abusing me again, which, many times, was also correct. My mother would always tell me about her anxiety as the years rolled by, "I was afraid to leave you alone with Toby for fear he would kill you." In my mind, I now ask her, "Then why did you leave me alone with him?" It would have prevented many traumas I experienced at his hands. The correct version, the secret, was something my mother never knew. And there was a lot more that she never knew.

My Life Begins

Beginning with my birth in 1934 during the Great Depression, when almost everyone was underprivileged, I arrived as a blessing to my parents (and established my life's purpose of helping others) just before the landlord planned to evict us from our home. The landlord took pity on us and let us stay because I had arrived. My mother, Emeline Gertrude (Ine, for short), was a homemaker and a writer of romance stories for pulp magazines. My father, Fred Harris

Simmons (Ted, for short), owned and managed a friendly restaurant in the college town of Granville, a New-England style community in Central Ohio.

During the Great Depression, students from Denison University in Granville and other patrons charged for their meals when they ate at the restaurant. But later, they could not pay their bills. President Roosevelt declared a bank "holiday" in 1933 because of the Great Depression when citizens made runs on the banks and withdrew their money. Dozens of banks closed before this event. Then, we could not pay our debt.

We were poor, and a wood-burning stove inside our living room's fireplace gave us heat. Wrapped in several blanket layers, I lay in my buggy next to the wood burner during the day. I slept in my crib in my mother's room while Toby slept in my dad's quarters at night. I never thought to ask about this sleeping arrangement. A fire started on the stove when I was almost three months old. Smelling the smoke, my mother opened our room door, and smoke came rushing in. She shouted for my dad, who rushed out of his room, and ran downstairs and out of the house, leaving my unfortunate mother to get my brother and me out alone.

She opened a window and yelled to a neighbor to call the fire department, as we did not have a phone. Then, she covered our heads as she picked us up. She tucked each of us under an arm and carried us downstairs. But the fire cut off the door my dad had exited. The house was dark, and somehow my mother made her way to the back porch. After she located the door key, she dropped it. She felt around on the floor in the dark but found it again. I can only imagine what kind of panic she experienced. When we were safe outside, a neighbor came with a garden hose, and the fire trucks arrived. That night we stayed with Mrs. Frank Burkhaw, another neighbor. After the fire, our house needed repairs, and during that time, we stayed with my grandmother, Anna Lawton Fate (or Gramma as I called her), in the village of Plymouth, Ohio.

One of the oldest communities in Ohio, Plymouth's original name was "Paris." In 1815, the first settler arrived, and Paris was big enough to become a town by 1818. In 1834, the officials changed its name to Plymouth to avoid competition with other Ohio towns, also known as Paris, because of the planned construction of a railroad to go through it.

Huron and Richland counties divided the town through the middle, with Huron County on the Northside. Gramma's house was in Richland County, and my mother, Toby, and I eventually lived on the Huron County side. The population was around 1,500 as I grew up there.

I never verified the story of the fire with my father as my parents divorced in my fourth year, and I had minimal contact with him throughout my life, but when we were together, this incident was the farthest from my mind. I guess my first conscious impression of my father, though, was that he was a coward.

My next impression of my father was that he was an angry man. Later, while growing up, my mother's venom spewed out frequently about all my father's shortcomings. Once, when my anger interfered with a goal, my mother told me I must have inherited his temper. That led to my years of repressed anger, along with the suppressed memories of my sexual abuse. Somewhere along the way, I developed the attitude when I was enduring a psychological or emotional injury *that it really doesn't matter.* If it didn't matter, it couldn't hurt. And it didn't because I was in denial of my feelings. But for many years, I wasn't aware of this perspective.

After our house was repaired, we returned to it until my parents separated and my mother sought a divorce. This action occurred during a period in history when not many people divorced.

Our family life resumed in Plymouth with my grandmother when we left Granville permanently. At first, still in my crib, I shared my mother's bedroom. Later, I had a tiny closet-sized room with a roll-away cot. It had a window and a closet but nothing else. There was a wooden playhouse on the lawn at the side of the house, and I'm not sure if it was for Toby and me or just me. The playhouse had tiny windows with window boxes and a front door. It was a place to use my imagination and play house with my dolls.

My mother was born in 1909. World War I (WWI) would have affected her during her childhood, just as I had in my youth during WWII. She lost her father (my grandfather), Harley Fate, a morbidly obese man, through death when she was around seven. She had an older sister, Mary Jo, and felt judged and sometimes ridiculed by her and their mother after her father's death. But as adults, my mother and aunt became best friends. My grandmother, a single mother, had raised them.

A chubby girl, my mother told me she had played girls' basketball by boys' rules while in high school. And in more modern times, when I was in high school, I had to play by girls' rules, which wasn't much fun. Someone feared that boys' rules would make the game too active for female bodies. My mother was a 1920s flapper and enjoyed two years of college at Denison University before marrying my father. She had two marriages but only one divorce.

My mother also told me my brother was challenging to manage, as if I needed to be informed. He picked on me right from the beginning. My mother said she was so proud of me one day when, as a toddler, I waddled up to Toby while he was playing with his toys on the floor, and I grabbed his hair and would not let go. That ability to defend myself personally didn't last long, and it never came to my defense when I needed it while growing up or as a young adult.

When I was about two years old and sitting in my highchair, I pointed to a bottle on the counter and said, "dwink." Toby got it for me, and I drank some of it. Horrified, my mother found me drinking from the bottle labeled "turpentine." She grabbed me and took us to the doctor, who told her I might go blind. Tears of guilt rolled down her cheeks at what he said. And how would I have felt years later if he had been right? The doctor then discovered that I had not gotten the turpentine into my eyes. I would not go blind, after all.

When my parents separated, I was four, but I don't remember it. I don't recall the move to my grandmother's or how I felt about it. Recently, a colleague regressed me to that time using hypnosis. In a trance, I cried and kept calling out for my father. I called, "Where are you, Daddy? I can't find my daddy. Where is he? Where are you?" This regression made real the feelings I must have had about him not being in my life then. He visited once or twice, but I believe my mother made it difficult for him to do it often. Or perhaps, he moved on and had no time for a relationship with me.

I don't know why I never asked him or my mother about it, but my "why" questions have always come too late to get answers. He had two more families and produced five other half-siblings, a daughter by his second wife, plus two daughters and two sons by his third wife, Rosemary, who, my dad told me, was paranoid schizophrenic.

My mother worked as a secretary at the Fate-Root-Heath Company, part of which my great-grandfather, John Daniel Fate, and his son, my grandfather, Harley Hiram Fate, founded. We were part of the Fate family. The JD Fate Company merged with the Root, Heath Company in 1919, three years after my grandfather's death. Products of the three companies, or the Fate-Root-Heath Company combined, included Silver King Tractors, clay machinery, lawn-mower grinders, Plymouth Industrial Locomotives, and the first Plymouth car, among other products.

In due course, someone informed me that Chrysler Corporation purchased the rights to the Plymouth name of the automobile, man-ufactured first by our company in 1910, for only $1. Chrysler wanted our car name even though they did not build their Plymouth auto-mobile until 1928.

When I was almost five, I contracted Scarlet Fever. It must have been soon after moving into my grandmother's home, as I was still in my crib. I don't know why I continued to sleep in a crib at four. In the 1930s, Scarlet Fever called for quarantine, much like COVID-19 today. We had to post a quarantine sign on the front door, warning people to stay away. Only the doctor could visit.

My mother somehow was allowed to come and go as she went to work, but she was not allowed near me when she came home. I stayed all day alone in that dark room with the shades drawn. We had heard stories that the illness could make me blind or deaf if not in a darkened room. I read later that it is possible that Helen Keller lost her sight and hearing from scarlet fever. My grandmother cared for me and was the only person permitted to get close. I wanted to be near my mother and could only see her in the doorway. I felt so deserted and abandoned by her, but I didn't know then that that was what I felt.

My grandmother, Anna, was a strong and independent woman. She was born on December 28, 1880, during the Victorian era. She and her two sisters, Harriet and Jessie, became orphans when their parents died in 1887, which caused a move from Sturgis, Michigan, to Three Rivers, Michigan, where their mother's parents, Jacob and Ann Slenker, raised them. Their mother, Emma Slenker, and a sister, Gertrude, died from diphtheria. A railroad accident killed their father, Henry Herbert Lawton, the same year. Eventually, the three sisters ended up in Ohio, and my grandmother ended up in Plymouth, where she worked as a milliner, a proper vocation for women then. At least three generations of women (my grandmother, mother, and me) lost a father early in our lives.

Anna married my grandfather, Harley Fate, in December 1903, but I never knew him because he died in 1916. My mother married my father in June 1930, and about three months later, in September 1930, my grandmother married Charlie Heath, a Root, Heath Company partner. It turns out that Charlie was gay, and she unexpectedly chanced upon him and his lover in her home, which was quite a shock to her.

My mother told me that this discovery eventually led to a divorce, and I always believed this until my father told a different story in a letter in the late 1980s. He said my grandmother stayed married until Charlie died when my dad invited her to stay with our family. His message about this secret comes later in this trilogy, revealing another secret.

When my mother told me Charlie's story, she gave me a copy of *The Well of Loneliness*, a book written when a gay person received a psychiatric diagnosis for being gay. She never told me it was my grandmother's copy, which I only recently discovered when I opened the front cover and saw her signature. Whenever I read a book in my younger days, I only looked at the first page. And it appears my grandmother was trying to understand her husband's behavior.

My grandmother was an excellent cook, as I believe many of the women of her day were. I especially remember her fried chicken and large-wedged French fries, the like of which I have not encountered since. My most treasured treat was the kuchen she baked at Christmas and other holidays. Loads of brown sugar, along with other ingredients, comprised its topping. It was a delight to see her carrying this culinary gem to our house.

I observed several things when I stayed with her various times while growing up. She appeared to be trying to appear cosmopolitan as she would smoke but never inhale. She would take a puff from a cigarette and blow out a cloud of smoke that surrounded her like a cloud of fog. I saw her drink beer while entertaining her friends with card games. Many nights she sat at her desk in her sitting room playing solitaire. She taught me how to play. I also remember other times when we played Parcheesi. Gramma read me fairy tales almost every night and sang songs like "Three Little Fishies." She helped me feel loved a little bit.

I kept my dolls in the "playroom," where my grandmother sewed and ironed. On Saturday nights, when I stayed with my grandmother, she took me to our small movie theater, which held Bingo games after the movie, the price of which was only a dime. I was fortunate in those days as I won something almost every time we went. And I never could understand how the owner made any profit.

Two incidents occurred long before my brother abused me that were harbingers of what was to come, although I wasn't aware of them. I had a favorite dress I liked to wear. It had been handmade by the kindly old lady, Mrs. Burkhaw, across the street from where we lived in Granville. She was the lady who offered us a place to stay after the fire. I think that wearing that dress reminded me of happier times.

One day around the age of five, I was wearing it. It was a sheer dress, and I wore it with an underskirt but nothing underneath the top. Toby and a neighbor boy were playing in the yard close to the playhouse. Toby said to the other kid, "Look at Penny, and you can see her nipples." They taunted and teased me. I didn't understand what they were saying, but I was so embarrassed after they ruined my day, and I never wore the dress again. This event appeared to be the beginning of Toby's sexual awareness. The second incident occurred after moving to Shiloh when I was eight.

CHAPTER 2

FAMILY

I don't believe an accident of birth makes people sisters or brothers.
It makes them siblings, gives them mutuality of parentage.
Sisterhood and brotherhood is a condition people have to work at.

—MAYA ANGELOU, *"CONVERSATIONS WITH MAYA ANGELOU"*
WITH JEFFREY M. ELLIOT (1989)

Toby and Me

My brother got off to a bad start in his life. Well, maybe I did too, but I didn't behave as aggressively as he did. He was a baby when a housekeeper gave him gonorrhea, but I never learned how that happened. Although I have imagined that she sexually abused him, I can only guess. My parents divorced when Toby was six, but he had already headed down the road labeled "difficult child." I can slightly understand my mother wiping her hands clean of him and getting him out of her hair at other times when he was older. Growing up, I never had that luxury. I wonder today if he might have had attention-deficit hyperactivity disorder (ADHD). He had many of its symptoms which I will elaborate on later.

When he was nine, my mother sent him to military school at Castle Heights Military Academy in Lebanon, Tennessee, a year after his two-month vacation at a boys' summer camp in Michigan. I didn't know why, and I thought it might be for discipline, but I also thought he was privileged and loved more than I was.

Years later, I dreamed of going to a boarding school to get away from Toby or have the same opportunity. To make up for his going away to a different school, my mother enrolled me at a small country school in the tiny town of New Haven, about three miles north of Plymouth, during the year he attended military school. As a psychotherapist today, I had my own ideas about his departure, and I thought he needed more love than he received. I also heard stories about my grandmother chasing and beating him with a broom. I don't remember ever witnessing that, but regardless, I recall little of my life then.

My stepfather-to-be, Miles William Christian, was an instructor at Castle Heights. My mother, grandmother, and I visited Toby once in the spring he was there. We stayed in a Tourist Home (the older form of Bed and Breakfast). But I recall my mother coming back one night from a date with Miles and saying, "Miles asked me to marry him." I was eight then, and with romantic interests in movies I'd seen or soap operas my mother listened to on the radio, I asked, "Did he get down on his hands and knees to propose?" Miles, eight years younger than my mother, was one of the most handsome men I'd ever seen, next to Clark Gable. During the summer following this visit, he followed after my mother and lived near Plymouth.

The following is an excerpt from my Sexual History Journal. It was not until the late 1980s that I could be in touch with and express what I felt about my various occasions of abuse:

February 23, 1989: *Mother encouraged me to swim in the pool where all the male students swam; however, I had no swimsuit. Someone provided me with a pair of male swim trunks to wear. Again, my chest was bare. I was more aware of being modest this time and felt even more embarrassed. I guess it didn't prevent me from going swimming. I doubt I would expose a little girl of mine like that* [if I had one] *without getting her a tee shirt or some other means of covering up. I can see how my physical or sexual boundaries were being eliminated or weakened. And I feel angry about that.*

On the Fourth of July that year, when I was still eight, I visited my two cousins, Jay and Joyanne Herbert, in Mansfield, Ohio. Jay was my age, and Joyanne was two years younger. Joyanne and I were walking across the back of the couch, imitating tight-rope walkers. I lost my balance, fell to the floor on my back, and pulled her right onto my left arm above the elbow, breaking my arm. I was in the hospital for a whole week for that injury. Medical aftercare was undeniably different back then (1942) and cheaper.

During my convalescence, my grandmother appeared every day like she did when I had Scarlet Fever, but there was no visit from my mother for three or four days. As usual, I felt rejected and not very important to her. When she did come, she announced that she and Miles had eloped. It delighted me to have a new father. As much as I could tell, my mother was genuinely in love.

Miles took a job at the Fate-Root-Heath Company. In those days, before any conflict between us, I called him Daddy because my biological father appeared not to care enough to be in my life. Following hospital rehab, they gave me a puppy because of their marriage and for what I had gone through.

So, now a family of four, we found a house to rent in Shiloh, Ohio, about four miles east of Plymouth. We had an icebox kept cold with ice blocks, plus a cistern in the kitchen where we pumped water. Toby and I played in an abandoned retail building next door. It was infested with fleas, and I ended up with bites and scars all over my legs from playing there. There was a dairy down the street where we got free small bottles of chocolate milk. I also remember an old horse buggy stored somewhere that we played with. We either pulled the carriage like a horse or rode in it.

Another life-altering incident occurred while we were living in Shiloh. I had taken piano lessons for one or two years, starting in the first grade, and I would sometimes practice and sing verses attached to the tunes I played. One day my brother came downstairs and handed me a chocolate bar, saying, "Here. Eat this. This chocolate bar will help you sing better." I ate it, but I kept running to the bathroom all day and was mighty uncomfortable and busy for a few days. The chocolate turned out to be Ex-Lax. I adopted the belief that I had no talent as a singer from that time forward.

I was afraid to sing out, had a closed throat and mouth, and was critical of my singing. It wasn't until I was 65 and took a singing workshop with Claude Stein at Omega Institute in Rhinebeck, New York, that I discovered I could learn to sing. I then took singing lessons from Norma Codespotti at the Beck Center in Lakewood, Ohio, and continued with her later at Baldwin Wallace College's Prep Program in Berea, Ohio. I studied for several years, moving from an alto to a mezzo-soprano. I wish I had taken lessons earlier in my life, but I am so glad I finally learned to open my throat to sing. Singing was another way of "finding my voice."

Then, a subsequent sexual-intent incident occurred with Toby. It was in Shiloh that my brother's introduction to sex first came, as with many children, innocent enough, I would guess. But when I reflect on our ages, we were past the age of "show me yours, and I'll show you mine." But that's how it started when we were eight and ten. It had transitioned to, "Let's draw pictures of each other down there." Somehow, he made it clear we were not to tell mother. This event started a secret I would never reveal publicly until now. I don't know what happened to our drawings.

But then, a significant event occurred that changed my life. It influenced my emotional reactions repeatedly throughout my life until recently. It started by giving me a reprieve from my brother's abuse progression. The event was the United States' involvement in World War II. My new dad joined the Navy as an Ensign and moved up the ranks to Lieutenant Commander when discharged from the Navy. Following his training at the Great Lakes Naval Station near Chicago, the Navy stationed him at the U. S. Naval Base in San Diego.

My parents packed up Toby and their things and left me behind with my grandmother. I was eight and felt rejected, abandoned, and disconnected from my family, although I didn't know what these feelings meant then. I did not understand why or what I had done for them to leave me behind. Later, when my mother explained it, I comprehended that it was because of Toby's unruly behavior, but the situation had already damaged my psyche. Still, what kind of excuse was that? Why couldn't my mother handle us both?

She said they did not want to leave Toby with my grandmother due to his bad behavior and thought it best to have him where they could keep an eye on him. That doesn't explain why they didn't take me (even though I may have been better off not being around Toby). Now, only as an adult do I understand their dilemma.

My grandmother tried her best to make it unique for me, but that rejection left my life with painful rejection and abandonment issues. That became my "hot button." I already had some of these problems because of my dad's lack of involvement with me. So, as a result, it conditioned me to continually seek approval and love from others as I went forward in my life.

My family stayed in California for less than a year, but their move didn't improve Toby, just as his military school had not. I felt excited when my pregnant mother and Toby returned. Mother bought a house in Plymouth for close to $10,000 on the Huron County side. I do not know where she got the money to buy it, but it might have been a loan. My stepdad did not come home for another two years as the Navy stationed him aboard an attack transport ship, the USS. *William P. Biddle,* in the Pacific. He assisted with the landing craft on various islands during the war.

After their furniture arrived, I was untying a package when Toby hacked my hand with a knife, leaving a scar on the knuckle of my right hand. That was just the beginning of what was to come.

Toby beat me up whenever he felt like it, but sometimes, like other brothers and sisters, we were chums. One night, we sneaked out the door of my room onto the roof and climbed down a trellis to visit friends in the neighborhood.

When I was in the second grade (before Shiloh) and before Toby went to military school, he enticed me to play hooky with him. But I did not know that was what we were doing. We left in the morning but stopped short of the school to play with a couple of friends who had not yet started elementary school. When it was time for afternoon classes, Toby said, "Come on, Penny, we have to go to school."

I said, "But I don't want to. I'm having a good time here."

"Well, that's up to you. But I'm going."

My decision got us both into trouble. We ended up in the principal's office after being discovered. Black licorice was smeared all over my face, and I guessed I was in trouble and cried. My mother was invited, and later, she told me it was all she could do to keep from laughing as she watched my tears making tributaries through the licorice on my face. Where did I get the money with which to buy the licorice? The day before, I had taken a fifty-cent piece off the student's desk behind me, not comprehending that I was stealing. I also had to own up to that and offer to pay it back.

Once, during the day, after Toby's return from California, we sneaked off with swimsuits under our clothes to go swimming in the creek running by another friend's house. I could not swim yet and almost drowned when I slipped on a mossy rock, and the rapids carried me into deeper water. I flailed my arms, trying to stay on the surface. The boys hurriedly swam and assisted me to the bank on the other side. As I crawled out, I pulled a rock off a snake that slithered right by me into the water. I was so startled that I fell back into the water. The boys retrieved me again. My mother never knew about this situation since we allowed our swimsuits to dry before going home. I had another secret to hold, but this event made me even more determined to learn to swim, which I did whenever I got to a swimming pool. I learned by watching how others swam.

When did the molestation begin? Most of it is a haze in my mind because of the repression of my memories. I had thought it started as I physically matured and developed breasts around 13 or 14. Toby would always grab me when no one was looking. I cannot tell you any details, but I know he assaulted me. I can now close my eyes and see his erect penis and a makeshift bed on the floor of his closet, but nothing else. One wall and a clothes closet separated our rooms, and Toby had created a peephole in the wall to spy on me when I dressed. After I learned about that, I got dressed away from his view.

The following is from my out-of-focus memory: Behind our house in Plymouth was a large, old two-story barn where we played. I recall jumping to the ground from the empty hayloft, and one time, I stepped on a rusty nail protruding from a cast-off piece of barn siding. Someone put me in a wagon to get me to the house as my foot had a hole in it and was bleeding profusely.

My memory seems to be only a fantasy or imagination of what happened in that barn. I can see the scene when I close my eyes, but it is indistinguishable. What appears to have happened was that Toby invited some town boys to watch us have sex. In my mind's eye, I see them lined up against the barn wall on the second floor, observing us demonstrate sex on the dirty wooden floor. Maybe they even took turns. I do not know if this happened, but I think it did. Why else would I have this hazy memory? My stomach turns to think it might have really happened.

This dim memory implies that I was a willing participant. I never felt willing, not with all the fear I experienced when alone with Toby. Recently, while trying to make sense of this insufficient memory, I realized this incident might have happened much earlier, perhaps after my family's return from California. I would have been nine and, for sure, not likely to remember much from that time. I am picturing Toby picking up where we left off with the drawings; he may have experienced sex by that time. It now seems likely that Toby introduced sex to me when I was too young to know any better or to remember. Then, when I got old enough to know it was wrong, he assaulted me and chased me to the bathroom when I refused him.

I intend to add a few historical events throughout my story to backdrop the era I lived in when some of my experiences occurred. When the abuse began, Harry S. Truman was a two-term president inaugurated in 1945. The Korean War started in 1950 and ended the same year Truman left office, in 1953, when I enrolled at Kent State University. Dwight D. Eisenhower, also a two-term president, followed Truman's presidency.

Then, there is serendipity. While working on this memoir, at this writing, I retrieved some file boxes from my storage locker, where I stored much of my lifelong writing, journals, letters, and other keepsakes, to see if I could locate past journals with my life or thoughts. I reached in, pulled out a spiral notebook, and looked inside, and I found some torn-out pages and some typed ones from my adolescent diaries. This discovery helps validate that what happened in the barn was real and that I did not imagine any of my foggy memories.

I do not say precisely what happened, but there is enough information there that I can now know. I will sprinkle some diary entries throughout the following pages to validate my memories as they relate to my story. Or I will comment on what was happening during my anxious adolescent years. I have not edited the writing of my forgotten memories in high school; they remain as I wrote them with the language I used then.

As an example of Toby's abusive behavior, I wrote the following entry when I had just turned fourteen on January 3, 1948, having experienced my first menstrual period a month earlier. I had just entered high school.

January 20, 1948: *Today, Toby came into my homeroom yelling at the top of his lungs, hitting me because he said I told somebody about a truck, and we were called down to the office. I was bawling bad. After my dancing lesson, he came downstairs and in a really nice voice, he says he's sorry. I almost fell over.*

The following is one entry that vaguely validates the barn incident:

February 6, 1948: *We played Shiloh tonight. Kenny didn't walk me home. John Root* [a second cousin of mine, Toby's age] *called me over to his table and said, 'Do you remember _ _ _ _?' I acted dumb. Oh, I could have murdered him. He said it in front of Kenny, Dean, and Billy. OH! OH!*

Here is another validation:

March 6, 1948: *I went to Carol's party tonight from 8:00 to 12:30. Miles had to call and tell me to come home. I went in a hurry, but he wasn't up, so I expect I'll hear from him in the morning. Kenny bought me a coke on the way down, and I'm going to the show with him tomorrow. Gee whiz, Vale had to open his big mouth about things, and Kenny knows about Neil and me, and Toby & me. And none of those experiences I could help, and I don't want to do it, and Kenny is probably going with me to get it.*

The following was an addendum to the above since it was the next day:

March 7, 1948: *Mother bawled me out good this morning, and I can't go out as late as I did. Kenny must be mad at me or something. Kenny said he was going to take me to* *the show, but he didn't, and he didn't even sit with me. I was mad at the world after Luther League.*

Here is one more entry:

March 21, 1948: *I went to Sunday school today, and Kenny payed a little more attention to me. Maybe I'll get him back. Larry and Ish were riding around on their motorbikes, and Larry had to bring it up about Toby and me. Oh, dear, what a world!*

From these entries, I believe the barn incident happened, maybe more than once, and Larry, Vale, Neil, and John Root were there, and possibly Neil participated. Since I don't recall or have any entries about this for the remaining years of high school, I think it faded in all the memories of everyone involved, including me.

Later in the year, I had another entry about the above:

October 24, 1948: *I went Halloweening tonight, and a couple of boys got fresh; even Kenny said two things I didn't like. I'm going to tell him my secret and tell him to go if he wants to or stay. I hope it's to stay. Then I'm going to tell my mother, and I hope she doesn't do anything to me. I want to be good, not bad. I love Kenny, and I want to go with him, but I'm scared he doesn't want to love me but to _ _ _ _ me.*

Once, we visited our cousins at Mifflin Lake (near Mansfield, Ohio), where their parents had a cottage. We loved whizzing around the lake in their rowboat with an outboard motor. On this occasion, Toby and Jay trapped Joyanne and me on a small island. Toby had influenced Jay into his evilness. I recall Toby saying, "Okay, you two have to fuck us. If you don't put out, we won't let you off the island." I do not remember if we did, but somehow, we got off the island.

Memories are strange. Some things we recall, but some traumatic experiences seem lost forever. And maybe that is a blessing. While writing this, I visited Joyanne, who adopted the name Azasha, in California. Earlier, I had asked her if she remembered anything, and she didn't but recalled Toby making her take her clothes off once and getting on top of her.

I recall my mother leaving me alone with Toby repeatedly and my running to the bathroom for safety by locking the door, not wanting him to touch me. Running, my heart pounding, adrenaline, cortisol, and norepinephrine coursing through my synapses, I screamed in terror. He refused to leave me alone, even knowing I wanted none of it. Sometimes, I have wondered if these experiences led to my chronic pain. I never recycled those stress chemicals of fear that coursed through my body. I never balanced them or dealt with them in any healthy way, as I now believe they settled into the cells of my muscles.

In another diary entry, I wrote:

August 20, 1948: *Dean was here tonight and passed the football with Toby. Earlier in the day, Dean honked as he went by, and Toby was with him and frowned. I stayed outside all night until Mother came home from uptown. Toby scared me.*

I felt safer out on the lawn than running to the bathroom and locking the door, as I did not have to encounter him. I don't know where my brother Fate was.

Around fifteen, I got another reprieve from him when he dropped out of school to join the military, and I had peace for the next year or two. Toby didn't bother me anymore when he returned. He had gotten our biological father, Ted (who had enlisted in the

Army as a Captain and ended up as a Lt. Colonel), to help get him discharged before his service ended. By then, I had repressed all the memories of what Toby had done to me. When he returned, Toby ended up in my senior class at school but never graduated with us.

Mother and Miles

Parents are the ultimate role models for children. Every word, movement and action has an effect. No other person or outside force has a greater influence on a child than the parent.

—BOB KEESHAN (*CAPTAIN KANGAROO*)

When Miles returned from the war, I was a short, spindly 11-year-old with long reddish-brown hair, deep hazel-green eyes, and many freckles covering my face and body. Around that time, we all went to Tennessee to visit his mother and brother, Buck (who was my age). I am unsure of the following sequence, but perhaps it occurred soon after returning from Tennessee. Mother had become overwhelmed with the three of us kids, even though I was her built-in babysitter, and my brother Fate was about two years old before he met his dad for the first time.

Making an insightful analysis of Miles' return, now, as an adult, I can understand what was going on between my mother and him; however, as I lived through it, I didn't. War-weary, Miles arrived home looking for relaxation and a lack of responsibility. Family-fatigued; my mother was looking forward to having a man in the house to handle the three of us, who presented her problems daily. A lot of that distress was because Toby provoked me, and I attempted to fight back. Also, there was the occasional drudgery of raising a baby who cried and needed to be fed and diapered, among other things. Miles had become a different person, as had my mother. They never quite returned to the chemistry they first felt for each other, although, through the years, they developed a more profound love for one another.

All this caused my mother to have a problematic depression or a "nervous breakdown," as she called it. I was about twelve. She saw a psychiatrist and took the train from Shelby to Cleveland to see him. Her psychiatrist didn't want to hospitalize her but recommended she go away somewhere for a while. She went to Florida by herself, but I don't know where.

While she was gone, which was traumatic for us, Miles hired a local woman to keep our house and watch us kids. I don't know why my grandmother wasn't selected to care for us, but I think she would have been a better choice. The most disgusting thing about this woman was that she never got the dishes clean when she washed them because crusty dried-on food always lingered on them. Doing dishes was still not one of my chores.

During this period, Toby continued in his wayward ways and did something terrible, upsetting Miles. I don't remember what it was, but I remember the aftermath. Toby told Miles that I had done it. And without due process, when I came home from school for lunch one day, he grabbed me, hauled me to the backyard, took a limb from a tree, turned it into a switch, and whipped me with it up and down my back and legs. I returned to school full of shame, with bloodshot eyes from crying and huge welts on my back and legs.

Up to this point, I had idolized Miles. When he was in the Pacific, he sent me personal V-Mails (Victory Mails), made a necklace for me out of small beach shells, and sent me an authentic grass skirt from Hawaii. He was my stepfather, but I called him dad or daddy. But now, I wanted to hurt him as much as I was hurting. My anger at unjust punishment and how it happened caused me to get even. So, I began calling him "Miles." To this day, I don't remember my mother ever spanking me, let alone whipping me. However, she issued other cruel and unusual punishments to teach me a lesson.

One such occasion occurred after we had moved in with my grandmother. Toby and I had taken all her freshly laundered and ironed clothes out of the dresser and thrown them on the floor. She filled a bathtub with cold water and made us get into it. I do not remember this, but she beamed with pride every time she told this story for thinking of this punishment.

Another occasion happened when I was a teenager. An extremely heavy snowstorm had deposited a couple of feet of snow on the ground. I invited Janet and Molly, a couple of my friends, to take mutual photos of each other in our bathing suits in the snow. I was freezing inside the house a few days prior, so I raised the thermostat to increase the heat while standing by the register to get warm. Thus, my mother got annoyed when she saw us outside, exposing our flesh to the elements. She locked me out of the house with only my Pea Jacket over my swimsuit, with my bare legs exposed between my coat and boots. Fortunately, Janet's house was just behind ours on the next street, where I warmed up until my mother decided to let me back inside.

Now, back to my mother on her healing sabbatical to Florida. She finally returned, and you might say she had gotten religion while she was gone—well, not precisely religion, but spiritualism, a different belief. It was something new in her life and gave her hope and a reason to go on. While there, my mother encountered various spiritualists, including Arthur Ford, a leading psychic, medium, clairaudient, and founder of Spiritual Frontiers Fellowship. He became her life-long friend. She began trying to develop her mediumistic skills by doing Automatic Writing. I remember her showing us the results of the writing that disembodied spirits allegedly did, entities taking control of her hand. (In some circles, there are stories that evil disembodied entities can assume control of a person's life from the same exercise.) Her experiment transitioned to table tipping which needed a "circuit conductor." She enlisted Miles for the job.

Over the years of my mother and Miles' work, they produced volumes of messages and lessons from "highly evolved spiritual entities from beyond." In the early stages of their work, my mother told me about Toby coming home one day while they were tipping the table, and the spirits controlling the table chased him out of the room with the table. My brother confirmed that that had happened, but I had difficulty believing it. While writing this book, I discovered the beginning of my mother's memoir that retold this story.

Later into my adulthood, they initiated a study group of friends who came to their house to meet their spirit guides and discuss the guidance they all received. I never followed in her footsteps, but I was interested in any messages for me. Instead, I ultimately became a student of the metaphysical broadly. On occasion, however, I have listened hard to hear the messages from my guardian angels in the past few years. When I connect with them, I accept that their message comes through my thoughts. I don't have time to do this when I am too busy.

After graduating high school, my mother self-published a book called *The Dams Can Break*. It is autobiographical, including some of the above. Her book tells the story of a depressed protagonist's visit to a spiritualist community and her discovery of Spiritualism, ultimately lifting her from depression. [*I have more to say about her depression in Book Three from my discovery of a tiny notebook.*]

As time passed, my parents began to heal from their extended separation and the challenges our lives presented. My mother and Miles razed the barn and built a tennis court in the backyard where they played tennis. I tried to play tennis with my mother but got worn out quickly and felt I could never keep pace with her. I always thought I was a good swimmer and tried to swim often, but I was still amazed at my mother's endurance as a swimmer since she rarely swam. She could outswim me, even though she was a chronic smoker.

My mother also played the piano very well. I remember the comforting and soothing strains of Beethoven's *Moonlight Sonata* while lying in bed at night, and tears sting my eyes anytime I hear it played. She even took lessons on the accordion in my late teens and played it splendidly.

CHAPTER 3

HIGH SCHOOL

*In school we learn that mistakes are bad, and we are punished
for making them. Yet, if you look at the way humans are
designed to learn, we learn by making mistakes. We learn to walk
by falling down. If we never fell down, we would never walk.*

—ROBERT T. KIYOSAKI, *RICH DAD, POOR DAD*

Brain Development

There are so few occasions I can think of in my life where I had an
early or regular beginning. Mostly, I have been a late bloomer in
so many circumstances, possibly because I had an early beginning
to school. My birthday falls on January third, so the School Board
allowed me to start school with other kids whose birthdays came
within the year before mine. I was five.

In retrospect, I was not as prepared for many situations in my
life because my brain had not developed enough to make proper decisions. I fell short of making them due to the circumstances I found

myself in before being mentally prepared to meet them. This possibility helped establish events I was not mature enough to handle.

I was puzzled over being irrational and having roller-coastering emotions. I have searched mentally for the cause of my adolescent and young adult impulsiveness and the risks I took, such as giving in to peer pressure. That also includes the inability to think about my actions' consequences or see other viable options.

I did not know my problem was brain development. In recent years, science has discovered more about brain development. Interestingly, in children and adolescents, reason and judgment do not develop fully in the prefrontal cortex until somewhere in our mid-twenties.

As I understand it, when young adults approach that milestone, most negative qualities come under their control. That discovery explains the many early miscues and abysmal choices. But I have no explanation for continuing to make poor decisions past the age of brain maturation. It also appears that those who abuse alcohol and drugs in their teen years will manifest a developmental delay and appear to be the age at which they started abusing substances before and after experiencing recovery. They still need to allow their brains to mature, even after 25. When I decreased my alcohol intake, I began to make better decisions. But also, maybe it all had to do with the repression of my traumatic experiences.

Sex Education and a New Secret

I started to get insight into what sex was about from the boys at school. In the eighth grade, another girl and I went to our lockers on the second floor of our small high school during the intermission of a basketball game. It was there we encountered a couple of male classmates. The boys barricaded the stairs at either end of the floor.

We couldn't get away to rejoin the fans at the game. Every time we tried to go down one or the other staircase, they would run there before us and prevent us from leaving. One said, "We'll let you go if you promise to fuck us." There was that vulgar word again. I now wonder if they were one of the boys in the barn. Did they know what Toby did to me? I do not have an answer other than in my previous diary entries.

We consented only to get free. I seized this experience to choose Toby as my confidant, so I told him about the encounter. He informed my mother, and the next thing we knew, the other girl and I were in the principal's office with the principal asking, "What did the boys say or do to you?"

I could not answer because I did not know what to say. I could not say, "*Fuck.*" Neither could my friend. We did not have the vocabulary to explain the experience. Nor did we have parental information about such events and knowledge of handling or taking care of ourselves. As a result, we could not propose an appropriate discipline for the boys for what they did. The authorities dropped the entire incident. And we never had to give in to the boys because we blackmailed them. We told them, "We've been to the principal's office about what you did to us, and we can get you into trouble." My question now is, what about Toby tattling on us? You would think he would have been fearful of being found out. Maybe he didn't want anyone encroaching upon his territory. I'll never know.

My sex education, delivered by my mother, was on menstruation. She wanted me to accept it naturally. She supplied me with little booklets informing me what it was all about. Her mother and sister never told her and taunted her during her first period, and she did not want me to go through the same thing. My menstruation commenced in the twelfth month of my thirteenth year and was without anxiety.

My mother had no brothers, so how could she know or suspect that an older brother would molest his little sister when that never happened to her? My life would have been different if only she had told me about sex or given me the proper vocabulary and all the other things modern parents express to their kids today about predators. Most importantly, these parents warn their children early in their lives to tell them when someone touches them inappropriately or uncomfortably. My childhood undoubtedly would have been altered, as would my adulthood.

My sex education also came from my classmates and chums, which only gave me a little knowledge. Even though my mother had given me those booklets, I still had no logical idea how babies were made or born. Remember, I grew up in the 1940s and 1950s with no televisions or computers. Where was I to obtain this information?

As if Toby were not enough, as I continued developing my secondary sex characteristics, I became the focus of Miles' attention. At the age of 14, at the same time as my diary passages, I was excited one night when Miles suggested a "date." All young girls want a date with their fathers, right? We planned to go to a movie in Willard, a mid-size town approximately six miles away, which we did, but on the way home, Miles pulled the car over to the side of the road and parked it. I didn't know what he was doing or what he had in mind.

In my teenage diary, I wrote:

February 27, 1948: *I went on a date with Miles tonight, and he felt around and kissed me several times ... He sucks and sticks his tongue in your mouth. We went to the show at Willard. He told me a lot of things I never knew. He said* *when he came back from the war that my mother would not let him kiss her or anything. Something had happened to him, and he said he would never tell, and my mother made it worse. He worried and went to work, and he wasn't supposed to _ _ _ _ for six months.*

My memory of this event had always suggested that he pulled me over to him and placed a very wet kiss on my lips with his mouth wide open, which made me feel he was swallowing me. As far as I recall, no boy, let alone a man, had kissed me yet. Then his hands began exploring my body. I felt scared, disgusted, and confused. I grimace when I recall it. This man was the person who took my father's place, but what was he doing to me? He was married to my mother!

Thoughts of what Toby was doing popped into my head. I reminded him, "You are my father. What are you doing?" That seemed to stop him. I think he may have been embarrassed as my words seemed to snap him back into sensibility. That did not stop his future advances, however. Somehow or other, he made it clear that I could not tell mother because of what it would do to her. In any case, that was the family rule, "Don't tell your mother. She won't be able to deal with it." I think he asked me more than once to have sex with him. These attempted seductions occurred until my first marriage. In my *Recovery Journal*, another journal started in the late 1980s, while engaged in thoughtful therapy, I attempted to understand my initial process in the following entry:

March 28, 1989: *It* [His attempts] *allowed me to share my deepest, darkest secrets with him. The family rule was not to tell my mother anything for fear that it would upset her. Of course, the more I shared with him, the less I could share with my mother, and, I think, the worse I felt about myself -* **I must be bad, or I must be wrong.** *I also must* *have thought I was bad because of the attempted seductions, and I may have felt responsible for them somehow.*

At the time, I did not have the consciousness to see the connection to the following situation. It was as if Miles were being punished by the Universe even though I was the one who felt punished. The next day, following his first attempted seduction, my teen diary entry reported:

February 28, 1948: *Mother and Daddy had a wreck today. The car is beyond repair. That means no more joy rides. Darn it, everything has to happen to us. Why does God have to pick on us? Why did I have to be born into a family with bad luck? Toby even felt me up today. I struggled and threatened to tell Mother and went back on my promise because I was scared. I was going to have Kenny down and then go to the midnight show with him. After what happened, I couldn't ask. I asked to go to the free movie but couldn't. Kenny wasn't even at the regular show. Oh, Woe! Woe is me. Everyone is against me.*

Even though I wrote about the wrecked car, writing this entry was one way for me to deal with what Miles had attempted the night before without my writing about it.

In a way, I could slightly "blackmail" Miles following his initial attempt. I think he knew it, as he would do all kinds of things for me if I asked. That didn't stop the discipline; it only got him on my side in issues with my mother. But as I said, he seemed to try to get me to be available to him at times. When I was 21, he helped me obtain my first car. It was also a secret from my mother about where I came up with the money when I had had no job, and I told her it was from my penny collection. He was my confidante. But neither was I able to tell him what Toby had done to me. There I was, holding onto all these secrets.

Love or Romance

As a freshman and a sophomore, I took acrobatic ballet dance lessons because I had taught myself to do backbends, handstands, cartwheels, flips, and other movements. In today's world, I might have been a gymnast. Because of these skills, I tried out for cheerleading and got elected by the student body to be a cheerleader, an honor and privilege I maintained throughout high school. My activities helped me focus away from what was happening at home and assisted my attempts to appear ordinary in every way. I was on the senior basketball cheerleading team during my freshman and sophomore years. We did not have a football team until I was a sophomore, but I got elected cheerleader to the football team as a sophomore and a junior. Still, the votes relegated me to the junior or reserve cheerleading team in my junior and senior years.

My mother was an excellent tailor and made all my basketball cheerleading uniforms. *[I now believe her making things for me was part of her love language.]* I loved out-of-town games, as I got to ride the school bus to them. Riding the bus was especially lovely when Kenny, my sometimes boyfriend during my freshman and sophomore years, was on board, and I got to sit with him.

I found it challenging to understand Kenny, my continuous favorite. He always ran around with his sidekick, Ish (short for Ishmael). They would drive through the alley next to our house and stop below my bedroom window. My room was above my parent's bedroom, which prevented us from talking. I desperately wanted him to kiss me, but he seemed shy, like me. He was not a threat to me sexually, as friends reported that he had sex with a girl of questionable character in Willard. He would put his arm around my shoulders at movies and on the game bus, which thrilled me. I felt all fuzzy and warm. He went into the military during the Korean War when I was a senior in high school and had started dating Lyle K. from Willard. He would sometimes bring home Lowell D., his chum from the service, when on leave. I dated Lowell several times and wrote to him at some point.

Speaking of boyfriends, it seemed I found myself in love with a different boy every week of the year. Yes, these were crushes, but I was in love with the idea of love. I got that concept from the movies of the 1930s and 1940s. Many were romantic, and they ended with "happily ever after." I felt love-deprived due to my circumstances and my biological father's abandonment. Also contributing was my family leaving me behind when they went to California. I wanted the romance I saw in the movies with someone's arm around me, holding my hands, or kissing me.

Since those movies didn't show or mention the couples having sex, I didn't know that sex followed the turning out of the lights, the innuendos they made, and the fade-to-black or another scene. It was the same thing with the sad love songs of the time. These songs included: *Again, Bewitched, Bothered and Bewildered, I Wish I Didn't Love You So, I'll Be Seeing You, The Very Thought of You*, and *My Foolish Heart*, to name a few. I can now see what the crooner was longing for so many years later, but I was clueless then. I thought they wanted what I wanted, love. Of course, they wanted to be loved, but they also wanted sex, which did not interest me.

The following entries from the same discovered teen diary demonstrate my angst over finding the love I desperately wanted.

March 3, 1948: *I went to the show tonight, and Kenny came. He put his arm around me, and I felt very warm. Oh, boy, do I love him. I hope he comes back, and I can ask him in. Oh, I want to be loved so much. I just yearn for it more than anything in the world, and if I get it from him, I'll be happy or from anyone. I just want the love of someone whom I can love back.*

[Please read "love" as love, not sex.]

March 5, 1948: *I was so mad at Mother because I wanted to go to the show tonight, and she wouldn't let me. I cried my eyes out. Cripe, everyone else is loved in this household except me. Oh, do I hate this cruel world. I made some fudge tonight, and for once, it got hard.*

March 14, 1948: *I went to the show today, but Kenny couldn't put his arm around me because my mother was coming. I wish something would happen to my parents. They're (awful or unfair). I love Kenny, and my mother won't let me go out much. He came down tonight, and so did Ish, and we messed around* [looked for things to do]. *Miles is so mean. I don't like to wish for such bad things, but I need somebody. If only my dad would come back. I wish. Oh, gee, what a life.*

April 11, 1948: *Gee, do I miss the kissing I got last night. Boy, I know whom I want now. I eliminated every boy until I came to Dean. He's the one I want, and I'm going to work for him until I get him. All four of my lover boys were at the show. Tom, he's too small* [young]; *Kenny, too bull-headed; Des, too fresh; and Dean, too bashful. I can't wait to get a kiss from him. Kenny and Ish are standing in front of my* *window right now. They want my attention, but they aren't going to get it. I'm through with them. I want Dean.*

August 10, 1948: *I know why I don't have any boyfriends because Toby lies about me. I found that out from quite a few people. I wish I could do something mean to him, but there isn't such a thing as you could call him.*

August 11, 1948: *I haven't much to say except it rained today, and I went to the inside free show tonight, and no exciting boys were there, darn it. I wish Toby would leave me alone.*

August 12, 1948: *I went to the show tonight, and I didn't see anyone anywhere. I'm getting unpopular again. If Toby doesn't leave me alone, I won't have a friend in the world.*

August 18, 1948: *I went to the show and spent my last cent. I'm not going anyplace now until the carnival. Toby made me mad tonight in front of Dean, too. He says, did I figure out a way to catch a boy yet? I could have cried. He makes me very mad.*

August 19, 1948: *I wish Toby would quit tormenting me, and I could get a boyfriend. I need one so bad. I love Dean because he's the right boy, and I like Des because of how he kisses. I want either one, or that's all. Please give me one.*

August 26, 1948: *I went to the carnival again and helped the Girl Scouts a little bit. Then I went with Bill M., Jerome T., and Marilyn L. I sat in the back seat of Ronny's car with Bill, and boy did we neck. I really enjoyed it. I knew I should get home early but kept putting it off. Miles was* *looking for me, and when I got home, boy did I ever get a bawling out.*

September 19, 1948: *Kenny was mad at me, but we made up. Toby was uptown, and he made me mad. He hit me. Everyone was trying to get away from him. I hate his guts. Kenny finally brought me home.*

December 7, 1948: *No teenage thing tonight, and boy, was I in the doghouse. Beak and Red, Carol & Harvey, Kenny & I went out for a ride and parked. We didn't get back till 11:00. I had fun, though. Kenny had his arm around me, and I held his hand or vice versa. I was so comfortable, but then when I got home, of all stupid things, I was locked out. I rang several times, and Miles came. He said I couldn't go out for a week and had to stay in from the basketball game, but I had fun with Kenny while it lasted. I could have kissed him, but I didn't have the nerve.*

My first intense love came in the summer of my fifteenth year when a carnival came to town. It was just before my junior year in the late summer of 1949. I met my friends; we went on rides together and did all the fun things we could find. One of the most handsome men I had ever met was at the Ferris Wheel. His name was Lee, and he ran the Wheel. He was extra friendly to me and began letting me ride for free. Before I knew it, we were talking about dating. He arranged to walk me home at night and even kissed me.

A booth at the carnival made ID bracelets, and Lee got me one printed with the words, "Lee loves Penny." Remember that this fair would only be in Plymouth for four or five days. But we kept in touch, and when we expected them to be in a town close by, my friends and I visited them. My friend, Janet, dated one of the other men. They all knew how I felt about Lee, so it wasn't a secret from them, but it was from my mother. Eventually, I told Miles, who told me I should not get involved with Lee but not say anything to my mother. Soon a conclusion came when my friends told me a secret they had withheld from me.

One night, Mary Jo, another friend, said, "Penny, we want you to know what we found out about Lee. Red told us that Lee is married and that the authorities threw him into jail in the last town the carnival was in because of something to do with his marriage." I started to cry and left my friends. I cried all the way home. I had a broken heart. I thought I had found the love I was seeking, that I was a special girl to him and that we genuinely had something together. I sobbed all night long in the darkness of my room until I couldn't breathe through my stopped-up nose. The following day, I emerged from my bedroom with red, swollen, and bloodshot eyes, depressed about another boy/man letting me down. I thought, *So much for love! Would it ever be mine?*

Not long after, I wrote this love story for *True Confessions* magazine. I showed it to Mr. Bishop, my English teacher, who rewrote it. I submitted his version, but the magazine never accepted it. Again, my mother never knew about this, but I guess she would have if the story had gotten published.

My School and Summer Activities

I participated in numerous other activities, such as the Glee Club, Future Homemakers of America, Girls' Athletic Association, the Girls' Basketball Team, and cheerleading throughout my high school years. During my junior and senior years, I was active with the Annual Staff and other activities and performed in the junior and senior plays. These plays fostered my desire to become an actor. My extra-curricular activities kept me away from home and thinking about what I endured there.

When I was 12, I started babysitting (an activity I pursued throughout high school) outside my home with three young children. Babysitting my younger brother prepared me for this initial occupation.

For some of my summers, my parents sent me to Camp Pittinger, a seven-day YMCA Camp in Tiffin, Ohio, but I never got to go for a whole summer like Toby did. When I was sixteen, I became a junior counselor at Pittinger and attended a day camp for a couple of summers. The day camp was in Shelby, about eight miles south of Plymouth.

Also, when I was 16, for travel or sightseeing, I went to Niagara Falls, New York City, Boston, and Plymouth Rock with my grandmother, her sister, and her niece. A year later, I went with our senior class upon graduation to Washington D.C., Atlantic City, and New York City.

Traditional Customs and Practices

While growing up, we children learned to respect our elders as best we could. We addressed them as Mr. or Mrs., along with their surname. We gave our bosses the same respect as we grew into adulthood. I offered this same regard to my elders through graduate school in the 1980s. It was the same thing about women wearing dresses to work until I encountered women wearing slacks one day. I disapproved of this at the time but found it was not long before I started to wear them myself until that was all I wore. We also said, "Please," "Thank you," and "May I?" Men held doors open for women, opened car doors for them, and held their chairs at a table to help them move closer to the table. We felt honored and cared for with these little courtesies.

We lost graciousness and something important to our culture or socialization when these refinements fell by the wayside. The world since my childhood has become caustic, coarse, vulgar, and disrespectful.

Also, certain objects and customs have disappeared from our lives, which is mainly suitable. We talked to others on landlines as we had no mobile phones or voicemails. Instead, we did not have computers but typed on typewriters very carefully because we feared typing errors, especially if we had carbons underneath the top page. Our typing was to be as error-free as possible. We went from White Out, a correction liquid, to manual correction tabs to spiral correction tapes placed on electric typewriters when we graduated from manual typewriters. We did not have copy machines. Instead, we had messy, inked mimeograph machines. We hand-wrote actual letters to one another and mailed them. Gas and transportation were inexpensive, but that might be relative to the amount of money someone possessed. I remember it was $0.28 a gallon when I was a teenager, but it had been even cheaper.

CHAPTER 4

ADOLESCENCE

*We have to acknowledge that adolescence is that time
of transition where we begin to introduce to children
that life isn't pretty, that there are difficult things, there are
hard situations, it's not fair. Bad things happen to good people.*

— LAURIE HALSE ANDERSON, IN *(SPEAK LOUDLY: A CONVERSATION
WITH LAURIE HALSE ANDERSON ON TOPICS SUBJECT
TO BOOK BANNING)* BY PETA JINNATH ANDERSEN

Teachers and Me

My junior year came along fraught with unhappiness. I'm unsure why because Toby wasn't around me any longer since he had enlisted in the Army. There were indications that I was troubled throughout my high school years, but most of it occurred in my junior year, as I was somewhat rebellious and broke the rules frequently (oppositional, defiant). Perhaps it was due to the strain of my repression or maybe the loss of energy from keeping secrets. In the late 1940s and early 1950s, no school counselors or social workers were available in small towns, at least not in my small school. There were only 28 students in my graduating class. And I don't think any teacher knew why a child or adolescent would act out. But troubled children call out for attention and desperately want someone to ask them what is bothering them. Troubled children do not know how to explain what is bothering them because they do not know how to say it. All of this applied to me.

Although Guy Bishop helped me with my first story and submitted it to a confession magazine, it didn't exonerate me from his discipline. Once in my junior English class, two dogs were going at it outside the classroom windows, and Mr. Bishop, a young instructor, went to the windows and pulled down every blind. I don't think he knew what else to do. Another time in that class, Gusty Ray, who sat behind me, snapped my bra strap. I turned around to tell him, "Leave me alone. Don't do that." But I was the one who got into trouble mainly because I couldn't say anything to Mr. Bishop about what Gusty had done. I was too embarrassed. Mr. Bishop sent me to the principal's office. I just sat there. The principal did not punish me or ask me what had happened. Boy, what a relief! I wouldn't have been able to tell him either.

One time in Mr. Samaha's Algebra class, I was reading a *True Confessions* magazine hidden inside a notebook. He came over to my desk and asked me to give it to him, but I put it under me and sat on it. The next thing I knew, he was pulling on my arm, trying to move me off it so he could confiscate it. He eventually gave up. Occasionally, I babysat for him, and he appeared puzzled by my behavior.

An illustration of my troubled existence is found in the discovered torn-out pages of my teen diary written in my junior year, at age 16 in the spring of 1950, as follows:

May 9, 1950: *Dear Diary: I worked tonight at Fackler's* [a children's clothing store], *straightening boxes and things. I got $2.00. Zeke walked me home and kissed me several times.*

May 10, 1950: *Dear Diary: I stayed home tonight. Today in algebra class, I was restless and wrote a poem.*

> How I wish I were out gallivanting
> Through woods now enchanting
> But here I sit in Algebra class
> Boring, restless, sitting on my A_ _.

I meant it as my ankle. Samaha took it away from Sammy Hutchinson and said, "The things that these girls write about nowadays." I would not speak to him anymore.

May 11, 1950: *Dear Diary: Today, Mr. Samaha showed that poem to everyone in creation, and I got really mad at him. After algebra class, he told me to wait and come outside the room. Samaha said he apologized for taking it and even for reading it, and he wanted me to apologize for writing it. That's such a stupid thing to apologize for. After school, I was walking down the hall, and Samaha asked me if I was mad at him. I didn't answer him. He kept asking me that, but I wouldn't speak to him.*

May 12, 1950: *Dear Diary: Today, Mr. Samaha talked to me all algebra class. He thought something was bothering me, and he acted like a father. I made up what I did tell him, and really, it did bother me. I didn't like the Junior-Senior Banquet. The dinner was good, but the rest of the evening was boring because all of us girls went stag. I bawled, but I* *don't know why. I guess I was lonesome for Lowell. I went home with my mother at 3:30.*

May 15, 1950: *Dear Diary: Boy, I sure got Samaha mad at me today. I was chewing gum in homeroom. (Samaha never told me to spit it out before, but he did today just to make me mad.) I said, "No."*

He said, "Did you hear me?"

I said, "Yes."

"Spit it out."

"No."

"You come in after school."

"Okay."

"You heard me. You come in after school."

I said, "Yes."

And in homeroom this afternoon, Beak had strewn yarn all over the room. Samaha was mad. Then he said, "The next one that opens his mouth is going out."

Me: "Don't look at me like that. I didn't do it."

"Get out."

"No."

"Get out."

"No."

He started pulling on my arm, and I held on to my seat. "Don't ever come in here again. I never want to see you again."

But I didn't leave. And Mr. Samaha again said he didn't want me there, so I didn't go to algebra or go in after school either. I was with Tom again tonight, and he walked me home and kissed me goodnight.

May 16, 1950: *Dear Diary: I stayed home tonight. Today, in the morning, I stayed in the basement for homeroom. I was supposed to report to Mrs. Lanius, and I was counted absent. Bishop asked me if I was tardy because my name was on the absentee list. Coming from history class, Samaha said, "Penny, … Penny, … Penny. You sure are making it hard for yourself. You're to report to Mrs. Lanius' room from now on." I just hate him.*

Mary Jo said that he said in algebra class when I didn't come in again today, "Where's Penny? I just can't stay mad at anyone."

I ended up sitting in the typing room behind Mrs. Lanius' classroom. Mrs. Lanius, who taught English and typing, was my best teacher in high school, but her enormous girth and the way she presented herself made her a formidable presence. I would never have thought about acting out around her or in her classes. It makes me wonder why I did with the male teachers. Some of the other kids from homeroom stood up for me and came to keep me company. Shortly, Mrs. Lanius arrived in the typing room and asked why we were there.

The others answered, "We were kicked out of homeroom."

She said, "Go directly back to your room right now!"

I didn't leave. Mrs. Lanius said to me, "Why are you still here?"

"I really did get kicked out of homeroom." She allowed me to stay, but I didn't stay long.

This situation was probably like today's in-school detentions. I do not think they called it that, then.

Drinking and Smoking

Then, in no time at all, it was summer. After getting my driver's license on August 31, 1950, I gained some independence at 16. Miles had been my primary instructor. But on many guy dates, I would shift gears or even steer the car while sitting close to my date. So I definitely had some practice.

A young woman, adopted when a child, lost her legs at differing lengths to a streetcar injury when just a little girl. Her prosthetics reminded me of dolls' legs, fitted and strapped on her stumps very uncomfortably. Dorothy was overweight, swayed on her prosthetic legs as she walked, and had over-bleached blond hair. She was too impaired to drive. If only Dorothy could have had today's prosthetics, she might have been able to operate her car herself. How different her life would have been if Dorothy had had that freedom.

Her family lived south of the town square, next door to Janet. When I got my license, Dorothy's father asked me if I would drive her to different places, including a bar and restaurant nearby, using their car for her greater freedom. I relished the idea because it allowed me to practice driving and increased my independence by allowing me to be inside a bar before being of age. Of course, Dorothy would slip me some of her drinks after I started to drink. It also allowed me to help someone less fortunate.

At Ruggles Beach on Lake Erie's edge was a dance pavilion about a 45-minute drive from Plymouth. It had a delightful crystal ball hanging in the center of the dance floor that spilled slivers of light throughout the hall as it spun to vibrations from the music of the Big Bands playing. That made it very romantic to dance. I took Dorothy there frequently, mostly in my seventeenth year. Her parents also had a summer cottage in the neighboring community of Mittawanga. Our abandoned Girl Scout troop, which morphed into a club called the Zodiac Girls (because there were 12 of us), stayed for a week at their cottage. As a Girl Scout troop, we had planned to vacation there and had bake sales and other fund-raising efforts to finance our trip. We just continued that effort until we had raised enough money to go.

In that cottage and at Ruggles Dance Hall, I learned to drink and smoke under peer pressure from some of the Zodiac Girls, and I could not say no. At Ruggles Dance Hall, I added three-quarters of a glass of coke to the 3.2 beer I was attempting to drink since I could not stand the taste. Eventually, I could drink the beer straight and even liked the taste. But with smoking, everything within me resisted it. I coughed and got dizzy but kept pushing on until it didn't bother me anymore.

I had to be 18 to drink, so I told everyone I was 18, but I probably looked 14. It seems the authorities did not check IDs in those days. I even met and danced with a couple of young men who I believe were also lying about their ages, even though they were probably old enough to drink. I met Jack H. from Lorain that week. He was an honorable and upstanding young man who would teach me a valuable ethical lesson four or five years later that helped me grow up. We mutually lied to each other that summer. He was probably 18 but said he was 21. We spent a lot of time with each other that week. He introduced me to, and read passages from, a poetry book called *This Is My Beloved* that fed my hunger for love and romance.

Crisis

I read my mother's letter while still at the cottage. She stated that the Plymouth residents heard rumors about us and reported that we were drinking and smoking (all true). She pointed out that I had said I would never drink or smoke. Something else in the letter made me feel like I was being rejected and abandoned again, which brought on rebellion, so I decided to do the abandonment and never return home. I told Jack and asked if there were any apartments in Lorain where I could live while finding a job, and he stated that there were. In response to my mother's letter, I wrote the following letter, telling her I would not be coming home, and I sent it back with another unsuspecting guy from Plymouth.

July 7, 1950:

Dear Mother,

Here's an enclosure of the two dollars you sent me. I don't want any of your damn money if that's all you think of me. Boy, you sure are dumb if you believe everything Toby says. So is every other dam mother in town. Boy, if by now you don't know Toby better than you do, you'd better give up.

I suppose Toby told you I was drunk. I know he must have because he said that about every other girl up here. It's not a bit true because Mrs. Schreck said she would ship home the first girl who was drunk. No one has been drunk. Sure,

I've been drinking. At least, I admit it. Everyone else up here has been too. I haven't had as much as half the other girls have. I can't hold as much. I was a little dizzy once or twice and sick once, but, by gosh, you've got to learn sometime, and experience is the best teacher. Last night I drank some beer. I can't stand the stuff anymore, and I'm not going to touch it. That's the truth too. I learned to inhale also, and I've never smoked so much in my life. I can't even stand the taste or smell of a cigarette now. I haven't smoked one all day. Everyone else around here is having nicotine fits. I can't even stand it. I'm probably just tired of it. Yes, I bet you believe me.

You hate me. Always when I wanted something, you never gave it to me. You didn't have any faith in me. You know how girls turn out when their mothers don't have any faith in them. I haven't done anything yet, but you probably wouldn't believe me. Always when I wanted something, you preferred to give it to Toby. Hell, you've been giving him stuff all his life. Has he appreciated and shown that he really cared about it? No. Well, why should I? I'm getting tired of being chosen last in this family. First, it's Fate; then, it's Toby. I come last. I don't see why you even keep me around if you don't like me. Well, just help me find the place, and I'd be glad to go. Maybe I'll find someone to love me there. It's a wonder you bought me those clothes. But don't worry, I'll pay you back or return the clothes to you.

Don't tell about the other girls drinking, or they'll get into trouble. I don't even want to come home. I've met many boys up here. They all think I'm 18, and I'm not telling them anything different. One of them said he could get me a job in a restaurant in Lorain. Don't be surprised if I don't come home. You don't want me to anyway. I always did want to be different, but I'm only human.

Toby probably didn't tell you he was so drunk that he got thrown out of Ruggles Sunday night. He got knocked in the jaw by one of the guys so that he would go, but he wouldn't go. I don't know why I was sticking up for him. I acted like I was drunk, but I was civilized in the bar when I realized what trouble I had caused. I did that because I wanted to be with Bob S., which is the only time he'll go with me, either when he's drunk, or I'm drunk.

Don't worry about me if I don't come home. I'll make out. I even look 18.

Your only daughter, Penny

*P.S. You never let me use my real name. I would like to use Miles' name, but you don't understand. My decision is all your fault. They also say kids go wrong when their mothers and fathers divorce. You won't even let me see my dad. Even if my dad is bad, I still love him because he **is my** father. You liked your father. Well, I like mine, and I want to use his name. I think Miles understands. He tries to make me feel good. He lets me drive, but you don't want me to. I'll never get to drive the car alone. Even if you bought Toby 3 or 4 cars, you'd never even start to get me one. All the kids here are with me. I thought they didn't like me, but they were also crying with me. I love them, and I hope they love me. Molly, Sally, and Beak are the only ones that don't drink because they can't stand it.*

On the last day of my vacation, I said goodbye to my friends from the Zodiac Girls explaining that I was not going home but running away to Lorain to get a job. I told them, "Jack is taking me there and out on his father's sailboat on Lake Erie when we arrive."

While sailing and with nothing to distract me, scary thoughts about my decision to live in Lorain penetrated the pleasantness of the sail on the lake. I thought about how unloved I felt in my family and my lack of experience in the real world. I did not know what kind of job I could get or how I would pay for an apartment and live alone. I was afraid of Jack wanting sex when I only wanted love. I hoped my mother would feel sorry that she didn't love me when I was no longer around.

I felt terrified and thought it was too late to turn back. I had never been on my own. I recalled my vacation, the drinking, and being encouraged to smoke even though I coughed and got dizzy when I did. I am so glad it wasn't drugs, which are far worse than cigarettes, but that was not a big problem back then.

I could not go through with it, and it wasn't too late. I told Jack that I wasn't 18 and wanted to go home. He said he knew and would take me home and help me ease back into my family.

We drove to my house, and Jack opened the car door for me. I told him, "It will take more courage than I have ever had to go inside." He validated the courage I had already shown by going to Lorain, confessing to him, and my decision to return home.

My family was in the kitchen with supper ready. I took a deep breath, swallowed hard, skipped gaily into the kitchen with Jack at my heels, and introduced him. My parents seemed genuinely excited about seeing me, and there was no mention of either letter. At that moment, I felt loved but puzzled.

The next day I went to the boy who had taken my correspondence for my mother. He wasn't there, but his mother asked me to wait. When she returned, she held my letter and told me, "My son didn't get a chance to deliver it."

I took the letter and said to her, "That's okay. I told mother all about my vacation, nonetheless."

As I walked away, I looked at the envelope and saw that someone had opened it. I wondered if the boy's mother had told my mother but maybe decided not to. But I knew I would never have the answer to that question.

This incident was another time when I didn't find answers to burning questions such as, did they open the letter, read it, and decide that it was not a good idea to give it to my mother? Or did they give it to my mother, who returned it to them to give back to me? Here was another secret held possibly by my mother but also by me.

What Will the Neighbors Think?

After this summer, I was a high-school senior. Since I did not get elected as a football cheerleader, I auditioned for the new marching band and got to play at the football games. Somewhere between my junior and senior years, I borrowed a trumpet from a friend and taught myself to play it. It wasn't the most incredible thrill because it was awkward holding the mouthpiece against my lips in the cold while the trumpet bounced off them while marching.

My junior year's misbehaviors continued into my senior year but were not as abrasive. Joy Bethel (my first-grade piano teacher and high school Spanish and music teacher) permanently kicked me out of Glee Club for misbehaving. I recall that Mrs. Mock would get upset with me back in freshman home education class because I refused to follow the cooking and etiquette training protocol. As I reflect on my high school behavior, I repent of my actions and wish I had not perplexed any of my teachers. I apologize to all of them wherever they are. It was not the way to behave. I also wanted the voice and language to release my secrets and tell someone about them.

On the positive side, because he was kind, I had a crush on our senior-year football coach and shop teacher, for whom I also baby-sat. I worked in his shop office typing during school hours throughout my senior year. When I graduated, he gave me a compact that I cherished.

Even though my mother never told me anything about sex, she expected me to know something about it. One time in my senior year, when she was off to a bridge party, my boyfriend, Lyle K., from Willard, picked me up from play rehearsal and brought me home. No one was there, and my younger brother was at my grandmother's that night. My family had no television, so Lyle and I chose to be romantic, sit in the dark, and cuddle. At least, that is all I had on my mind. My mother unexpectedly came home early, and when we heard her at the door, I sent Lyle out the back door but not in time.

My mother came inside and was furious about the lights being off and whatever she thought was going on. Of course, nothing was happening. She said, "What will the neighbors think?" *I don't know,* I thought. But wasn't that a teachable moment? I'm sure she jumped to the conclusion that I was doing something sexual. She could have taken some time to instruct me about handling myself in such situations. Why was she more concerned about what the neighbors would think than my brother had done to me all those years? Of course, she did not know, but I wish I could ask her today. And now that I think about it, this is the sort of comment that creates shyness in someone. Those who are shy and anxious are always worried about what others think.

As far as Lyle was concerned, we didn't have to "do it" in my darkened living room. My friends preferred the back seat of a jalopy to the comfort of a living room, where discovery might be likely. Once, we went with another couple to the cabin of a relative of Lyle's. We were in a separate room by ourselves and tried to have sex. Thankfully, he could not get an erection. This occasion was to be my first sex of choice. Lyle probably would have been the man I married if I hadn't left Plymouth soon after graduation. I had dated all the Plymouth boys I had a crush on.

In the early 1950s, it was anathema for an unmarried girl to get pregnant. One of our classmates did, and she was the center of the town's gossip for a while. But it did not bode well for her for some time then. She ended up dropping out of school and married her boy-friend. They were still together, the last I heard.

Predators and Other Ilk

No sexual assault story is complete without referencing the disturbed characters populating our world. They could be considered troubled men who are misogynistic, depraved, or predatory in one form or another.

One day in my sophomore year, as we were assembling for a class and the teacher had not yet arrived, for some unknown reason, a boy, Eugene M., as he was going to his seat, made a fist and struck me in my right breast. The pain was unbearable, and it appeared no one saw what he had done. Again, I could never tell any adult about it because I still had not learned the language. A couple of years later, another boy, Bob, slapped me for no reason when my gang of girls gathered outside Janet's house, which was next door to Bob's. These experiences should have made me a little leery of boys and men, and they probably did.

Some sleazy men lived in our small village of 1,500-plus people. There was a man in our town with a bad reputation. None of us kids knew anything about him, but there must have been some reason we used the phrase, "Are you ready for Freddy?" regarding him way before there ever was a Freddy Krueger. We all were afraid to walk by his house. The gossip we heard was that he kidnapped little boys. He may have been known as a pedophile or suspected of it today.

One man also may have been a pedophile but was an exhibitionist. It seemed that wherever we girls sat in the movie theater, he would sit in our row. We called him "Mr. Thingamajig." He always wore a hat he placed on his lap during the movie, and his hand would sneak underneath it and appear to agitate it. We would try to move to another row whenever he got close to us. It seems no one ever reported him. Other adults would have known what he was up to, but no one seemed to come to our defense.

Another man who lived in Plymouth always looked like he had a crush on me and even resembled Miles a little bit. Over the years, this man would stand behind me at public social gatherings. I felt very uneasy, mainly because he was married, and his wife was not far off. As usual, I did not know how to deal with him either.

And One More

After high school graduation and slightly over three years following our movie "date," Miles arranged for me to be a clerk typist at the Fate-Root-Heath Company. He had moved from a draftsman after the war to a salesman of industrial locomotives by then. I am not sure what position he held at my high school graduation, but he eventually managed to work up to the CEO and Chairman of the company's board. One Saturday morning, I had chosen to sleep in because I got up early every morning for work. He came into my room and said, "Penny, get up and do some dusting while your mother is shopping."

Egad! Toby was no longer the pursuer; Miles was. Although he did not say it, I suspected he had something clandestine on his mind. Besides, I didn't know where this dusting or cleaning of the house had come from. Mother had never had me do either. My chores involved dishes and my own clothes ironing. I didn't want to leave the bed in front of him in my pajamas. I retorted, "I won't get up until you leave the room."

By then, I was sitting up in bed with the bedclothes clenched high to my neck, and Miles reached out and slapped my face hard. There was no call for that! Embarrassed and shy, I didn't know if he did that because of how I replied or because he knew that I knew what he was up to and was ashamed, but he put the onus on me. Any way you look at this situation, I had a right to privacy and not be seen in my pajamas.

I shouted at him, "I hate you!" These were words I could never take back, and I never did. I just had to go on despite them. He left the room, and I got up. After dressing, I went downstairs to dust. Like everything else, this situation was never discussed again, so the secrets continued to build.

Quite possibly, I would not have had it any better with my biological father, according to Louise, my half-sibling. She ran away from my father's third marriage home in her teens. Eventually, we met as adults when she was in her first marriage and shortly after the end of mine. Later, she shared a secret that our mutual father sexually abused her from about three or four. She was the only one who knocked my dad off the well-constructed pedestal I had placed him on while growing up.

A New Enduring Guy Friend

During the summer of my seventeenth year, following graduation in 1951, I continued going to Ruggles Beach. I eventually met Jack M. from Cleveland. He became a lifelong friend, never pushing for sex whenever I dated him. He was a cameraman in the burgeoning television days and later became a local television station's manager. You will hear more about him later.

CHAPTER 5
LEAVING HOME

Leaving home for the first time is like going through the birth canal one more time. It is like losing the delusional warmth and security of the womb to find yourself naked in a strange new world while seeking ways to clothe yourself to achieve once again that warmth and protection permanently. It is like swimming in an abyss as you pursue the way to pull yourself out.

—Penny Christian Knight

On My Own

I had been living pretty much on my own most of my life. But isn't that true of all of us? It is something to think about. Even when we are with someone, we're still on our own. However, with the larger picture, the macrocosm, or the Source, we are never actually on our own or alone. But most of the time, we are not aware of this aspect.

While still in Plymouth and dating Lyle, I continued working through the summer. My mother wanted me to leave Plymouth and, I think, not marry Lyle. Knowing how important it was to have those skills when she divorced my father and had to support us kids, my mother made her plan for me because she wanted to ensure I would always have a means of taking care of myself financially. She desired to provide me with the needed skills to earn income when I needed it over time. So, she enrolled me in a business school, Dyke and Spencerian Business College in Cleveland, Ohio, to become a secretary.

When fall came, my mother and Miles loaded me and three suitcases into their car and drove me to Cleveland to be on my own for the first time at 17 years and 8 months. It was 1951, and Harry S. Truman was president. The world event that continued to loom large was the Korean War started in 1950, my senior year in high school. Some of my friends were in the military and already fighting there. And later, I encountered soldiers traveling on the trains I took back and forth to Shelby to go home to visit.

From my rediscovered teen diary, written a few days before departing Plymouth to be on my own for good, I wrote the following about Lyle and me:

August 24, 1951: *I was with Lyle tonight, maybe for the last time in a long time. It was so hard to say goodbye. We clung to each other desperately. Then I started crying. He kissed my tears away. When I brushed his cheek, I could swear he was also crying. Finally, we said goodbye. I sure hope I love him. I know he is the first boy I ever cared for, really cared for. I hope he's my mate because I don't want any other. He told me to look around. I don't want to, but I will, and I hope I don't find anyone else.*

Upon leaving home, I didn't know it was the fifth of fifty or more moves in my life, although some were only short stopovers. I wonder how my life would have gone if I had married Lyle or if the Universe had decided I would not experience all I have. I guess I already know the answer. It was my Heavenly assignment or spiritual contract to undergo most, if not all, of it because the people and events we are supposed to encounter will appear at the right time.

My New Home

My mother found a women's rooming house for me in a former brick mansion converted for that purpose and which the business school had recommended. It was like, yet dissimilar from, a college dormitory. Most of the 22 to 27 women who lived there shared a room with one roommate, while the larger rooms held three women. The house had three floors and even an old servant's quarters in the back, where some of the women lived, but there was only one room for one person, which was on my floor. My room was on the third floor, where all the windows were gabled. Closet space was limited, so I hung my few clothes on an over-the-door closet bracket.

Ten of us shared one bathroom with an old-fashioned claw foot tub, no shower. We all shared only one telephone (landline) in a tiny alcove off the hallway on our floor. We signed in and out on a register on a side table in the front hall next to the front stairs so our landlady, Mrs. Grundel (Mrs. G), would know who was at home and would be there for dinner. There were no hours, and we all had keys. It was not very structured for someone as young as me. For only $15 a week, we received breakfast, dinner, our bed, and a shared laundry room containing the new "automatic" washer and dryer.

Mrs. G's

*Nothing or no one had equipped me for what I encountered at this rooming house. It was the best of times, and it was the worst of times. I was 17 years old and unprepared for life alone, but I had moved into a laboratory for learning. I often get an image that we were all reincarnated prostitutes from a brothel of the past, not that we **were** prostitutes or carried on in that way, but just that image flashes into my mind. My fantasy probably has a lot to do with our landlady, Mrs. Grundel, or "Mrs. G," as we commonly referred to her, who reminded me of a madam. Her room was right off the front hall of our former, old three-story brick mansion. I hardly remember her being fully dressed except when she left the house, but she usually appeared in a loose cotton-floral housecoat.*

Further, she seemed never to be without a cigarette which dangled from the corner of her mouth with the ash the length of the cigarette itself. I marveled that the ash never dropped and practiced trying to do the same, but with little success. She was loved and feared. She was the first to greet our visitors, and the men had to wait in the hall, not being allowed upstairs.

I lived at Magnolia Manor (my self-created name) between September 1951 and August 1953, when I left for Kent State University in Kent, Ohio. At Kent, I had the assignment to write a personal essay for my freshman English class entitled "The Spot I Call Home." It related to Magnolia Manor and to my initial experience of leaving home. The essay follows:

Two years ago, I left my home in the small town of Plymouth, Ohio, to find my way in the world. I moved to Cleveland, Ohio. I thought I was leaving home for good as I had enrolled in a two-year secretarial course at a business school. The only time I would return home would be on some future weekend.

I thought it was permanent during my first month away from home. My mother and father weren't around when I wanted to run to someone. It seemed like a big load of responsibilities had been placed on my shoulders. I couldn't take it all and wanted to give up and run home. Home to me, then, was the warmth and understanding of my parents. But then I discovered, or so I thought, that they weren't as understanding as I had perceived them. They wouldn't let me come home, not even for a weekend. Oh, how persecuted I felt! My parents didn't want me anymore, and I no longer had a home to go to.

In someone's first month in a new place, getting acquainted and making new friends takes time. So, there I was, thinking no one loved me.

What was wrong with me? I discovered it was homesickness. However, it seemed a little worse because I thought my parents didn't want me. I didn't want to go to business school either. I did not know what I did want.

Finally, they let me come home for a weekend. I was so happy that I forgot that I had vowed never to return. I went home, and I was shocked! It wasn't the way I had anticipated it. It had changed; my hometown had changed, but most of all, I had changed, and I didn't know it. I had been getting accustomed to my life in the place where I lived and beginning to love it.

So, I went back to my little rooming house with 27 girls, back to my landlady, who always got on all the girl's nerves, but actually, she was nice. I must admit we all were wrong about her most of the time.

I found that my life was better than in my old home, and I could hold responsibilities on my shoulders. I just found my life more wonderful, more livable, and more fun. I found it so much fun that I didn't want to return to Plymouth.

I stayed in Cleveland and got fed up with business school because I never liked it and quit after almost nine months. I could have gone home, but I didn't want to then. I left school without my mother's permission. By this time, I had grown somewhat independent. I got a job and went to work. My parents didn't know it until a week later. I held my position for 15 months until I decided to attend Kent State University.

I had found my home in Cleveland, living with 27 girls and women, sharing their problems and interests. My friends were there. My job and life had centered within my small four-walled room, which I called **home.**

My first room at Magnolia Manor was small, with one roommate, BJ. I soon moved across the hall to share a larger room with two other women. Nancy, who also registered with me at business school, was one of them. Thank God! There was someone with whom I could study. We had a small desk by the gabled window to do our homework. Mostly, we sat on our twin-size beds to do so.

I wrote in my teen diary about my first day there.

September 1, 1951: *I came to Cleveland today. Already, I like it. My roommate is BJ (Betty Jean). I met quite a few girls today, Jean Tucker, Carol, Sue, Mickey-17, Lillian, and Marian, and they're all swell. I certainly like them. I don't think I could live in a better place. BJ asked me to go to the movies tonight, and then her favorite called and asked for a date. BJ was really nice and asked me to go along. His name was Jerry. We saw "On Moonlight Bay" at the RKO Palace. Then we drove around and went to a bar and came home. I had a swell time, and I'm glad they asked me to go along.*

The other women were of varying ages and from different backgrounds. They were mostly employed as businesswomen, mainly as secretaries and sales clerks. These jobs, including nursing and teaching, seemed to be the only professions available to women around the 1950s.

Many of the women were dysfunctional, and some dealt with mental illness. I think we were a repository for social services to dump troubled teens. At some point, BJ informed me that the very day I moved in, she had contemplated suicide. The following is a portion of a letter I wrote when I was 23 or 24 and married. I wrote it to a young woman from Plymouth as she contemplated moving to Cleveland. I had determined by then that I had had a good experience living there:

Some were secretaries, some were students from different schools, some were from many different occupations, some were good, and some were bad, but I would never change those two years for anything. I learned more about life, people, happiness, and unhappiness in those two years and grew up faster than I could ever have grown in Plymouth.

The girls come and go. The undesirables usually leave pretty fast. There was an orphan of 16 who tried committing suicide. She even drank ammonia in front of me. Her tongue was swollen and ulcerated as a result. It didn't kill her because she didn't drink enough. I had to take the glass from her and report her to the landlady. I heard she tried something else, and the welfare agency had to put her into an institution. In my estimation, the kid needed love and affection, and no one could give it to her. She didn't want to live because there wasn't anyone who cared. Oh, if only there could have been someone.

We also had a few streetwalkers, alcoholics, thieves, and lonely girls, and they all made it exciting to live there.

I learned a lot about men from the other girls, how to act on dates, and how to take care of myself if there were any wise guys I might date. [Today, I would question this statement.]

The Neighborhood

Western Reserve and Case Universities were not far from where we lived (the university section of town). They later (1967) merged and became Case Western Reserve University. And within a long hiking distance (walking and buses were our only transportation) was a college bar hangout, Moe's, which the college kids and our group visited. The owners didn't need to worry about the décor. Students dripped paint on the walls in various strange and repulsive colors. The wooden chairs and tables were the bare minimum needed to seat people. At 17, I would go there with some of the "older girls" from my house, and we would drink beer, but with 3.2 percent alcohol content for me. Sometimes I would drink too much. When that happened, and the world was spinning out of control, I might spend the night on the bathroom floor shared by the 10, hugging the commode. [*The thought of doing that today is disgusting.*]

I had to learn how to navigate the new neighborhood from Magnolia Drive, where I lived. It took three or four long blocks to reach a shopping area, restaurant, and Moe's in one direction. In the opposite direction, there was a medium-long block to get to a local bus that could carry me to Cleveland's center or downtown area and the location of my business school.

They Are Here, Too

On my way home from somewhere one day, I was about to cross the street to Magnolia Manor when a car drove up to the curb. The trees lining the road produced shadows upon his vehicle. The man inside asked me for directions to some other street in the area. I looked in the direction I was pointing as I explained. I could see into the driver's seat when I turned around and saw the man caressing his exposed erect penis. He asked, "Why don't you get in and show me?" Images of Toby chasing me flashed through my mind, releasing a smidgen of my repressed memories. I made an excuse that I was late and fled to my house as fast as possible across the street. I was concerned that I showed him where I lived, but I had nowhere else to go. **I wanted to get behind a heavy, locked door as soon as possible for safety.**

As far as I knew, it was a period in history when there was no news about perpetrators. I was not likely to know about it if there had been because I didn't read newspapers then. We didn't have television and did not listen to the radio. No one had ever told me what to do in such situations, but my instincts paid off when I left the scene as quickly as possible. Was it my instinct or my experience that informed me? I don't know. I only guessed that there was another "dirty old man." Today, we know too many women and children have disappeared due to this particular kind of encounter with men.

On other occasions, I saw men (like Mr. Thingamajig) pleasuring themselves in public. Once or twice, riding on a city bus, I saw men doing so. A couple of years later, I worked a temp job in downtown Cleveland. From about ten stories up in a very tall building and from my office window, I saw a man jacking off in an alley behind a building. These men turned my stomach and added to my earlier traumas.

Moving toward civilization, as I called it, we would walk past several fraternity houses, mostly converted mansions, from Case or Western Reserve University. Occasionally, on my walks, I met some of the guys who lived in them. Over time, I met and dated a couple of fraternity brothers. One was Cole F., who came in and out of my life for about 44 years until I lost contact with him. Possibly he passed on close to the end of the century. At other times, I would meet guys at Moe's, where we would start to talk, and then one or another would ask for a date.

In a rediscovered journal, I found the following entry, which describes well what it was like living at Magnolia Manor during my first year. Mainly, it is about my relationship with one of our female residents, possibly the origin of many of my poor choices.

Irene

Irene was a quiet girl when she came to Magnolia Manor. But we heard tales about how a man had seduced and stabbed her when she was 12, and she was 17 now. It took a couple of months, but we got to be friends.

She was from a semi-wealthy family who gave her anything she wanted but the one thing she needed, love and affection. We all tried to provide friendship to her so that she would know she had friends.

Irene was a beautiful girl about 5'4" tall. She had blond hair, which she always had done in the proper hairdo. All of us were envious of her way of taking care of her hair. We were also jealous of her clothes with the perfect figure upon which she wore them. She had everything. We were envious, yes, but we had our parent's love. However, when someone has a lot, we want that too. She wore heavy makeup but not so you would notice it too much. When she dressed for a date, she appeared to be the age of 23.

When she came to live at the house, she was still attending high school and a senior. But in December, she tried to commit suicide and was taken to a hospital to be cured. But could she be healed?

Her mother and father had gone to California to live, leaving her without love but with money.

She started getting depressive. Then one day, she slit her wrists. Well, that night, when I got home from business school, she came into our room looking for BJ. She looked pale as a ghost and was wearing a long-sleeved sweater.

But below the sleeves, Nancy and I saw the white bandage wrapped around her wrist. She found BJ and told her. Then I knew BJ wouldn't confide in all of us, so I went to talk to her. I talked her into telling me, but she told me to keep quiet about it. I promised, but what else could I do when I wanted to find out why she was so pale?

That night when Nancy and I came in after a date, Irene was in the bathroom talking to BJ. BJ told me that this was Irene's fourth attempt to kill herself. She tried to slit her wrists; she jumped out of a window; she tried sleeping pills. I was shocked. Of course, Nancy wanted to know, and I told her that nothing had happened. She had a short sleeve bathrobe on, exposing the bandages on her wrists. She didn't try to hide the fact, however.

The next day when Nancy and I came home from school, Irene walked around on the second floor, crying, and we asked her what was wrong. She came to our room to tell us and explained that her social worker was taking Irene back to the hospital.

She had been in it once before. We cried for her because we felt sorry for her. Maybe it would be good, but those hospitals never take care of their patients as they should, and they don't give their patients the friendship they need, as Irene needed ours.

Many of the girls in the house condemned her and said she needed a good spanking, but deep inside me, I knew that girl required something else.

About a month later, the doctors released her from the hospital against their wishes. She had told her mother she would never see her again if she didn't take her out. So, she came back with us. On the first night she was back, she went out with her boyfriend and got in late.

I was sleeping so nicely, but pretty soon, I heard, "Penny. Penny." I woke up and almost screamed. There was BJ as white as a ghost wearing something on her hair to protect her curls. That was enough to make anyone scream.

She told me to come into her room because she needed help. Then I saw Irene. She was lying on BJ's bed. She had no makeup on, and she had just washed her hair, but she hadn't combed it out yet. She looked very young this time. She was sleeping but in a very troubled sleep. BJ said she might get violent, and we'd have to hold her. I had to remember she'd be strong if she did become violent.

It was 1:30. We sat terrified, scared to do anything. All of a sudden, Irene started thrashing, and BJ and I just looked at each other. We were supposed to sit up with her until her mother came. Then she quieted down again, and we relaxed a little more.

Then Irene sat up. We thought, this is it; this is it! She looked around the room and stared at us with glazed eyes. Then she lay down again. This time she went into a more restful sleep. Then she had her head covered up, and BJ said it looked like she had stopped breathing, so I went over to see if she was ok. I was scared to get near her for fear she would wake up. She was all right. It was four o'clock when her mother came. BJ came into my room to sleep.

The next morning, we woke up, and Nancy couldn't understand why BJ was in our room; I told her it was because she had a nightmare and came to sleep with us.

Irene had said the night before, when she asked BJ for help, that she felt like screaming really loud and beating her head against a wall, and she didn't know why.

Then Irene came out of BJ's room, and Nancy couldn't understand that. Then of all things, someone called Nancy on the telephone, and she went to answer it and saw Irene's mother. Then she returned and said, "What's going on around here? BJ's in our room. Irene is in BJ's room, and some woman is there." We finally had to tell her about what was going on, but we told her to keep quiet if someone in the house got scared.

On the next night, almost the same thing happened. She got in late, and her roommate came upstairs after BJ and me. BJ said she wouldn't go down and couldn't take any more. So, Nancy and I went down. Irene had a terrific headache, but she didn't know Nancy and I were there. She was babbling away and said something like she was putting something over on someone. "I'll kill myself." Her roommate didn't think she would get violent, so we went back to bed.

I felt so sorry for that kid. I could just imagine what she was going through. The next night BJ came into our room to sleep because she didn't want Irene to disturb her. When Nancy, BJ, and I were all settled with the light out and the door locked, there was a knock at the door and a voice whispering, "BJ. BJ, come out here." No one wanted to move. Then Nancy got up, turned the light on, unlocked, and opened the door. Sue jumped in and yelled, "Boo." Nancy fell to the floor.

Then Irene decided to go to California with her folks and rest up. She was gone for a month and returned as a new girl. Then she decided to get married to her boyfriend. So, they started planning the wedding. Irene went to work. But his folks didn't want him to get married. They were having trouble with that and had a fight and were supposed to be through with each other. Irene was going out to walk the streets and pick up anyone she could. Luckily, I didn't have a date that night, and as I would have been the only one at home, I asked if I could go with her. She said yes.

We went to a movie. Then, we went to a bar. Several characters tried to pick us up on the way, and I was scared that Irene would accept. But she didn't. Then two guys asked us if they could buy us drinks. She said yes. Then they sat down. We found out they were off-duty cops from another town. If they knew how old we were, they could have turned us in for drinking underage. They must have been around 30 and wanted to take us home. We said, "We only live two blocks from here." Irene said, "You can walk us one block of the way, and we will go by ourselves the rest of the way." They said okay. So, they took us halfway.

Then we went home, and I said to myself with some relief, "Well, I at least got her back safely." But as we approached the house, she told me she was going back out again, and there wasn't anything I could do about it this time. She went out and didn't come home until around 5:00 p.m. the *next day. We called her boyfriend, and he came over, and they made up.*

Irene once told me about what happened to her when she was 12. She said the man was a married man who lived across the street from where she lived. He used to take her over there. He was a dope addict. Irene knew a little bit about dope but not a lot about it. Then he grabbed her one day and gave her the needle. She didn't realize it was dope. Then, he seduced her. And when she said she would tell, he stabbed her in the stomach.

They took him to court and charged him with being a dope peddler, taking dope, rape, contributing to the delinquency of a minor, and attempted murder. They sent him up for a good long time. His family blamed her, which drove her into a nervous breakdown. She tried to kill herself and failed. Her family sent her to the hospital for a cure from the dope and her breakdown. But she still took dope. Her boyfriend and I were the only ones who knew.

Then, she started saying she wanted to die and that no one liked her. But her parents had been kind to her since she had gone home, and she didn't think anyone was her friend. I told her I was and that she never had to worry about me. And the kids in the house liked her. Well, now, she's in California, and her boyfriend is on his way out to marry her. And she said she was in love with him and couldn't wait until he got there. I hope she will be happy. She sure needs it.

The two experiences that greatly influenced my life were caring for Dorothy while I was in high school and my experiences caring for Irene. They revealed my compassion for others and my desire to help them. I learned a lot going through my experience with Irene. Perhaps both influenced my decision to go into clinical social work and counseling in mid-life.

Another Sexual Assault

Around a year or more after moving into Magnolia Manor, I was raped. I recently recalled this buried memory because I didn't know what had happened then. It transpired on "just" a date. I do not remember his name, but I will call him Scott. I don't recall where I met him, but he was a DU (Delta Upsilon) fraternity brother from Western Reserve. Ironically, Mandel School of Applied Social Science (MSASS), CWRU's current newest social-work school building, stands on the very spot of that DU house. I attended MSASS at a different building when I attended CWRU. As was usual in the 1950s, I went to a few fraternity parties at the DU house, as elsewhere, and of course, there was drinking. In those days, I would drink until I was high and sometimes until I was sick. But I had never passed out.

Recently, much press has been about high school girls or college women attending fraternity parties, passing out, and getting raped. The explanations offered by the men are that it was consensual sex. But there is a warning that if someone, a woman, is impaired from drinking, she cannot possibly give consent. And there is also the question, what if a man slipped a date-rape drug into that woman's drink? That might be hard to prove for a long time afterward.

Now back to me and my date at the DU house. I had never passed out in my drinking career before this night or since. But one night on a date with Scott, it appeared I had done so or had gone to sleep or blacked out. When I came to, I was in the back seat of his car outside the fraternity house. I don't remember getting in there. We were sitting close together, and I was experiencing discomfort in the region of my genitals. I felt horrified that I must have had sex with him or that he had taken advantage of me, maybe even raped me; however, I was unsure. I felt utterly bewildered.

As an aside, I never consciously had sex with any of my dates throughout this period. So, I could not say anything to Scott or anyone else. I felt embarrassed if it were true. If I had confronted him, which I didn't dare to do, I would have been embarrassed if it were not true. I didn't want anyone to judge me for having sex. So, I ignored the whole situation and pretended it had not happened. I felt ashamed. This sexual assault is another secret—never revealed. I never told anyone. Never! I still feel shame. I'm angry he took advantage of me, and I'm mad that I didn't understand alcohol and its effects. I'm annoyed that no one ever protected or educated me about handling myself with men like this.

Only recently, I began to wonder if he had put knock-out drops in my drink, and I am now sure of it. I don't know what it was, but knowing that Scott had raped me, I want to ask him, "How could you take advantage of me like that? I trusted you." It enrages me that so many men take advantage of us women in this manner. I'm not sure what this experience did to my psyche, but it was a part of my sexual assault journey throughout my younger life, and the experience became repressed like all my other assaults. And I feel outraged about it now.

CHAPTER 6
FINDING MY WAY

Now I was entirely on my own, paying my way,
making up my mind. Nothing can be more significant or give
a person a greater feeling than being independent and free.

—PENNY CHRISTIAN KNIGHT

First Full-Time Employment

Around May of 1952, I quit business school (secretly from my parents) and was hired for my first job as a clerk typist (shipping clerk) at National Screw and Manufacturing Company, following eight-and-a-half months into my two-year course. I quit school because I was envious of and influenced by all the employed women at Magnolia Manor who had income. I also didn't find the study conditions there ideal either. About this job, a year or two later, I wrote the following autobiographic essay for college English at Kent State:

> *Now I was entirely on my own, paying my way, making up*
> *my mind. Nothing can be more significant or give a person*
> *a greater feeling than being independent and free.*

I kept my job for 15 months when I decided to go back to college to realize some of the ambitions that I have had all my life. I want to be an actress on Broadway. Also, I would like to be a writer. I have the desire to create. I have the ambition, but I don't know whether I have the talent.

One thing I don't like about Kent or any other school is that you cannot be independent. I feel like a little kid with rules that make decisions for me. I am independent and can take care of myself, as I have proven within the last two years of being autonomous. [Of course, I now question the accuracy of this statement.]

At National Screw, men appeared to focus their attention on me. I walked through the manufacturing plant and past the many men working there to get to the shipping department. The men whistled or hummed musically with every step I took, *"da-da-da-da, da-da, da-da, da-dump da-dumpedy-dump da-dump."* I felt very self-conscious walking past them, but there was no way to avoid it. Maybe I should have been pleased they paid attention to me, but I wasn't. It was just more unwanted attention.

While working there, I joined the other women from Magnolia Manor for beers at Moe's at the end of the day. Some days following too much drinking the night before, and because I was hungover, I would lie down on an old couch in the Ladies' Room during my breaks at work. I found it more challenging to get up and go back to work, and I sometimes took advantage of the company by staying there longer than I should have, but no one ever said anything to me about it. I am not proud of this, but it was a time when my drinking was unbridled.

Dating

As time passed, I dated other college men and an occasional military man home on leave. I met another nice young college man, George G., who was also in my life for a short period. Then, sometime again around 2016, I found him on Facebook. I cannot remember in what order I dated these young men.

So far, I haven't found any other written material to chronicle these two years at Magnolia Manor other than those above and a few entries below that I will now share about what happened around my second year at Magnolia Manor:

August 23, 1952: *Sue went out with Vinny, I went out with Mike, and we went to the Richmond movie. The parking lot attendant took us to a bar, and I had two slow gins with ginger ale, after which we went to the show and got out at one o'clock. The DU house was supposed to have a party, but it broke up at 11:30. We went there, had a bottle of warm beer, and sat on the sofa in front of the fireplace. Joe F. brought us a bottle of cold beer, and then Sue and Vinny left at about 3:30 while Mike and I fell asleep. We woke up at 4:30 and walked home, getting there at 6:00.*

August 24, 1952: *I ironed today and met some guys from the Phi Gamma Delta house as Norma and I walked past. They showed us their bar. Then six of them drove us home. Jerry P. called and said he would call back in 10 minutes, but then Cole from the Phi Gamma house called, and I told him to call back in 10 minutes. But Jerry called, and I went out with him and Angelo. We went to a drive-in movie, and I got in at 3:30.*

September 28, 1952: I do not have any journal entries to share about this date. I remember my mother calling. She struggled to tell me, but I interrupted and finished her sentence. "Gramma died?" She had been diagnosed with colon cancer and had had surgery. Everything, allegedly, was proceeding well. But something went wrong, and she died. She was 72. At the funeral home, I remember touching her body in the coffin. It was cold and hard. I shivered. That was not my Gramma, who was warm and soft. She was my first loved one to die, my first profound loss. I had lost pets, but this was different. I hurt inside and cried frequently. I didn't have the tools to understand death or work through my grief then. Eventually, I did.

Back in Cleveland, my life continued. At Moe's, I met Gil Q., one of the bartenders. He was short, handsome, friendly, and protective and lived close by in a small off-campus apartment. He worked at Moe's to help support his education at the Ohio School of Podiatry (Chiropody) in the area.

We became exclusive in our dating. We did not have sex, but I remember dreading having it on sweltering days, knowing it was inevitable. The thought of having sex when it was hot was a big turn-off for me. It was the idea of having sex that turned me off. I was indeed not like others who eagerly looked forward to it. And by this time, I had almost forgotten Lyle. Gil was very old-fashioned, and when I was dating him, I was not yet wearing makeup, only lipstick. He was against my wearing any makeup. His control soon became a problem after I went to modeling school and learned how to apply it. He told me not to wear it and was categorically against my modeling, period.

We talked about marriage at one point, and I started to get cold feet because of the control issues (only I did not know then that's what they were) and decided to break up with him. In those early years of dating, it appears I was more capable of arriving at an intelligent decision regarding selecting an appropriate mate than with my later choices. Or perhaps, it was that I was too afraid to commit.

October 15, 1952: *I went downtown tonight to Billy Tilton Modeling Agency and paid $50. When I returned, I met Gil at the drugstore, and we went to his apartment, where I watched him shave. Then we went to the Commodore Bar to watch TV fights and came home at 11:30. Gil wants to marry me. Don wanted to marry me. Kenny wanted to marry me, and Lyle wanted to marry me. Someday, if I never get married, I sure will kick myself for not taking one of these offers.*

Since I didn't dare to break up with Gil in person, I wrote the following *Dear John* letter, which shows a lot of my mental processes regarding permanent relationships then:

Dear Gil,

Well, honey, did you have a lovely Christmas? I hope you did; more than anything, I wish you did. I hope you have a really Happy New Year, although I'm not sure you will after reading what I must say.

Oh, darling, I don't want to say it. I've prolonged telling you this for so long, and since I'm a coward, I must write this rather than telling you, and besides, if I told you, it wouldn't come out the way I wanted. So, darling, remember, whatever I say, I still love you, and I always will. Oh, I just can't say it. Please hold on, darling, because this is going to hurt.

I want to break up again for two main reasons, which I will tell you. Please take this as a man and don't do anything you'll regret. I know you told me never to break up with you again, but I think it is best. In my opinion, our marriage wouldn't be too good because we are two entirely different personalities and make. I love you, darling, and I will miss you something awful because I miss you already.

My desire to break up is why I have been acting as I have for the past couple of weeks because I didn't know what to do. I've been driving myself crazy because I know I love you, but I also know we don't get along very well. That is why I cried that night, besides what else you were talking about. That is why I have been as tired as I have, too, because I couldn't sleep from thinking about you. So, you see, darling, it is just as hard for me as it is for you.

I also hated taking the bathrobe you gave me because I knew what I would do. Oh, but I love the robe. Everyone here is crazy about it, but if you want me to return it, I will. But I would like to keep it. I gave you the lighter because I love you and wanted to give you something to prove that I love you too. Please keep the lighter, and don't lose it.

I'm such a lonely and mixed-up girl. I'm just like all the rest of the girls up here. Maybe I'm like this due to my upbringing, or I'm just scared of love or marriage. I wanted it so, but when we started going together again and arguing, I was less sure. I would still like to marry you, but I just don't know with conditions the way they are. I just don't think it would work. I can't change my habits, just as you can't change yours.

All I ask is, please don't hate me. I'm just an immature brat. I wish our relationship would have worked because it would have been lovely. I still can't realize it because it's just like you did the breaking up the way I feel. I feel so awful about it and know I am probably making a big mistake. But I am so dumb that way.

I wanted to let you have me that last night, so I could have made you happy. That is why I went as far as I did, but I couldn't when it got right down to it. I love my virginity too much to give it up, I guess. But I wanted to make you happy, but I didn't. Maybe someday, we could try again if you are still single and still want me when I'm grown up in a couple of years. You said this was my last chance, however.

But you can fall in love more than once, so don't say you'll never marry. Maybe you will find someone a hell of a lot better than me. Perhaps she will do what you tell her, but I can't. She will make you a better wife than I would. I guess I am career-minded, and you won't let me have that.

One reason is, well, I don't know if you realize it, but it's your telling me what to do. Maybe I notice it too much, but that's how it is. The first couple of weeks we started going together again were okay. I don't know what happened, but you told me what to do. Not so much what to do, but either you asked me not to do something, or made me feel like I'd better stop, or wouldn't I do that for you.

I wanted to do things for you and even tried, but I failed because I couldn't break the habit of how my parents raised me. You said once that if we were ever to get married, I would have to give up my independence, or we wouldn't get married. I can't give it up because it is one of my qualities. You will have to take me as I am or not at all. One of the things I know you didn't like about me was my wanting to wear makeup. Nobody has ever said anything against it, and practically everyone loves it on me but you.

As I see it, we wouldn't have a happy marriage because we argue too much, and when I get married, I don't want any arguments. I've seen too much of what they do to people. I want to have a marriage like my mother and Miles. They have discussions on some things, yes, but not severe ones. They never tell each other what to do, and I just can't see them telling each other what to do. You can't change a person. Like, I'm not trying to change you. Not once have I tried except for you playing poker.

You are supposed to love me for what I am, not what I could be with your help. If I want to change, I will change but not with coaxing from someone else; I have to do things for myself because I'm independent. So, that's where you made your big mistake in trying to change me. I have changed in some ways. Like I quit drinking, but most of that is because I wanted to lose weight. I've tried to stop smoking, but it's too hard to stop.

Marriage should be 50-50. There never should arise a time when either one or the other must tell the other what to do. I've given a lot, but you haven't given anything. Like you won't dance specific dances and won't try to learn some. You know how you feel about that. That is the same way I think about makeup and things.

You also think women are trying to be like men, but we aren't. Short haircuts, for one thing, are because it is style, are simpler to take care of that way, or are more comfortable. Jeans or slacks. Women don't wear pants to be just like men, but because pants are more comfortable to wear. The voting process is because women want a hand in saying who will govern them. You always seem to think women are trying to be like men, don't flatter yourself. I want treatment as an equal. There are few dainty women left in this world. Women must learn to stand up for themselves like I had to this Sunday. So, darling, please understand everything I say.

I've noticed another thing that is different about us. You don't like to do the same things I do, like that basketball game in Plymouth. You didn't want to go because you didn't know them, but I can enjoy almost anyone's basketball game. Like you don't like to dance, I love it. You don't care about swimming as much as I do. Or any sports like I do. You never seem to talk about your younger days to me.

You see, Gil, there is too much difference between us. Think it over. Look at some of the things I have pointed out. Don't you agree? I feel you love me more physically than mentally because if you cared for me mentally, you wouldn't keep trying to change me. You never try to tell me to make changes physically, so that is why I figure you love me more bodily.

I wrote and told my mother my problem, so she answered, and I didn't follow her advice. I will repeat half of her letter, so you know what she thinks of the situation. I will also write to you about the message that my brother wrote to me. Oh, Gil, I sure wish it would work, but I guess I am through trying anymore. I will take your advice and move home for a while. I sure need it, and I should leave this house, too, but I guess I'll never learn.

My other reason for wanting to break up isn't as strong as the first reason. If I become a model, I will want to continue with it, not quit after getting married. It means so much to me because this is something I've wanted all my life, and if I can make a hit at it, it will be what I have been trying to obtain for so long. If I stick to it, for one thing, it will be the first time I have stuck with anything. That's why I can't give it up. And if I can't get to be a model in Cleveland, I want to go to New York City, go to a modeling school there, and maybe be a model. Then I can have my name in the paper. That is another ambition of mine. So, with my plans, we couldn't get married for quite a while. So, when you come back, I won't be around to see me, but you can call me if you want to talk to me.

It's not that I want to date anyone else because I don't. When I return to Cleveland after Christmas, this kid I know in the marines is home on leave and wants me to go out with him. He knows our situation, so I told him I might. After he leaves, I'm not going to go out with anyone. I may even just move out and away from here. Maybe go to New York now or go home and save money. I'm just running away from things as I always have done. Don't you agree that I need a psychologist?

That was the end of our relationship, allowing me to begin pursuing a modeling career and remain independent. But I should have been this objective about my future relationships when I chose to marry any of my husbands. I now ask, "Whatever happened to this grit?"

Modeling

A paradox! What was strange was that I didn't like the attention those men in the factory gave me, but I wanted to improve my looks to gain attention. So, during my first year at my job, I decided to go to modeling school, primarily to improve my looks. Billy Tilton's Modeling School and Agency offered a 10-week course that met once a week. Applying makeup was one of the lessons, and learning to walk a catwalk for fashion was another. I walked the short hallway on the top floor of Mrs. G's with a book balanced on my head to improve my posture. The school owner, Billy Tilton, told me I would never work as a model because I was too short to be a fashion model at five feet, three-and-a-half inches.

That was the wrong thing to tell me because of my rebellious nature, as I have mentioned before. Under my breath, I said, *No way. I'll show you I can model professionally.* It turns out that I became a slightly successful independent Cleveland model who competed for modeling jobs with his agency's models. Free-lance modeling was my first entrepreneurial enterprise, and I was the product.

The question was where or how to start as someone of 19 years of age with no experience. Billy Tilton, the Modeling School, nor anyone else I had ever known had prepared me for how to handle myself in a world of lustful men. As you can tell, I wasn't the wisest girl in the world all the time, and I was plain naïve. I answered an ad for a photographer, Johnnie, seeking a model for an industrial product. That photo appeared in the newspaper. It turned out that I was pretty photogenic, and I would, over time, get various modeling jobs with this photographer, who also became a mentor to me.

Not the Life I Imagined

Next, I answered an ad for a photography club. The club was located somewhere in downtown Cleveland, and it occupied a large room at the end of which was placed a massive roll of white paper for a backdrop in front of which I would stand. There was an array of photography lamps strategically placed for the best lighting of a model. This sort of setup I would encounter many times throughout my modeling career.

One of the photographers greeted me when I entered. I noticed various men standing around playing with their cameras. The man said, "You can take your clothes off behind the folding screen in the back." I thought, *No one told me I would have to model nude! Now, what am I going to do? I'm too afraid to leave, and I'm also scared to stay.* But I decided to make the best of it, grit my teeth and bear it. No pun intended here, *and whether it makes any difference between undressing behind a screen and standing naked in front of photographers.* I knew models who posed in the nude for art classes, but on this job, it was unexpected.

I left my high heels on, swallowed hard, and moved out and into position to pose. Without knowing how to take care of myself and never knowing how to say no, which I should have done when I discovered this situation, I found myself standing naked in front of a group of ogling men. I heard the click, click, click of cameras following the turns I made at a command from somewhere, "turn to your left, turn to your right, look over your shoulder," and so on.

The bright lights blinding my eyes prevented me from seeing their gawking and peeping stares. These lights became a saving grace for me. As the photographers shouted for me to turn, I might stop to hold my hand over my eyes, shielding them from the bright lights and to see what the men were saying. But unknown to me, one or two photographers in the group were into porn. They snapped illegitimate shots of me, making me look as if I were posing, such as a frontal view, which was illegal. That's when those rotten apples took their illicit photos. More about this later.

If it is true that we relive our childhood issues or traumas again in disguise (and we do in repetition compulsion), then how reminiscent of the town boys lined up in the barn. Of course, I did not understand this then and did not know this undertaking would end like this situation did.

The theory of repetition compulsion, discovered by Freud and other prominent theorists or therapists, has transformed slightly. As I understand it, repetition compulsion appears to be a childhood situation or behavior repeated over time by a person who had experienced trauma or something similar in childhood. There is an unconscious pressure to repeat the experience or deeds. The victim may unconsciously pursue the need to repeat the situation to learn an intrinsic lesson involved in the original circumstances or find a means of healing from the early trauma through empowerment or understanding. This doesn't explain how a person does something unknowingly as I did here, but I can guess that if I repeated the situation, knowing what to expect, it would be to find healing from the circumstance.

The camera club made it easier to occasionally take off all my clothes, or partially, in the future with Johnnie's selected shoots because I felt I could trust him due to his status as a professional photographer.

Little did I know or understand in those days about my body (or other women's bodies) being exploited; however, this was my modeling debut. It propelled me into many additional jobs with my clothes on throughout the years I modeled.

While on sales trips, Miles would stop in Cleveland to take me to dinner. By then, I had successfully suppressed the memory of his attempted seductions. He, by this point, had become a trusted confidant or mentor. I confided to him that I was modeling nude, and he told me that the pictures could end up on calendars that would inundate the Fate-Root-Heath Company in my small hometown of Plymouth, Ohio. His concern was that my mother would find out, which would be destructive to her. Here it was again, not to tell my mother. His solution was to suggest I go to college, a campaign he took to my mother.

Off to College

Surprisingly, my mother, disappointed and devastated when I quit business school, was open to the suggestion and tried to enroll me at her alma mater, Denison University, in Granville, Ohio. I took an admittance exam and performed poorly on it due to being out of high school for a couple of years or not using what I had learned (use it or lose it). They denied me admittance, which angered my mother so much that she stopped donating to their university.

Next, we explored Kent State University, and they had no such admittance torture to go through. So, I registered in the Theater Department due to my desire to become an actor.

It was the fall of 1953 when I started at KSU, the Korean War had ended, and many veterans also began attending Kent State. Dwight D. Eisenhower was another two-term president who left office in 1961.

During my year at Kent, I appeared in a few plays as an ingénue. Otherwise, life proceeded uneventfully while there. I acclimated to university life, met other guys to date, and competed against sorority girls in a beauty contest. Their sororities supported them, but I was a GDI—God Damm Independent. Even so, I was a runner-up. I lived off-campus with a couple of other "older" students in the home of a married couple with children. As for me academically, I was on the Dean's List in the first quarter, but my grades slipped to average during the subsequent two quarters due to my integration into college life and acting in the various plays.

During my year at Kent, an opportunity arose on spring break for me to go to New York City for an interview with Richard Aldrich, a theatrical producer, to become an apprentice at his professional summer stock theater, The Cape Playhouse on the Cape in Dennis, Massachusetts. There would be work with and around various well-known movie and stage actors.

Mr. Aldrich was a friend of Eleanor Whitney, a high school chum of my mother and aunt, who had had a brief operatic career before marrying Cornelius Vanderbilt Whitney. She recommended me for an interview, a process from which he chose ten apprentices for the summer season. Before meeting in New York City, I read *How to Win Friends and Influence People*. I applied some techniques during my interview, but I will never know if Mr. Aldrich selected me to be one of the ten on my own merits or if Eleanor Whitney had influenced his decision.

Eventually, I learned that about a year after my summer stock apprenticeship, Mr. Aldrich had become the Economic Counselor of the Embassy in Spain and Director of the United States Operations Mission, ICA. I have often wondered why he chose that transition.

CHAPTER 7

IMPRUDENT CHOICES

To do or not to do are not the right questions.
The question should be, "What will be
the consequence of my choice?"

—PENNY CHRISTIAN KNIGHT

Lessons

A brief journal excerpt of my summer stock experience follows:

> *It was the beginning of a delightful and exciting summer,*
> *and as I tried to fall asleep in my little roomette on the NYC*
> *train to New York, my stomach did flip-flops. This trip was*
> *my first long trip away from home alone. I suddenly felt so*
> *grown up and realized that, at last, I had blossomed into*
> *womanhood.*
>
> *Later, questions ran through my mind as I rode the day*
> *coach from New York to Massachusetts: What will it*
> *resemble? Will I like it? I noticed a few other girls riding*
> *in my car, and I wondered if they were going to the same*

place. I speculated whether the people coming to meet me would recognize me.

Immediately, as I stepped onto the platform at the train station in Yarmouth, I recognized the Playhouse station wagon and truck accompanied by three boys to greet me. I slowly walked over to them, and two girls from my train car did the same. The tall, thin blond-haired boy asked us if we were the girls headed for the Playhouse, and we answered we were. They loaded our gear into the truck and us into the station wagon. Once on our way to Dennis, I discovered the names of my companions. Woody Price was the driver of the station wagon. The cute girl with the small scar under her right eye was Sarah Woolsey from Chicago, having just completed her freshman year at Sarah-Lawrence College in New York. The other girl, Ellen Smith, was tall for 17 years and had just graduated from a high school in New Jersey.

We drove to the rear of a darling little cottage and piled out of the car. It was the apprentice cottage and would be our home for the rest of the summer. We entered the small house through the rear, which was the kitchen. It had been converted from a back porch and was replete with a sink, dishes, table, and icebox. Next to the kitchen was a bedroom containing two beds. The next room was our living room, and a bathroom was also downstairs.

Upstairs, we found two bedrooms; the one on the right of the stairs had three comparatively comfortable beds with a tiny closet. I chose that one. The bedroom at the head of the stairs had a couch bed and a double-decker bed with a nice walk-in closet. We also had a bathroom with a shower upstairs.

It was 1954, and I was 20 years old. I looked forward to working as a technical apprentice at The Cape Playhouse for the whole summer with great anticipation and excitement. During the summer, I met and fell in love with a young man from Boston, Ben R. He was working at the theater's campus restaurant for the summer to earn money to attend Boston College. Ben was Jewish and had served in the Korean War. He had the brightest eyes and the most brilliant smile of pearly whites I had ever seen. I think that is why I fell for him. His brown hair was short and curly.

As an apprentice, I got to work in various capacities to taste all aspects of a theater, from washing construction flats to becoming the backstage manager to working in the business office to chauffeuring stars appearing on the boards. We even selected, performed in, and presented an apprentice play of our own. And while doing all this, I was experiencing my romance.

I worked hard that summer. I intended to attend the American Academy of Dramatic Arts in New York City in the fall. Falling in love created a dilemma. Should I go to Boston to be close to my beloved at the end of the summer, or should I go to New York to seek my acting career? With advice from my then-ten-year-old brother, Fate, I chose to go to Boston.

When our season ended, and our work was finished, I moved to Brookline, Massachusetts, with Ben's help and settled into a third-floor walk-up extended-stay hotel owned by a Rabbi on Beacon Street. There was one large room with a bed, dresser, table, closet, and private bath. I shared a small community kitchen down the hall. The cooking implements were sparse, so I usually bought and warmed up various canned foods such as La Choy Chow Mein. It was not easy for me to choose a healthier diet.

If Only I Could Say No

Although I was still interested in acting, I wanted to pursue modeling in Boston. Before looking for a job, I took my portfolio to visit a modeling agency. I was very timid and had to push myself forward to do these things, even though I had somewhat come out of my shell during the summer. I had more comfortably pursued modeling in Cleveland, where I had lived, but I was unfamiliar with Boston.

Before going to the agency, I stopped for a Coke at a drugstore soda fountain for time to gain some courage. A man in a suit approached and sat next to me.

"And what are you doing here, young lady?" he inquired.

"Oh," (I was always too frank and honest), "I'm looking for some modeling work, and I am going to the modeling agency," I said shyly. [*Today, I don't recall its name.*]

"Let me see your book."

"Here." I could not see any reason not to let him see my modeling collection. He turned the pages while looking at my various photos.

"These are very nice. My name, by the way, is Larry Maturi. My brother is Victor Mature, the movie star, and I can help you get some work and possibly into the movies if that would interest you." He even resembled Victor Mature.

I had not told him that I was interested in acting, too. "Yes, yes, I would," I said eagerly. "And my name is Penny Christian." Excited, my heart started beating rapidly as I imagined this was my big break. Many stars, at least some stars, had allegedly been discovered on a soda fountain stool, but I never believed it would happen to me and in Boston.

"Well, okay, I'll hold an audition for you. Come with me where we can have some privacy." [Imagine the Wolf and Little Red Riding Hood.]

I thought he had an office nearby, but he drove me to his home. He had me pose and walk in his living room as if on a runway. But after that, he said, "Take your clothes off so I can get a better look at your body." *[How naive can anyone be?]* I discovered that I could do this because of my nude modeling experience, even though I wanted it no more.

Then, he touched me. I felt full of fear and could not move or speak. There was no place to run to and lock me in safety. He fondled my breasts, caressed, and kissed them. Next, he moved to my genitals, kissed me there, and stroked me with his tongue while I stood frozen. Feeling like a statue, I could not move or respond because I was paralyzed, mentally and physically. My early sex abuse would not allow me to react sensually to any stimulation. I was afraid to say no for fear of what he would do to me, so I had to let him have his way.

Thank God he did not attempt to penetrate me, but all of this was bad enough. After he was through with me, I was then able to move. I got dressed, and he took me back to the drugstore. I took a subway train home. I felt so mortified. But also, I felt lucky to still be alive. "It could have been worse," I told myself, with my usual, "It doesn't really matter." I never did get to the modeling agency after that.

But it did not end there. I had innocently given Maturi my phone number, and he called ceaselessly. I had to go down the hotel's three flights of stairs to receive his calls on a public phone. I felt everyone knew what he had done to me, burdening me with shame and embarrassment. I didn't know how to get him out of my life, but I still felt I had to be kind to him. Finally, I knew I had to find a way to leave Boston and go to New York City. Sure that relocation would end his calls, I decided to run away.

I might have stopped his assault if my childhood molestation had not occurred, but I had no voice; therefore, I could not or did not know how to say *"no."* That word was never accepted or acknowledged while growing up. Just as in learned helplessness, I had learned that no one could hear it.

Toddlers seem to learn the word *no* and say it a lot until their parents get upset with hearing it so frequently, and they tell them to stop it or somehow instruct their child to stop saying it. The word *no* is the most essential word they can learn, but they also need to determine where they can use it.

I can see now that he was a wolf in sheep's clothing, and I was like Little Red Riding Hood. If only I could have seen that then. I was way too trusting and naïve.

While writing this book, I researched something online when I found some articles on "tonic immobility." Tonic immobility is when the body becomes rigid and motionless during sexual assault or rape, just like mine did with me. I was not passive; **I was temporarily paralyzed!** Surprisingly, I had never heard of this before.

In one of the studies, I read that 88 percent of sexual assault victims experience this condition in which the body becomes paralyzed. It appears to be instinctual. The sympathetic nervous system responds to the trauma and fear engendered by the assault. During this survival response, the conscious mind shuts down from its ability to choose what it should do (such as fight back), and then the *freeze instinct* kicks in as a third alternative to the fight or flight response. **This paralysis is considered normal and healthy.** If a victim appears as dead prey (paralysis), the predator will not be interested (animal studies). If my predator had any thought of penetration, he might have lost his interest due to my lack of response.

After discovering this information, I became eager to share it with other survivors. This information seeks to eliminate guilt, shame, and unwarranted self-accusations. (In my case, I felt that I might have led him on by undressing to his command and then rationalizing it.) Both could eventually lead to depression, anxiety, and PTSD (Post Traumatic Stress Disorder).

Aftermath

Following my encounter with Maturi, I did my best to suppress the experience and its effects. As usual, I told no one. It was another secret to torment my body at some level. I never revealed anything I had ever experienced as a victim to anyone. Was this eating away at me internally? I did not know to whom to communicate these experiences or where I could get help. I felt such humiliation, so I put it away from me as best I could. *It doesn't really matter,* I told myself as usual.

The only reminder of what had happened was the constant daily phone calls from that man I now know was a predator. In those days, television was a distant luxury, and neither was the media present to warn young girls and others of the dangers of talking to strangers, even when someone is 20 years old. The only warning I ever received from my mother about anything sexual was that all men wanted was sex and, of course, "What will the neighbors think?" Well, that was indeed true in this case.

It was also the same with Ben. He wanted sex, too. But, when I was wrapped in his warm arms, begging for his passionate kisses, yearning for stimulation from my genitals, I finally wanted sex, too. But, with Ben, the first real sexual relationship of my choosing was a colossal disappointment. On my bed, within my room's privacy, Ben made love to me in the only way he knew. As I've heard the phrase stated, he was "on-again, off-again Finnegan," Perhaps it was premature ejaculation. Maybe he was so excited to be with me that way, but if that were the case, I think he would have been able to prolong his climax with time. I did not know then what I needed in the way of stimulation.

I didn't know how to communicate what I liked because I had no clue and would have been too embarrassed to request anything anyway. I was also internally fighting my mental demons from the childhood sex abuse that prevented me from enjoying sex as I fantasized every other female I knew, or had heard of, enjoyed it. Why not me? It just wasn't as superior as it should have been. Perhaps I needed a man who understood my body even when I didn't comprehend it. As for my mental demons, I had never told a soul about my early sex abuse or the Maturi molestation, mostly because I had repressed it.

What is that song? *"I can't get no satisfaction."* It was the beginning of the end for Ben and me. There was another thing that was going on for him. I am not sure if his parents were Orthodox Jews or Conservative, but they gave him an edict when he told them about me, a Gentile and a Christian. They told him they would disinherit him if he insisted on marrying me. They also asked him what kind of parents I had who would allow me to travel all over the country alone. Remember, this was 1954. Considering what had happened to me, I wondered the same thing. His parents' position disturbed him greatly. He said, "I can serve our country in the military, but I can't even marry the girl I love." His sister stood up for him, but that didn't help much.

He started doing weird things that were scary to me. For one thing, while upset over his parents, he tore the transmission out of his nearly new car by driving too fast and stripping gears. And on another occasion, one night, as we sat in my community kitchen, he took out some dollar bills and rolled them into objects looking like straws (something like cocaine users use to snort cocaine). But then, he would light them with a match and burn them up. This behavior frightened me, and I began to create an escape plan. From him. From Maturi.

I decided to proceed to New York as I had initially planned, although it was too late to enroll at the Academy. Since I never got to the modeling agency, I worked in the Loan Division of Norfolk County Bank at Coolidge Corners in Brookline. I was assigned to collections, another tough job for me as I hated to ask people to make payments on their loans. I had been living in Brookline for about three months.

I contacted Mr. Aldrich, the producer I had apprenticed for at The Cape Playhouse, to ask if he thought I had any talent. He affirmed that I did and suggested the Allerton House for Women at 57th Street and Lexington for lodgings. He also set me up for a clerk-typist position in the office of a theatrical attorney, David M. Holtzmann.

Before relocating to New York, I also had to prepare to leave Boston. Initially, I tried to get out of my room obligation. I still was not of legal age (21 in Massachusetts), but I had signed a lease agreement accepting financial responsibility for my lease term, which ran monthly. It was still early in the month, and I had the remainder to pay, and the rabbi would not let me out of this contract. I couldn't afford to pay him and move to New York, so I arranged to sneak out.

I had made friends with Jim and Nancy, a slightly older couple who occupied a suite at the basement level. Steps led up and outside onto the street from their level, and I could entirely bypass the lobby. But I had to somehow get my trunk and suitcases down to their level without being seen. They would help me out onto the street and into a taxi. And the rabbi wouldn't see me because I would not have to go through the lobby. And that is what we did. The night before I was to leave, Jim helped me down the back stairs with my trunk. It took a couple more trips to take my three suitcases down, and I had only one bag left that I could carry when I was ready to leave. And I started early in the morning.

Survival

In addition to being afraid to tell Maturi I was leaving, it was the same or more problematic telling Ben that we were through and that I was ending our relationship. I was dreadfully afraid of hurting him, as I was with almost anyone I knew. This fear always kept me in relationships long after they should have ended. Instead, I told him I had to go to New York to get the acting bug out of my system, which was also correct. Unfortunately, that kept our line of communication open, allowing him to visit me in New York. Still, I was stuck on how to break up with him. Next, I resigned from my position at the bank.

The taxi took me to the train station. Somehow, I got my luggage loaded. My Boston experience was like a nightmare with all the anxiety of my exit from the hotel. This included the pressures I didn't know how to deal with.

Life in New York was not all I had imagined it to be, either. In the 1950s, New Yorkers seemed aloof to me. Maybe it was my shyness, but no one ever offered a "hello" or "how is your day?" Neither did I because I didn't know how to start a conversation with a stranger. Even on the elevators, also today, where no one anywhere speaks, there was silence as I ascended to the floor of my tiny room. I barely remember it. It was not anything extraordinary. There was a bed, dresser, small table, and a chair with an adjoining bathroom. The room seemed to be about 9 feet by 10 feet or smaller. I recently Googled the room's size, and it appears it was 225 square feet, but I think that included the bathroom. There was one window where I could look out at the world to see if it was friendly yet.

Mr. Holtzmann's office was something else. By contrast, it was enormous. I felt like a Lilliputian moving through the thick carpet as if I were crawling in the tremendously tall grass of a jungle. I was unable to make friends with anyone there. A vendor brought a coffee and doughnuts cart around every morning. I was more inclined to talk to him since he was not as intimidating should I err in grammar or protocol.

These experiences describe my first week in New York. I think my tenure with Mr. Holtzmann was about two to three weeks. I felt like Petunia, the character I played in "I'm a Lonely Little Petunia in an Onion Patch," an elementary-school play in the third grade. Lyrics can be found at https://www.youtube.com/watch?v=1g9bzcB-ME_I. (Accessed May 26, 2019.) The title is the first part of the lyrics, which expresses how lonely I felt.

One night I found a movie theater. The movie playing was *Lili* with Leslie Caron. The character was lonely and naïve, and I over-identified with her. *Lili* reminded me of how my recent experience made me feel. While walking to the movie, I passed Van

Johnson, the movie star. He was walking alone, which excited me because he was one of my favorite movie stars. But I only nodded to him, wishing I dared to speak.

Ben came down from Boston on weekends and stayed at a hotel. Of course, I went to his hotel room, where we had sex as quickly as usual. I was relieved to see him leave, and he, at that point, was not helping my loneliness.

Then, something strange happened. I became very nauseous. I somehow hid it at work, but I ran to the bathroom to vomit when I got up in the morning. Nausea became a constant companion, and I wondered what was wrong with me.

I called Jim, assistant stage manager from The Cape Playhouse, who lived somewhere unknown to me in New York, quite a distance from where I was, and told him I needed a friend and someone to talk with. He told me how to take the subway to his place. When I got there, I found it soothing to be near someone I knew, with whom I felt safe. I explained my dilemma, and he was incredibly supportive. He gave me the name of a doctor I should see.

I visited his doctor, who gave me the fateful news: "You are pregnant!"

Pregnant? How could that be? I guess I don't even know the first thing about it. That also explains why my breasts are sore and getting bigger. Oh, my, what am I going to do now?

I had no question whose baby it was. It was Ben's. But what did that mean to all my plans for acting? Would I now have to marry him? I would never get away from him! How would I survive in this world pregnant? I shared some of this information with the doctor.

The doctor gave me a pill instructing me, "This medicine should start your period, but you should come back to see me if it doesn't." I went home, dutifully took the pill, and waited for it to take effect, which it did not. I was disappointed but decided against going back to see him. That was a life-changing decision because now I think that he or someone else might have aborted the fetus, and I would have been able to continue with my plans and stay in New York.

I thought hard about what to do. I was genuinely fearful about what would happen to me. I thought about writing my mother and telling her, but I wouldn't be able to do that because not being allowed to say anything to her that would be upsetting. Finally, I decided to write to her anyway and tell her I had a problem I could not explain. I communicated to her that I was no good. She wrote, "*I strongly feel your problem is that you are pregnant. We want you to come home. We love you no matter what you have done, just as we did when you were a little girl.*" My letter to her was the first time I ever let anyone in the family in on a secret, and it turned out okay. I did not have to suppress it as I did everything else that had happened to me in my life, even though I did afterward. And it felt good to hear that my mother loved me. I didn't remember ever hearing it.

So, off I went again, not escaping so much as surviving. When I made it home, I felt safe and not as lonely. We sat and discussed what to do about "my problem." My mother told me that she had aborted a fetus before getting pregnant with my younger brother. So, my parents decided that I should get an abortion because I could not become a single mother and put all my career plans on hold. Being a traveling salesman at the time, my stepfather had traveled to many locations where he could locate a doctor to perform the abortion. The abortion had to be done in secret because it was illegal then, but I did not have an opinion about it one way or the other. He found someone.

We went to a doctor's office somewhere out of town, and the doctor packed me with gauze and whatever else. He told me I would abort spontaneously in about three days. We contacted our local doctor, who said he could not participate in the abortion but was willing to look at the results and ensure I would not hemorrhage or whatever else might occur.

CHAPTER 8

A NEW DIRECTION

Being human means, you will make mistakes.
And you will make mistakes because failure is God's way
of moving you in another direction.

—OPRAH WINFREY (COMMENCEMENT ADDRESS
AT JOHNSON C. SMITH U., MAY 16, 2016)

Life Goes On

The time came, and I aborted. Mother put in a call to our doctor. If anyone was listening in or tapping the phone, she said, "We have the puppies for you to see." He came over from Shiloh, the small town where we lived when I was eight, and told us everything looked in order. So, life goes on. And we never talked about it again. It was a **secret, even from us.**

Members of Alcoholics Anonymous and other 12-step groups state that we are as sick as our secrets. Their fourth step involves a searching and fearless moral inventory of yourself, and the fifth step is to admit to God, yourself, and another human being the exact nature of your wrongs. These steps include mistakes other than secrets, but they could also be the secrets that compel a person to self-medicate by drinking or using drugs in the first place. I see this memoir as my fourth and fifth steps, even though I am not an alcoholic or drug addict. Also, as I unburden myself of my secrets, I feel lighter and less impeded.

I decided that I would never have sex again. No one had ever talked to me about contraception. Wasn't this another teachable moment? If someone ever told me about it, I would have asked, "What is that? How do I do it?" The easiest way for me then was not to have sex in the first place. And besides, it had never been pleasant. It was abusive; it was dirty; it was disappointing, and it was unsatisfying.

While I was at home, Ben kept calling me every day. We had one landline; cell phones were not available yet, thank goodness. I refused to talk to him and asked my parents to tell him I was out. Of course, I never returned his calls. Yes, he knew about the pregnancy, but not anything following it. Finally, Miles told me one day that I had to explain to Ben that it was over. I was scared to death to do so. Remember that I did not want to hurt anyone? It was frightening to think of how it would impact him, especially after he showed such a terrible lack of emotional control when receiving bad news.

I don't recall today what I said, but I know I stammered and stuttered. Ben got the message, and I could tell he was genuinely hurt, but I got no more calls from him. I hoped a lot that he would forgive me.

It was time for me to go in a new direction. The former one was no longer feasible at this point, it seemed. So, I contacted George, one of the young men I had dated in Cleveland just before college. George resembled Gordon McRae, the actor/singer. He and a friend had even visited me at the Cape Playhouse during the summer. George had always been a pleasant young man, and I trusted him. He had never imposed any desire he might have had for sex. He invited me to a New Year's Eve party in Cleveland and to stay at his house. I accepted with delight. One of the aunts who helped raise him after the death of his parents lived there. I felt I would be safe.

So, I took the train to Cleveland. Of course, I don't remember much about the party except that I had fun and probably drank a little too much. We started making love when we returned to his house exceptionally late in the evening. This time he wanted sex. My resolve about not having it raced through my mind. I liked George very much and didn't want to let him down. It never occurred to me that I would let myself down if I gave in. I did not want him to call me a tease. He was gentle and loving and didn't climax right off the bat. Up to a point, I enjoyed the lovemaking. But I did not experience an orgasm, which I never did anyway. Afterward, I fell asleep in his arms. That was nice. However, I was fraught with guilt and shame. I felt guilty because it happened after the abortion and my resolve never to have sex again. Two weeks had not gone by before I was again engaged in it. Shame because I continued to feel like a hussy and worthless. Would I ever enjoy sex and feel and accept that it was a natural way of life?

I have a diary entry from this trip dated **January 1, 1955:**

We now embark on a new and, I know, more excellent year. [I'm always optimistic] *Ah, yes, I had no hangover except being tired. George was in the same condition. We sat around watching the Navy-Mississippi game. Then we went to Snagel's house. Everyone came there. After the Rose Bowl game, we went to Cobb's house or apartment and had a snack. All the kids were there, but soon, they were going to a party. Three couples, Todd and Shirley, Al and Robin, plus George and me, went to see the midnight movie 20,000 Leagues Under the Sea. We came straight home after.*

And here is another entry from **January 2, 1955:**

I slept late and was very lazy. Al and his sister came over, and we went to Nancy and Dick's house. We didn't stay long as I had to catch my train back home, and George took me to the station. I watched TV after I returned home.

There is a mention of television. Even though I did not personally own a set, TV became available to others. These diary entries do not mention intimacy, but it occurred as described above.

After returning to Plymouth, I began planning to return to Cleveland to live and find a job and an apartment. On January 3, I turned 21 and could have my first legal drink. In short order, I achieved all these goals and became immersed in my life in Cleveland once again, as noted by the following diary entries for that time:

January 6, 1955: *I went to Cleveland today with Miles and spent an hour and a half on the phone. I found out Carol Barge was marrying Capt. Tyler and moving to Oklahoma. I looked at two places and took one with Genevieve F. on Hessler Road. It has six rooms-three bedrooms, one dining room, one kitchen, one bath, and one living room.* [This was in the same vicinity of Western Reserve University, where I had lived before going to Kent State.] *It is nice and only a block from Euclid, Moe's, and civilization. Drove down to Kent and saw Phyllis* [my former Kent roommate] *and the Roes* [my previous landlords]. *I stayed in Cleveland at Mrs. Diego's.* [I don't remember who this was].

January 8, 1955: *I bought a 1950 Chevrolet today. It is so wonderful to own your first car. Of course, it isn't my own, but it will be after I make my last payment. Payments are due on the 30th. I told my mother, and she was happy. I took Dorothy to the Pullman tonight and brought Kenny home.*

January 9, 1955: *I packed Miles' car and mine with all my junk, and we drove to Cleveland to my new address on Hessler Road. They left, and I did a little unpacking. I called Carol and went over after her, then up to Jan's apartment. After there, we went to Connie's apartment. We went to the Pizza Palace, took Carol home, and then Connie.* [These all were former residents of Magnolia Manor.]

January 10, 1955: *I parked in a no-parking zone and got a three-dollar ticket. I went to Lake City Employment Agency (employer pays) to look for a job. They're sending me to Carlings Brewery. I went to Frails'* [former high school coach] *for dinner and stayed until nine.*

January 11, 1955: *I went to Carlings Brewery* [not too far from my first Cleveland business job] *for my interview to be a receptionist and switchboard operator. And I got it. I paid my parking fine today.*

January 12, 1955: *I went to work and operated the switchboard at noon. It was a lot of fun, and I know I'm going to like it there.*

January 13, 1955: *I stayed home tonight. Operated the switchboard all night long.* [In my dreams.]

Was this all a new direction or a repeat of the one before? It was not long before the answer to this question revealed itself. I did not live in that new apartment for more than a couple of months, partly due to my much older roommate. I don't remember much about her, but she jeopardized my safety, if not hers. She went to local bars at night and brought home all kinds of strangers, and they had sex in her bedroom. This practice of hers made me a little uneasy, considering my background.

I found another woman my age, Pat, who also worked at the Brewery. She was also looking for a roommate. We found an apartment to share in Cleveland Heights. It was a three-room furnished apartment in an old brick building. The bedroom was at one end of the apartment, and the kitchen was in the middle, followed by the living room.

Pat and I got along well and became close friends. Later I asked her to be my matron of honor at my first wedding. In the meantime, we respected each other's privacy as much as possible within three rooms.

When Will I Ever Learn?

Soon after moving to the apartment and becoming reacquainted with my former friends, I visited Pops. He played my father in *Susan and God* while I attended Kent State. Being older, he had always taken the mentor or surrogate father role with me. He was another man I felt I could trust. His wife, also a friend, wasn't home. I wanted to share my summer stock adventures, Ben in Boston, pregnancy, and abortion. I needed his perspective on what I had been through by letting my secret out. It was like slowly releasing the air out of the neck of a balloon, a little bit at a time, to see how much I would tell him.

He prepared tea for me and asked, "Would you like some wine?" I consented to the wine to put me more at ease. It also loosened my tongue and inhibitions, and I told him too much.

Before I knew it, I soon took off my clothes and found myself in bed with him. I thought, *Maybe I trusted him too much. How did this happen?* What had happened to my great resolve not to have sex again? I was breaking it for the second time. Maybe I thought that with his being older and married, he might know how to make love and that I might at last experience some satisfaction in sex.

But guess what? I still got no satisfaction and felt only shame for what had occurred. This episode ended our relationship, and I thought I would never be able to face his wife again. My days in Boston had unleashed a false nympho in me, or I had become a naïve seducible target for men. I was far from being a nympho, so the latter seemed to fit.

A Surprising Modeling Restart

After working at the Brewery for a couple of months from the start of the New Year, I decided to go to a locally renowned hairdresser called Joe Portaro for a new hairdo. He also had a television show, and I told him I had modeled before. He bleached my hair blond and asked if I would be interested in modeling for him on television and learning how to apply makeup on patrons as he traveled around the local area. Of course, the break attracted me, and it sounded like another opportunity for me to be discovered. He paired me with Joanne, another "Portaro-made blonde," and we became his primary models. I learned from him how to do makeovers with various makeup tricks. Later, as a marketing promotion, he colored my hair a beautiful shade of blue. In retrospect, this experience must have been a Divine intervention, starting with the thought of getting my hair done.

I quit my job at Carlings and found a means of income with a couple of temp agencies filling my financial gaps (secretarial, the career my mother initially picked for me!). And I also began to free-lance as a model and had my job with Portaro. Once again, I was off and running to do work I enjoyed, with the prospect of some fame. But this is not a story about my careers, which only serve as back-drops and are incidental to the sexual assaults I suffered, seeking sex-ual satisfaction, or searching for someone to love me.

Also, I dated George briefly until my hair was colored blue. I went to one last party with him, and then we drifted apart. I kept trying to find modeling jobs independently by marketing myself (no agency involvement) and by word of mouth. Also, this year, Cole and I found each other again and dated sporadically.

Enter Stage Right—The Police

While modeling when I could, I was active with Portaro for a few months during 1955 but had to continue supplementing my income by working for the temp agencies. The temp agency assigned me to various secretarial jobs throughout Cleveland. While working for a company in one of the tall buildings downtown (the same office mentioned earlier from which I saw the man jacking off so far below), two police detectives walked through the door. I was alone in the front office. They introduced themselves and asked for me. I wondered how they knew who I was and had located me on a temp job and why they were looking for me. But, after all, they were detec-tives. They said, "We're working on a case where your name came up, and we located you. We would like you to come to the station to help us with our case."

They told me I was not being arrested, but I was curious about how I could know anything about their case. I asked my temporary employer if he would excuse me for the rest of the day. He signed my timecard, and I left with the detectives. On our way to the police station, I kept wondering who I knew or what could have happened so that I would be able to help them with their case. When we got to the police station, they took me to a bare interview room to show me some photos they had confiscated. That is when I discovered the reason they were looking for me. I didn't think I had ever done anything illegal, but they accused me.

They said, "We found your name written on the photos we confiscated from two men in a porn ring. Here, this picture shows you posing with this frontal view." Please recall that movies in this era did not include nudity and sexual display like today. I knew I had never posed like that, but someone had taken the photos secretly and unknown to me. Remember how I described my experience at the photography club? I started to sweat. My hands became drenched and began to shake as I commenced thinking that I was in deep trouble and that they might arrest me for being a part of this porn ring, which I was not. *Would they believe me?*

I said, "I didn't pose for that picture!" I told them about the photography club. "I know that it looks like I did with my hand over my eyes, looking like I was saluting or something, but I promise you, I never posed for this picture or any other photo you might conceivably have of me! If I could not hear someone's directions for a pose, I would hold my hand over my eyes because the lights were so bright that I had to shield them. That way, I could see what the photographers were saying." I didn't know if this made sense to them.

I explained the circumstances under which I had worked at the photo club. "I was just starting to work as a model and didn't know what I was getting myself into at that club. I didn't know I would model in the nude, but I was unaware of how to get out of it when I got there, so I took my clothes off and posed as requested. I would never have posed purposely like in that photo. They made me a victim of their illegal activity!"

I hoped the detectives believed me and prayed to God once again under my breath to get me out of this situation, and I would never let myself become involved again in making such poor choices as I had made in this case. Maturi came to mind. Scott came to mind. Toby came to mind, and at the same time, I wondered what mistakes I might make in the future.

"Okay," one of them said, "that makes sense. There are no other pictures here of you."

"How did you find out this picture was of me?"

"Your name was on the back of it."

"Okay. Then, am I free to go?"

"Yes. We'll take you back to your building. But we will keep you on file if you aren't telling us the truth, and we will find more pictures of you. But, for the most part, you can relax."

When I think about how things are today and how the internet circulates pictures in no time, I am so grateful this occurred long before such a thing was possible. I could see how something like this would have ruined my reputation before I was wise enough to worry about such a thing.

Serendipity

There were other curious happenings while I worked for this same employer in the same tall building. It appeared to be Fate or serendipity. Another day while working there, a solicitor walked through the door. He was selling beautiful large family-heirloom Bibles. We got to talking, and I discovered he was from Boston. I told him about Ben and my short adventure there. It turned out that he knew Ben. He informed me that Ben worked in Manhattan then as a shoe salesman. I found it so hard to believe, but I took his word. And I bought one of his Bibles. *Maybe I could be saved.*

A couple of years ago, I wrote the following just for myself when I realized it was an event that helped me grow more humanely than anything else. It happened around this same time when my modeling career was blooming.

I have a story to tell. It is about a man who traveled many miles through a snowstorm for a woman who stood him up for a date. She had given no thought to that man struggling through the snow to see her. Another opportunity appealed to her more, so she left a note on the door that she was sorry but had to go somewhere suddenly. The man also left a note that referred to a barrel of apples with one rotten apple inside, and he had picked that apple.

When the woman returned home, she found the note. Her conscience struck when she realized she was the rotten apple and never wanted to be referred to as such again. She began to feel compassion for the man who had traveled so far in a snowstorm to see her. She thought about how selfish she had been and how unkind she was. How could she go about her life without thinking of others and what they might be experiencing? That was a significant turning point in that woman's life. Afterward, she began thinking about what others were going through and became kinder, gentler, more caring, considerate, and compassionate.

This story is about me. The man was Jack, the young man who took me on his father's sailboat the day I ran away from home. His note made all the difference in my striving to become a better person because what he wrote effectively raised my consciousness.

Starting Over Again and Again and Again

Modeling was sporadic, and my work with Portaro began dwindling, so I had to take a full-time office manager position with a small company. I worked for a Jewish entrepreneur who may have been grooming me for himself from the beginning. He showed me the ropes for managing the office, which I later applied to run my own business. He also taught me how to make deposits, run to the bank, do general accounting, etc. I had learned some bookkeeping while in business school but was never very adept at it. But Sam (not his real name) taught it all to me. I even helped him with his public relations, went to trade shows with him, and helped him do his job in an affiliated association's beauty pageant. He would invite me to lunch frequently to discuss the business and other necessary things. I felt vital, and I was the only female working there.

Sam was married and had a lovely wife who stopped by the office often. I don't recall how it happened, but I believe it began with his gratitude for my work. I think he started to touch my hand or arm as a gesture of appreciation. At some point, he progressed to kissing me. He was not that appealing because he was older, large, and past his prime. But with my father's absence from my early life, I began to lean on Sam like a father.

After starting this job, my roommate Pat became pregnant, and I thought I could find her an abortionist through a person I met at a trade show where I had modeled. He was in the Teamsters Union. In return, the man asked for sexual favors from us both. I don't remember what Pat said, but I told the man I had an STD, and he let me off the hook. Whew! I was starting to get a little wiser, but I still had a long way to go.

Pat and I lived together until around the end of 1955. I then moved into a studio apartment with Sam's help and design. Now he could visit me whenever he liked. I cannot recall if we had sex, but I think we must have. It is amazing what one can do to block out unpleasant memories. It was a secret, even from me. I began to feel the shame of this arrangement, though, and quit my job with Sam and returned to Magnolia Manor, where I could afford to live independently again. It was the beginning of 1956 when my modeling finally began to take off big time. Mrs. G's seemed like a good starting-over place. It was safe, where no man could get to me without passing the house owner in her housecoat and long-ash-dangling cigarette. And that would not happen. I moved during the same year as Miss Cleveland and Jet Air Age pageants.

On my return, I shared a much larger room with an older woman, a beauty-products sales clerk at Higbee's. We did not share much in common. I didn't need to hang out any longer at Moe's, the college bar we all used to visit. I had been to college, to Boston, to New York, had an abortion, was, to some extent, a mistress, and was becoming a successful model. Life could be different now if only I could find the way.

Modeling truthfully is not as glamorous as it appears to be. It is a lot of hard work. A model might have to hold a pose indeterminately during a shoot while lights, shadows, and other items are arranged. These poses are one reason models need to be fit because a long-held pose makes a person stiff and full of pain. I was fit, but not by today's standards. I never worked out. Swimming and walking were my only exercise. I was fortunate to appear more fit than I actually was. But I was shapely and attractive. Being attractive, though, called forth all the lechers and predators in the businesses with whom I modeled.

Miss Cleveland Pageant

It didn't hurt for models to enter beauty pageants because they aided a modeling career. I participated in a few minor contests and came close to winning. But then came the large one, Miss Cleveland, a preliminary to Miss Ohio and possibly to Miss America.

The only talent I had developed by that time was acting. I had never learned to sing, but I did at age 65 when I finally took lessons for around six years. Perhaps I could have danced, but I quit after high school and did not dance in the interim. I could never twirl a baton successfully or play the piano or any other instrument then. However, when I was 35, I started violin lessons, which ceased after receiving my graduate degree in 1984 at age 50. Of course, the ability to afford lessons of any kind had not been available to me then. The pageant was five years after high school.

So, I decided acting would be my talent. And I looked around for something to perform. I decided on a prose poem called "I Am Man," created by my mother in the book she wrote and self-published called, *The Dams Can Break*. The poem had two parts: Man and Spirit.

I decided to stage and costume it using a choir robe for *Spirit* over my costume for *Man*. At the time, I was still living at Magnolia Manor, so it was difficult, at best, to rehearse anything more strenuous. I felt prepared at pageant time.

Many other contestants had sponsors or people to subsidize them. I didn't have that luxury and had to do everything on my own, the real story of my life. I found a one-piece yellow bathing suit suitable for the pageant. My dress was strapless with off-the-shoulder sleeves, a tight bodice that showed my well-proportioned body (36-24-34), and a full skirt with a hooped petticoat.

I was lucky to find a light blue-green evening gown that resembled (to me) the ball gowns worn by Scarlet O'Hara in *Gone with the Wind*. (This was my favorite movie, and I sat through this movie twice when eight. Because I was gone so long, my worried mother searched the town for me only to find me in the darkened movie theater, enthralled with Scarlett O'Hara and in love with Clark Gable.)

One of the judges was a photographer for whom I had worked. He had given me advice he thought would probably assist me when the judges looked at me. He said, "Play down your eye makeup because the judges don't like heavy eye makeup."

Well, I did not think I wore heavy eye makeup, to begin with, and I was in a quandary about whether to wear any. I trusted his word and thought I might have an advantage over some of the other women. So, I went without eyeshadow. Playing down my makeup was a huge mistake because all the other women wore heavy eye makeup. Sometime later, I learned how important it is to make up one's eyes when appearing on a stage because audiences (or judges) cannot see a person's eyes without eye makeup. The eyes just fade away. I could have added eyeshadow, but another error happened when I got ready at home and did not bring my makeup. Models always have their makeup with them. If only I had had an advisor.

A delightful woman, Sandra, and her police officer husband, Richard, organized us backstage. I tried to set up everything, so I could make quick changes. That is when I discovered I had left my hooped slip at home. This discovery sent me into a tailspin, and I began to weep, which caused what little eye makeup I had to run, making my eyes fade even more.

Sandra told Richard, who had brought his friend, Bill, a firefighter. Bill said he would run for it and try to get it back to me by the program's evening gown portion. I brightened a little and called my rooming house on a payphone backstage (no cell phone in the 1950s) to alert Mrs. G to get my hoop ready, so I would not have to walk on stage in a wimpy evening gown.

The firefighter came to the rescue, but not for a fire other than the one in my heart. He made it in time.

However, this tumult took the spirit out of me, and I wasn't my best with bloodshot eyes from crying plus no eye makeup. I did my best to pull myself together for the competition. I think I did a decent job on my acting, but hindsight tells me I should have introduced the piece as my mother's poem, and I should not have picked such a severe and unique piece to perform because of the somber nature of the selection.

Robbie, the Miss Cleveland title winner, went on to win the Miss Ohio title. She sang "On the Street Where You Live" from *My Fair Lady*. Robbie deserved the title, and I believe she had a sponsor. Robbie wore heavy eye makeup and glittered, and she sang well.

How did I do? Well, not so bad, considering all that happened that night. I was the third runner-up. How did I feel about that? Well, I felt proud, and it was decent publicity for me. Photos of contestants were in the papers, which probably helped my modeling career.

I met some delightful people. If I had decided to do so, I could have entered the contest again another year, perhaps with a different talent that I could have developed in the meantime and with heavy eye makeup.

Miss Jet Air Age Pageant

Following the Miss Cleveland contest, I entered a couple of other beauty contests that did not require talent. One was the Miss Jet Air Age of 1956 pageant conducted in Cleveland. I no longer recall what was involved, but basically, it eliminated the 80 contestants, and I ended up winning it. This contest sponsored enlisting 50 young Northern Ohio men into the United States Air Force. After swearing into the service while they stood on a dais in Cleveland's Public Square, they became known as the Jet Air Age Buddy Platoon. I appeared with them in my bathing suit and was known as their "mascot." Afterward, my court (runners-up) and I visited the 79th Fighter Group at Youngstown Air Force base and the Cuyahoga County Fair. My prize was a trip to San Antonio Air Force Base to visit the Buddy Platoon I sponsored. I had a stopover in Chicago for television and radio appearances and a motorcade in which I appeared riding in an open convertible.

In San Antonio, the mayor greeted me when I disembarked from the plane on my arrival. Instead of offering me the key to the city, he presented me with a certificate naming me an honorary mayor of La Villita, the original San Antonio. La Villita is a small community that has undergone various upgrades, from a tiny Native American settlement to Spanish soldiers' residency to European immigrant businesses and trades to the Arts Community, the last time I checked. At the time of my visit, I had the honor of being only the fourth person to receive this accolade, which would allow me to become mayor anytime I visited there, but I have not been back since. Another person who held this distinction was actress Dale Evans, Roy Rogers' wife.

Sergeant Sarkozy, an Air Force Public Relations person, made all the arrangements and accompanied me on the trip. While at Lackland, I stayed in the officer quarters. I dressed in a six-foot Airman's fatigues with sleeves and pant legs rolled up to fit my 5'3½" frame for photographs on the obstacle course. I almost jumped from the parachute tower, reviewed a parade in my honor, and Sgt. Sarkozy and others presented me at a local baseball game.

As for the parachute tower, I confess I was too afraid to jump, so the men hooked me to wires on the ground and hoisted me close to the top. Then they released me for a slide down the cables. I had never experienced a full-body thrill like that when the blood pumped wildly through my veins. I changed my mind about jumping, but there was no time for a second try. Upon my return to Cleveland, I discovered the title of Miss Jet Air Age of 1956 enhanced my modeling career and publicity.

Modeling and More

I met men during my modeling jobs to whom I was attracted, but inevitably, sex would enter the picture, and when it did, I maneuvered my way out of the situation and never went out with the man again. I guess you could say I was becoming slightly savvier. There was a rule I learned from other more experienced models that when going to a modeling interview in a hotel room, the door should be left open. That knowledge helped. But throughout my modeling career, I consistently encountered homely men with a gleam in their eyes, sweat on their brows, and hands that were too quick to touch or try to explore my body. At times, it was all I could do to continue modeling. I liked modeling. It was a way to express myself differently in diverse photos or on a runway. In a sense, it was acting. It even involved acting, which I loved because I could express myself creatively.

At one point, I became a TV moderator for a show called *Makeup and Live.* Another hairdresser related to Joe Potaro sponsored this television program. I was excited about this opportunity but found it difficult because we had to memorize the script in those early days of TV as there were no electronic prompters or cue cards as they have now. This job was not good for someone like me, who feared rejection and was anxious about carrying on a conversation. I think I could effortlessly do it today because that fear of expressing myself has healed.

From age 21 to 23, around 1955 to 1957, I auditioned for and won my first and only professional TV acting role. I was one of many secretaries (only one episode for each) for a private detective known as Johnny McQueen, the show's name, and it was written and produced in Cleveland at WEWS-TV. I think the series was the only one ever to have done so. I also appeared in one play on Cleveland's west side at the Lakewood Little Theater, now known as the Beck Center for the Arts. It was far from the east side, where I lived at the time.

CHAPTER 9

LOVE IS BLIND

*Marriage brings one into fatal connection with
custom and tradition, and traditions and customs are like
the wind and weather, altogether incalculable.*

—SOREN KIERKEGAARD (1813-1855),
DANISH PHILOSOPHER

The Family That Upset My Apple Cart

A lot took place in the year 1956. Eisenhower was still president. I was 22, and in July of that year, I met Ed H (10 years older). Ed was an iron and steel warehousing business entrepreneur who employed his mother and sister. I found him fascinating and fell in love with his mind. Ed always seemed to have great ideas. He was handsome but not outstanding. He had short brown hair and brown eyes.

I was naïve about his family and what I would undergo when married. I will go into more detail a bit further along in this narrative. His mother (Edith) was controlling, and his sister (Phyllis or Bunny) was cuckoo. From a professional standpoint, if I were to diagnose

Bunny today, I would say that she was probably bipolar and addicted to alcohol and possibly drugs. And if I were to assess Edith, I would say she had a narcissistic personality disorder. But I did not have that knowledge then. Allegedly, Edith accepted me into the family. But I never fully integrated into it. My relationship with them was fraught with difficulties from the outset.

In the meantime, Ed seemed to be proud of my modeling career and approved of it. Also, he assisted my success with great marketing ideas. That was to change after we were married.

Ed lived with his family in a two-bedroom apartment in an affluent complex where he shared a room with his mother, and Bunny resided in her own bedroom. That arrangement should have been a sign warning me against marrying him, but I didn't think much about it then. I guess I did not know much about a lot of things. In those days, I was still "unconscious." I probably would never have married him if I had been more conscious and self-assured. I seemed to have had more sense when younger. Remember my Dear John letter to Gil? After being married to Ed and experiencing his family, I now think about the peculiarity of that arrangement. Sex, of course, came with Ed, but being madly in love, it seemed appropriate.

Ed shared a party apartment with a confirmed bachelor attorney friend, separate from his residence. It was in a less desirable area of town, and the two threw wild parties. They held champagne and peanut parties, where guests threw empty peanut shells on the floor. Some party-goers got so drunk that they jumped into the shower wearing their clothes. I even remember someone hooking up a hose to a faucet and spraying others. We all were loud and unruly. Now, I wonder how the neighbors ever put up with us. However, all this craziness led me to believe Ed was fun.

But I am getting ahead of myself. I had more challenges to deal with before the proposal and marriage.

More Challenges Ahead

After the beauty contests and meeting Ed, it was time for me to move again. This time, I rented the upstairs of a double home in East Cleveland with my landlords living downstairs. They were a lovely couple, perhaps 20 years older, who eventually sold their house and moved to Hawaii. East Cleveland was a safe and pleasant city then, but it has slid into disrepute over the years. Now there are many abandoned buildings, from businesses to residential complexes. And the city doesn't possess enough money to run it efficiently.

I took two women from Magnolia Manor as roommates to share my expense. We weren't good friends nor became so, but we were friendly and cooperative. They moved out about three months later due to uncomfortable incidents that I will now explain.

Soon after moving into the house, I filmed and taped my episode of the Johnny McQueen detective series television production. Publicity for this TV show involved photo ops with the newspaper. The photographers posed me in a bathing suit while watering a plant atop a file cabinet. It appeared in the paper significantly, and my name was printed in the feature.

The next day, I started receiving phone calls from another kind of predator. I called him *The Whisperer* because he talked in a whisper. If there is such a thing as verbal rape, then I was raped. I can no longer repeat his words, nor do I wish to; however, today, I believe I can tolerate his language more effortlessly than I could then. He used the words of the gutter. I was 23 when these phone calls began.

When I answered the phone, The Whisperer would ask me what I was wearing and proceed verbally through the sex act in repulsive and repugnant terms. If I didn't answer, the phone would ring endlessly, 20, 30, 40, or 50 rings until I picked it up. It drove me crazy. I had difficulty leaving the phone off the hook because I needed to answer the phone to receive modeling calls. There was no choice but to respond to the phone calls. It was a real dilemma.

My roommates and I scolded and tried to make him stop calling by shaming him, reading him Bible verses, or hanging up on him after imploring him to end his calls, but he wouldn't stop. It became something I had to live with and dread. His phone calls made me ill and exasperated my roommates, who finally moved out. Ed and I now had privacy, even with my landlords living downstairs.

There seemed no way to end these calls. I was stuck, that is until I got married. These occurrences and the passes from the hot and sweaty men I encountered with my modeling may have pressured me into marriage.

Not long after my roommates moved out, another challenge presented itself. *Oh, God! I am pregnant again.* I knew this time without going to the doctor to confirm it. I still didn't know about contraceptives! You would have thought Ed did because he bragged about the 80 women he had slept with that he never had trouble satisfying. That was something he kept telling me when I could not be satisfied. Later, after we were married, he sent me to the doctor to determine if something was physically wrong, preventing me from having an orgasm. The doctor found nothing inappropriate with my anatomy. None of us knew or suspected that my sexual abuse might have had something to do with it. But, of course, they didn't know about my childhood as it had not emerged yet. I probably needed psychotherapy to resolve the issue, but that didn't appear to be an option then.

When I told Ed about the pregnancy, I hoped he would suggest we get married immediately. However, he had not given me any indication that marriage was viable for us. I assumed we were exclusive, and I thought he loved me. He was not excited about the news. He told me, "You will have to get an abortion." I thought, *"not again."* I wanted to marry him, and I desired to have a baby. I was ready, and I felt crushed. So, I had another secret to hold. And I felt rejected and dejected once again. He found another doctor who performed virtually the same technique as the first, but I did not have a follow-up doctor this time.

Earth Angel to the Rescue

Whenever I was in trouble, I prayed to God to save me. I would always tell Him, "If you get me out of this jam, I will not do it again," for whatever found me in trouble in the first place. God always seemed to answer these prayers one way or another. But I usually did not fulfill my end of the bargain. When I prayed for an answer, He sent me an earth angel.

I had met Robert, who worked in public relations, in my modeling adventures. He was a gentleman, respectful, and extremely pleasant. He did not seem to fall into the category of most of the other men I had dated or known. Robert wanted to date me, but I was involved with Ed; however, I occasionally stopped with him for coffee or a drink.

I always wondered why many women (myself included) are not attracted to men who have everything going for them and are pleasant. Robert was also handsome and talented. He gave me a gift. It was a book of free verse poems named *Archy and Mehitabel* about a cockroach, Archy, who climbed onto the typewriter at night and wrote. Archy had been a free-verse poet in a former life, and Mehitabel, the alley cat, had been Cleopatra. I held onto the book for years, but I reluctantly let it go when I began purging some of my books. While I had the book, it reminded me that there still were decent men in the world.

I called Robert when I found out I was pregnant and invited him over. By then, my roommates had moved. I confessed, "Robert, I am pregnant. Ed is responsible, but he won't marry me. He wants me to get an abortion. What do you think I should do?"

After a bit of thought, Robert said, "I will marry you and take the baby as my own." What an excellent solution to another discouraging problem. The only thing wrong was that I was in love with Ed, not Robert, and I told him I needed to think it over.

I ended up turning him down. Even though I didn't know it then, before reincarnating again, I had contracted with my Holy Council to be with Ed. Many times in my life, I regretted that decision. I sometimes wonder how my life would have turned out if I had chosen to marry Robert, and I imagine it would have been much different and better. He was an angel sent to resolve my dilemma, and I turned him away. Enough said.

Getting Married

Ed and I continued to date. Near the end of our first year of dating, when I received no proposal, I decided to return to New York to resume my modeling, hoping I might also break into acting. I made plans with various people, lined up an apartment with another model, sold my car, and broke up with Ed.

One day while modeling, I encountered some dirty old men. I became despondent when I considered that I might meet the same in New York City (like in Boston) and began to worry about the "casting couch." My life changed forever that day. I was virtually ready to leave Cleveland when Ed finally popped the question that night. I felt relief when I considered that I would not have to put up with more passes. Ed and I agreed not to have any wedding publicity to free me of the sexual leech who would not stop calling me.

Ed required that I convert to Judaism for him. He was a Reform Jew. At the time, I didn't know it was a requirement for a mother to be Jewish for the children to be Jewish, and I only learned about that years later. In my brief education regarding Judaism, I was required to read a certain number of books before converting. My transition had to occur before our small wedding on July 27, 1957, which we planned for three months following his proposal. It was the anniversary of our first date. Moving with Ed into our apartment and taking his name, the phone calls from The Whisperer ceased. But in the end, I was not free of this freak, even in the safety of marriage.

The Whisperer

A couple of months later, when I was pregnant, my mother-in-law, Edith, and I attended a maternity fashion show where I won the door prize, resulting in some newspaper publicity the next day. That is when The Whisperer resumed the calls.

Ed required two phone lines for his business. Somehow, the pervert caught on to that and would call me on both numbers. I figured that he was someplace where he had two phone lines at his disposal. It was not long before Ed wanted to take police action to catch the culprit.

So, Ed contacted the police, who told me to keep The Whisperer on the phone line to trace the call. They did not have the technology at the time to do it quickly. So, I had to listen to and incite The Whisperer to go on for as long as possible. The pervert was delighted, but it sickened me. I have wondered why it took so long to locate the caller. Could the police who were listening have been getting off on the content of the calls? It appears I was getting paranoid even about the police. Then, they told me to make a date with him, call the police, and have them stake out the meeting location. After weeks or months of evading or scolding him, this new plan questioned how he could sincerely believe I would keep that date.

We tried to catch The Whisperer in person by inviting him to our apartment, of all places. I called Ed, who left work to join me, and he hid in the bedroom. Ed explained the plan concocted between him and the police. He said, "The police will be circling the apartments this evening, watching for the perp to show up. I will hide in the bedroom with my gun. When he knocks on the door, I'll be ready to jump out when you open it. Then, you step aside, and I will shoot him."

I shuddered to envision a man dead, even this man, with his blood running all over our new carpet. I had been cooking chili for dinner, and it was slowly drying out on the stove as we waited. I should have turned it off because I was losing my appetite anyway, but I was not in touch with the whole situation's reality. We called the police, and they assured us that detectives were close by, offering me further protection.

I did not want all this! I only wanted to be left alone. Minutes seemed like hours, and hours, like days. But we waited, and my chili turned dry on the stove. I paced in circles, first one way and then the other. Then I heard footsteps on the landing outside our door. I held my breath, but whoever passed by soon moved up the stairs.

Although the police said these characters rarely make dates, The Whisperer must have smelled a trap. They get their kicks on the phone. He did not show up. However, I lived in fear for days and weeks afterward that he would show up when no one was there to protect me, with his now knowing where I lived. Thank God he did not. But he continued to call—repeatedly.

His calls persisted for ten months. We even tried changing our phone number to unlisted a couple of times, but The Whisperer discovered it every time.

Our attempts to stop or catch him continued even after tracing him through an antiquated phone system that required me to keep him on the phone for as long as possible. His discourse always sickened me.

Every day I was a victim of sexual harassment and sexual abuse. Additionally, I was pregnant and experiencing morning sickness. It was so unfair for anyone to ask me to go through this, and no one seemed to understand how offensive it was to me. Everyone around me was guilty of continuing it and not finding a solution. Perhaps I was also, but I had not yet learned to use my voice.

Then, my baby was born. But he died. Finally, Ed changed our phone number so no one could ever get it. And, finally, it worked. The Whisperer no longer called, and his calls ceased for a blessed three to four years until we moved into our first house.

In the meantime, I got pregnant again and gave birth to my son Michael in 1959. A year later, I got pregnant with my son Gary, whom I was about to deliver when we moved from our apartment into our house. It was 1961, and a new and exciting president, John F. Kennedy, took the reins of our government only to be struck down by a sniper's gun two years later.

One day soon after moving into our new house, the phone rang. I picked it up and said, "Hello." I nearly dropped the receiver when I heard The Whisperer on the other end. I thought, *I can't go through this again!* I called Ed, who called the police, and they returned to the tracing. The police were a little more efficient this time and traced the call to the Cleveland Plain Dealer newspaper. We realized that we had given out our number that day to the Home Delivery Department of the paper as needed in our moving plans.

Unfortunately, the police sent several detectives to catch the perp, but he must have seen them coming, as the calls ceased immediately and never again resumed. The police never apprehended him either, to my knowledge. That upset me because he deserved punishment for what he had done to me. I am sure I'm not the only one who received his calls, although he spent enough time with me that I might have been.

Marriage to Ed and the Death of Our Baby

The grass is always greener. Well, you can finish that. I had six years of independence to pursue various parts of my identity following graduation from high school, and I did just that before getting married. Then, I lost it all in marriage.

My marriage to Ed was no picnic. I also had sexual problems with him. I would have been happy just wrapped in his arms, even if I could not climax during sex with him. I felt desire, but I never could say what felt right or did not like. So, I would go so far, he would climax, and that would be it. Sometimes he would continue trying to stimulate me, but I either had performance anxiety, or the stimulation became excessive and began to defeat the purpose. That is doubtless why he thought there was something wrong with me. Of course, it didn't have anything to do with him. Nothing ever did.

Pregnancy occurred within the first month of our marriage. My pregnancy proceeded typically with all milestones. About a week or two after my due date, my water broke. We went to the hospital right away as the pains were close together. It was 1958 before babies were delivered or stayed in hospital rooms with their mothers. I gave birth within six hours in the standard delivery room. Afterward, in a private room of my own and all alone, I waited for the opportunity to nurse my baby. Lying in my hospital bed, I listened as babies were wheeled down the hall to their mothers for feedings. I heard their newborn cries. I wondered why they didn't bring mine.

Finally, Dr. Marv Whitman, my OB-GYN, and Ed came into the room. I asked why I had not seen my baby yet and how long it would be before I did. Ed asked the doctor to leave so he could talk to me alone. He said, "Our baby ...."

"Died?" I completed his sentence. I don't know how I knew, but I did. I was awake during his delivery. The nurses showed me all his toes and fingers were normal. He cried a good healthy cry. *How could he be dead!!!?*

New mothers stayed in the hospital following delivery for seven to ten days. On my first day, I picked up the phone to call a friend when the operator admonished me that I could not talk on the phone when the babies were out. I barely choked out, "My...baby... died!" She was apologetic. I began to think that this occurrence was divine retribution to Ed and me for having had the abortion. Now, we were not allowed to have any children. During that terrible time of grief, Ed gave me a note with the warmest sentiment he had ever given me.

We agreed to an autopsy on the baby, whom we named William after Ed's father. It revealed that William could survive inside of me. When it came time for him to live independently, he could not do so because the veins or arteries leading to and from his heart were mixed up. My doctor told me this kind of birth happens in only one birth in a million or another statistic.

What did we do with little William's body? The physicians asked us to donate it to science to study what caused the problem. In giving up William's body, I never got to hold him, say goodbye, or have closure. I just never saw him again. There was no grave for me to visit. There was only a profound emptiness within for many years from the lack of these experiences. Thankfully, hospitals do things differently today for other families who experience their newborn's loss.

Interestingly, I met a survivor of this sort of heart defect around June of 1999 when I participated in a theatrical play, and the survivor was one of the cast members. In my understanding of what she told me, the physicians discovered this issue while she was still in utero and performed surgery to correct the defect. It was serendipitous for us to meet. For my comfort, I would like to believe that our gesture of donating William's body to science created the young woman's chance to survive.

I took hypnosis training with a psychiatrist whose infant had a similar malady and died after living a bit longer than mine. And I am happy that after my loss, God blessed me with two healthy baby sons: Michael, the following year, and Gary, two years later.

Regarding Ed's behavior with me the year following our tragedy, he appeared to be as emotionally affected as I was, and we had the best year of our marriage ever. He treated me with respect and concern. I pursued another pregnancy, became pregnant, and carried Michael to full term. He emerged big and healthy. But Ed changed again. I noticed it during his first visit to my hospital room after Michael's birth. He became controlling again, reverting to the same behavior as before our loss. Things were different. He now had five mouths to feed, counting his mother and sister. We could not have any more fun.

CHAPTER 10

MARRIAGE TO EDWARD H. AND FAMILY

The purpose of our lives is to be happy.

—HIS HOLINESS, THE DALAI LAMA,
ESSAY IN *INDIA TODAY*, SEPTEMBER 30, 2021

My Personal Journal with an Account of My Life as Edward H.'s Wife

The following notes are taken from the Personal Journal I kept during my married years. They regard details of my marriage to Edward H. and convey my life with him, his mother, and his sister from our marriage's early to its latter days. These notes were written when I needed to release my thoughts and feelings, and I wrote them originally in 1960, three years after Ed and I were married. They are events taken from memory as they occurred and not necessarily as a daily or weekly journal.

Edith

This story began when Ed and I told his mother, Edith or Edie, that I would become her daughter-in-law. She told me then, "I will never be a mother-in-law type but will be a second mother to you; therefore, never call me your mother-in-law, just mother." Anytime I referred to her as my mother-in-law since that time, she became very incensed. "I'm not your mother-in-law. I'm your mother!"

I told her, "I can't introduce you or clarify our relationship with others unless I refer to you as my mother-in-law." I guess she isn't honored by the word. She should be proud. Maybe (along with everything else), it's because she can't face the fact that her son is married, and she lies to herself that I'm her daughter. I have always believed she didn't want her children married because she couldn't face being alone. This is evidenced, I believe, by her oldest child and daughter, Phyllis (called Bunny or Ba), being divorced and never having remarried. Bunny has had many opportunities, but her mother always interfered by pointing out all of a man's personal bad points, leaving Bunny to believe she thought of them. I have heard that Edie also stepped in on many of Ed's romances. I don't understand why she finally let Ed persuade her to let him marry me.

Perhaps this is because she had a chance to remarry and asked her children if they would like it (which is a mistake because children cannot rationalize a mother's heart, only their own). They opposed it. She may have tried to do the same to them because she missed her happiness. Who knows?

I was deceived right from the beginning by her wanting me to call her "mother" and by the following discussion Ed and I had before we were married.

"Honey," he said, "I owe my mother a lot because I told her not to remarry when she had an opportunity to do so and because she has invested a lot of money in the business; therefore, we must be kind to her because I owe her so much." First, what kind of mother makes her children feel they owe her anything other than respect?

People only owe their parents to do the same for their children, such as raising them, caring for them, loving them, and seeing them have every opportunity. This is how people repay their parents for raising them.

Second, when he marries, a man owes more to his mate and children, purportedly to make them happy, than he owes his parents.

Being a naïve and well-deceived young woman, I was led astray. Being in love with my husband, I set out to make Ed happy by biting my tongue and trying to keep his mother happy. [*Ed had found someone he could dominate, and he knew it before I did. At the time, I was a woman who could be dominated.*]

In all social circles [*in the 1950s*], I understood the woman and her family were responsible for all the wedding plans, and the groom's family were guests. I wanted a small wedding with both immediate families. Of course, there had to be specific relatives on Ed's side; therefore, I invited some friends, my mother's sister, and her husband. I chose a pregnant female friend [*Carol*] to be my matron-of-honor. It was not a formal wedding, and my mother-in-law wouldn't hear of it. With a pregnant woman walking down the aisle in front of me, she would feel disgraced by her relatives. For Ed, I chose my former roommate [Pat] to please Edie because I didn't know better. I have since learned that including a pregnant woman in a wedding party is acceptable, even at formal weddings.

My mother's arrival in Cleveland to find my wedding dress and arrange my reception with the caterer was the occasion for my mother-in-law's next treacherous battle. My mother had planned two days in town, one for me and one for my mother-in-law.

Carol my first choice for Matron of Honor, and I met my mother at the train station. We had lunch and drove to a suburban store to look at my wedding dress. My mother-in-law had selected it beforehand, but my mother didn't know, and I was afraid to tell her. But the saleslady slipped and revealed that my mother-in-law had ordered it from New York. It was a pretty dress anyway, and we decided to take it. Then we drove Carol home and went to the caterer to select our reception menu. We picked what we desired and sat down mother-and-daughter style to discuss what was coming. We had so little time to talk due to living in separate towns.

The following day, we tried to reach my mother-in-law, and it seemed we kept missing her. So, we decided to have lunch alone and shop for a suitable dress for my mother. I kept running to the phone to reach my mother-in-law. Finally, I got her, and she was noticeably short and curt and insisted we come to Ed's office immediately.

When we arrived, she started picking on my mother. She insisted my mother should have called when she arrived in Cleveland. She said, "Why wasn't I invited to select the menu for the reception? I have never been so insulted." We showed her the menu, and she declared, "It is not a good one." We told her three-quarters of the couples getting married had selected that menu. She couldn't be appeased. Ed and Bunny were angry with us, too. Finally, I had to get my mother on the train, and she left town crying.

What a way to begin a relationship between in-laws! Edith criticized me even more by telling me that we were utterly wrong.

To make matters worse, my mother-in-law went to the caterers and changed the menu to her liking, paying for the extra service and saying her relatives would laugh at such a menu. You have it; the wedding was for her relatives, not her children. Need I say I didn't enjoy my own wedding and reception? I hated every minute of it, and I even got ill afterward.

A long time later, and a short while ago, Ed and I finally discussed how unhappy I had been. He defended Edith. "She knows more about weddings and etiquette than your mother. The other menu wasn't any good. Your mother shouldn't care because Edith paid for the extras herself. She doesn't owe your mother an apology." Edith kept insisting my mother owed her an apology because my mother failed to call her when she arrived in town. What a terrible breach of etiquette! [*It seems she should have called my mother first to welcome her because Cleveland was Edith's hometown.*]

I selected my silver and crystal patterns. My mother-in-law knew what I wanted. So, when she sent the silver and crystal gift, it was a different pattern from what I wanted. It is pretty but not what I wanted, and it's also the principle of the thing. Her excuse was, "You are too young to know what you want" (I was 23). Ed also excused her by saying, "Well, you like it, don't you? What difference does it make?" (This occurred in our discussion not too long ago when I could no longer control my bitterness.)

I think it makes a lot of difference because, generally, you may buy silver and crystal only once in a lifetime, so you might as well get what you want when you buy it.

It has been that way with many items in our home, even when I told Ed I wanted a particular picture above our couch before my mother-in-law brought the plaque that now hangs there.

July 27, 1957 [Our wedding day]: *We had planned a two-week honeymoon and went to the Concord Resort Hotel in the Catskills at Kiamesha Lake, New York.* [It was closed in 1998.] *We stayed for only three days. Ed received a call from Bunny about a customer's cancellation of a substantial order, and he told me, "Pack up, as we are going home." Before I had the opportunity to adjust to being married and becoming a housewife, I was whisked back to Cleveland and into housekeeping. I indicated to Ed that I knew he was upset about returning and my being upset, but he only seemed to take it out on me.*

I had hoped perhaps that we could continue our honeymoon by staying in a hotel in Cleveland while Ed went to work during the day, and we could honeymoon at night. Instead, we moved right into our apartment, and Ed expected a home-cooked meal that first night (I didn't know how to cook yet) when I had no opportunity to go shopping or means to get there. He blew up at me for even expecting to go out to dinner our first night home. He gave me no opportunity to adjust to the whole situation. I managed to get to a store and picked up a couple of glass candle holders for a candlelit dinner. He ranted and raved about their cheap appearance. After all, they were not silver. I wondered what had happened to the man I thought I had married.

We never did get a complete vacation during our whole marriage. Sometimes we took three- or four-day weekends, usually on business or with someone. But we never got to go away together on a real vacation without business worries or alone. I began to feel that Ed was afraid to be alone with me. We took no vacations because he couldn't afford the time, and he didn't provide a way for me to go. The way things looked, we wouldn't vacation until he was ready to retire.

After Ed and I were married and settled in, my mother-in-law demanded my time. She took me to lunch several times a week but let me refuse, and I would hurt her feelings, so I sat through many a lunchtime when I longed to be at home working or with friends my own age.

There was a significant dispute the first Thanksgiving after our marriage. Ed and I went to Plymouth to celebrate with my parents. My Mother-in-law wanted to know why we could hurt her so much because this was one occasion that the family always celebrated birthdays together. Her birthday comes a few days before, during, or after Thanksgiving, but she celebrates that day. My mother's birthday is within a week away also. But after the fuss she made, I decided we'd spend one Thanksgiving with her, the next with mine, and so forth. Besides, what is wrong with celebrating her actual birthday? To have all the families together would be impossible and miserable. I gave in again. It looks like we would spend every one of them with her. At least, we did with the last two.

Edie had Ed and me with her all year. Couldn't she give up Thanksgiving? Edie also had us for the Jewish holidays. She was fortunate that my parents weren't Jewish, or we'd have fights over that, too.

Then, my baby, Mike, arrived on the scene on April 29, 1959. My mother-in-law must have thought he belonged to her. She went to New York while I was in the hospital. The day after I came home was Mother's Day. Bunny insisted we have a massive dinner because her mother was returning from New York that day. I was trying to nurse Mike and needed rest and no excitement, but I should never have attempted to nurse with this family around. I felt lucky to have a maid instead of a nurse to help out. A nurse would have walked out. As it was, Bunny didn't show up, Mike had to be fed when the dinner was ready, they all complained about the roast, and I was a nervous wreck.

The homecoming was for my mother-in-law, not me. I had to give up nursing because my mother-in-law dropped in every day. I had no rest and too much excitement, which Ed didn't keep from me.

The next thing that happened was Mike's first visit to the doctor when he was six weeks old. I was well enough to drive and had been doing so, but while discussing it one evening, my mother-in-law, cautious of what could happen, asked, "Who is taking you?"

I said, "Ed is."

He said, "If you would take her, Mother, I won't have to."

So, I was stuck. I couldn't get out of going with my mother-in-law.

Just as I suspected, things happened. Mike was scared upon being examined, and I believe it is essential to be there when a child needs his mother. My mother-in-law believed him to be hurt and started to pick him up. I said, as politely as possible, "Please, if you don't mind, mom, I'll do it." I saw her tighten up, but I tried to hear what the doctor had to say. I put Mike down and reached for his clothes to dress him, and before I knew it, she had picked him up. I sighed, gave her a dirty look, and turned my back before saying something I might regret. Finally, she got so angry with me that she put the baby down, got her things, and told me she would wait for me in the car. We tried to be as sweet as possible, but I could feel the animosity. My mother-in-law didn't say a word until we were halfway home. Then she started on how conceited, selfish, and dumb

I was, and never again should I ask her for any favors; never again should I ask her to babysit. "What an ungrateful wretch you are."

I tried to be as calm as possible and said, "Well, that's what happens when a baby enters a family; a mother and/or mother-in-law get upset over these little things."

"Well, I've tried never to be a mother-in-law."

Hah! I thought.

I saw then it was no use arguing anymore, so I kept quiet. My mother-in-law had never been anything else but a mother-in-law as far as I was concerned. And I had never asked her for any favors.

I told Ed what had happened that evening. He told me to call her and apologize, and I wanted to know for what. "If anything, she owes me an apology."

So, we didn't speak for a couple of days. Then I decided this wasn't good for Ed and called her to apologize, humbling myself to all her criticisms.

Our subsequent significant encounter happened the day after Thanksgiving, 1959, her birthday celebration. Now she celebrates twice a year! I had had a particularly rough day with Mike that day. It seemed as if everything had gone wrong, and I arrived at her home close to exhaustion. I remarked in an amusing way that I'd had it. This upset her.

Mike went through a few antics, and we put him to bed since we were late. He didn't want to sleep and cried, which was his habit. Mike had to be rocked and soothed to sleep. They catered to this, and he was getting spoiled. I was convinced that three nights of letting him cry would break the habit [*Dr. Bloomfield recommended it*], but no one would listen to me. Everyone insisted that his teeth were bothering him. I insisted that he was spoiled and that his teeth never troubled him. Then, I was unable to take it anymore and exploded. "I'm getting sick and tired of no one having faith in me as a mother or not listening to what I have to say!" Then, feeling somewhat ashamed, I began to cry.

Not realizing – and I should have – that I had again offended my mother-in-law, I went home with Ed and the baby. The next day, Ed asserted that I should call his mother again and apologize for my outburst. I wanted to know why I was not entitled to an occasional outburst since Bunny does it daily and Ed at least once a week.

To appease Ed, I called his mother, who would not accept my apology. I sobbed at the receiving end of the phone, insisting that the things she said were wrong. Ed finally told me to hang up as she was unduly cruel (this was the only time he ever stood up for me). She told me, "You have no right to blow up, and you should have better control of your emotions than crying." She had gone on and on, tearing me down spiritually, morally, and in other ways.

Our feud went on for a little more than a week, with Ed pleading with me to patch things up and with my saying that his mother certainly owed me an apology this time.

Finally, I again gave in and called her to come for a discussion where I felt I could tell her how I wanted things to run in my household. She convinced me, with her wiles, how young and ignorant I was of so many things. I let her go on as I got, or tried to get, the point across about how I wanted Mike raised. I told her I wanted her to enjoy him and that while he was in her home, she had the right to do what she wanted with him, but when I was around, my word was law. She then agreed but later forgot what I had said and continued doing things her way. I could go on and on about her, but I have picked the really agitating things.

Bunny

My sister-in-law is another story that I will make as brief as possible. She was very jealous of anyone in a relationship with her brother. She had a perverted sense of possession of him. She didn't want to accept that he was marrying me and wouldn't accept me as a sister. She continuously tore me apart and made me feel small and ignorant. She started with my looks, my clothes, and my personality. I used to feel that I knew something about these things, having been a popular model, but with her constantly nagging me, I began to feel maybe she was right. I began developing an inferiority complex. [*She was guilty of Gaslighting me.*] I had no one else to check my reality with at the time.

Whenever I was in her presence, I would quiver and quake, petrified to do anything for fear I would do it wrong. Even if right, it had to be wrong. She kept me in a constant nervous state. Ed should have protected me against her, but he failed to see anything wrong. Every time I talked to her, I waited for her to blow up and diminish me. I tried to fight back, but even with her, it was a useless battle.

Ed

I felt that if Ed's mother and sister had been out of the picture, Ed and I would have had fewer problems. This brings me to Ed. I thought he fell in love with me the way I was, but he was continuously molding me into what he wanted me to become. When I dated Ed, I had no false front. I was myself in every detail. Knowing this, he shouldn't have married me if he didn't like how I was. He even told me he married me because of my "potential." But with his pushing me too fast and his mother's and sister's bossing, I was becoming a person I couldn't respect because a part of me was false; also, I didn't think I was a bit of fun to be around anymore because I was so worried that I would do something wrong.

Before we were married, we had loads of fun and much in common. We were happy to do what the other person liked because we had fun being together. After being married for three years, it seemed like we had fallen into a rut. All we did was sit in front of the TV all evening, every evening of the week, save one, usually spent with our friends.

Ed was never grouchy with me before we married, and I felt so good about it. He seemed awful grouchy about everything, which was never apparent to his friends. On an evening when he was grouchy, a friend would call, and he was as sweet as pie, but when he hung up, he was grouchy again. (It seemed as if he could forget about it when he talked to a friend, but he could not forget it with me.) I always tried to be cheerful, but I had become sad from banging my head against this stone wall.

Suddenly, Ed started picking on the little things I did, which had never bothered him. It seemed he didn't like a single thing that I liked anymore. Our musical interests differed, and our tastes in every small thing. We didn't even want the same kind of house we used to want. This was another issue that had been hurting me. He kept promising me we would move at a particular time until he decided not to, and he kept pushing the date further back.

What made my job difficult was that Ed kept telling me how to do this or that. And why didn't I do such and such with the baby? I went to prenatal class; I read numerous books, talked to numerous mothers, discussed things with the baby's doctor, and spent 24 hours a day with the baby. Also, I have a long history of babysitting. I knew Mike and the best way he should be cared for. Ed had not had the experience, and I knew he was interested, but it came to a point where he demanded I do what he wanted. It got very irritating with him running my home, which was my job. His job was to run the office; I knew he wouldn't like me to tell him how to do that.

Sometimes I believed he wanted children only when he was in the mood for them because when Ed didn't like what Mike was doing at a particular time, he said, "Don't you think it's time for his bed?" He couldn't stand the mess Mike made eating, and I couldn't initially, but I grew to bear it because I knew all babies must mess in their food, especially if they're to learn. He insisted that the baby be a perfect adult child in every manner that it takes some adults a lifetime to learn.

Whenever we discussed the things bothering each of us about the other, I always came out on the short end of the stick, bowing, and kowtowing to Ed, admitting I was wrong and trying to do better. As a result, I was further becoming someone I wasn't. I was becoming bitter, resentful, and doubting my love for Ed. Worried about my future with Ed, I asked him three questions:

(1) "Are you happy?" His answer was, "Happy? No, and I never will be."

(2) "What do you want from life?" Answer: "To feed, clothe, and house my wife and children."

(3) "Don't your wife and children deserve something else?" Answer: "No."

In other words, he was thinking only of his moral obligations and not his spiritual ones. He didn't believe his wife and children deserve love, affection, and protection or him in his happiest state. I was baffled and somehow felt I had lost my security, and I don't mean financial.

> **November 4, 1957:** *Real trouble had begun, with me ready to walk out. But I was pregnant and couldn't go back to modeling. I saw the trouble and told Ed we should see a marriage counselor. He said then, and throughout the entire marriage, whenever this topic was brought up, "If we can't solve our own problems, no one else can!"*

In a letter to my mother at this time, I wrote:

I feel like I'm living in a cold display house, not a home, and I'm never happy anymore. If this continues, we will never have a home, and I hate to think of what it might do to our children.

Before we were married, we did a lot of things together. We had fun, and we lived. We talked about everything we could and would do together after marriage. Ed is grouchy and tired and plops down in front of the TV set, and we don't communicate anymore. He rushes through dinner to watch TV all night, and I don't enjoy my meals. He initially took the fun out of housekeeping for him, and now he has taken the fun out of cooking. Even when I make little surprises, I can't please him.

Is this all my imagination? Or is it due to depression from my pregnancy? Or did his attitude bring on my depression along with his mother's and sister's attitudes? I know this can't all be my fault, and any other woman would rebel under such circumstances.

He is so stubborn and won't listen to reason. The first year is the hardest, and I only hope something changes all of this. I wish I knew the answer, but I can't live under such circumstances for the rest of my life and be happy.

Perhaps I'm going through a depression right now. If so, you should disregard everything I've said. But if things don't smooth and straighten out, I will have to do something about them. We both know I hate to have this marriage fail, so I will do my utmost to keep it happy unless it is not within my power.

This excerpt shows how the marriage began, persisted, and worsened with the same primary symptoms. It was not within my power to keep it happy, and it dragged me down with it.

We would patch things up for a while, but it also became our marriage pattern. We would talk everything over, usually with my suggesting a marriage counselor and his not wanting to discuss anything after it was mentioned. Then we each agreed to try harder. This usually ended up with my agreeing that I was wrong and to do everything his way. I never could explain to him how miserable I was becoming or how unjust everything was. Things would be all right for a week, maybe two, but he would slip back into the same pattern of being grouchy and tired.

This situation continued throughout the marriage until I believed I did nothing right and was the cause of our unhappy relationship. I also believed I was inadequate in every area and would never be good at anything. I kept getting stepped on until I was pretty flat and worn.

April 22, 1958: *About a month before my first pregnancy's due date, Miles, my stepfather, came to town, but Ed was too tired to go out. This also became a problem when relatives came to town, which was not very often.*

CHAPTER 11

1961

Children bring us a piece of heaven on earth.

—Roland Leonhardt

My Diaries

[These diaries plus letters will tell most of my story throughout the following five chapters.]

July 15, 2004: I rediscovered my diaries written many years ago during the "end days" of my marriage to Ed. I decided to type them for posterity should my children want to know what caused their parents' divorce or learn how their lives may have been likewise affected. It might give them insights into how they grew up in their father's household if they, like me, could not remember their experiences. If they have no interest in reading these pages, perhaps other family members or historical societies might be interested. Time will reveal that. My Diary entries now reveal the further downfall of my marriage. My son, Gary, was born on June 9, 1961. So here goes....

The Strain of Daily Life After Three Plus Years

January 1, 1961: *We spent our first New Year's Eve at home last night. Mort and Shirley Kress brought their baby over, and we spent the evening playing Monopoly and Parcheesi. We watched the New Year come in on Times Square via television. Today was a lazy day. This afternoon, Mike went to Edie's, and we picked him up later. Aunt Ceil was there. The remainder of the evening was lazy. We went to bed at 11:30. Mike was restless from 12:30 a.m. to 2:30 a.m. and wanted Daddy.*

January 2, 1961: *Today, I awoke early and accomplished what must be done. I picked up Marty and Phyllis, and we met Jack (Marty's significant other) at Clarks Restaurant near Phyllis's for brunch. I got home at 2:00 p.m. and put Mike to bed as Ed was having trouble. We both lay down for a nap. Mike woke up around 4:00 p.m. He was cross and asked for Daddy. Later, at 5:00, Edie came over and stayed until 7:00 p.m. At 6:00, Ba (Bunny) arrived, and they left together. I'm beginning to think I married them instead of Ed. Bunny called later and told me to bring Edie's glasses outside in five minutes when she would pick them up. I told her we were both in our PJs. She got angry and told me to be out there. I got angry and hung up. Bob and Connie, from next door, ended up taking the glasses to her.*

January 3, 1961 (My birthday): *This day began like any other, with Ed waking in a bad mood, and it sure didn't seem like a birthday. My mother called this morning. I ordered Mike's Big Bed, went to Page Boy, and bought $135 worth of maternity clothes.*

We all met at Edith's for dinner. I told Ed about the clothes, and he wasn't too pleased about the price. Bunny blew up and had a tantrum. She slammed doors, screamed, then cried. When she calmed down, we ate.

When we arrived home, Ed blew his top over my buying Mike's bed because he didn't want to use up any more space [in the second bedroom] *for the bed. But I felt we had to get it for Mike's psychological security before we moved and the baby arrived. I played Mahjong at Nancy Herman's and won 49 cents while spilling and breaking a glass of cherry pop.*

January 4, 1961: *I picked up Norma for lunch, and after lunch, I went to Heights Furniture to buy a headboard for Mike's bed. After Ed had conceded to my buying the bed, he decided we had better get the headboard.*

January 5, 1961: *Mike and I stayed home today. The TV man came again, and Heights delivered the headboard.*

January 6, 1961: *I went to Page Boy to buy a maternity bathing suit because Mike and Phil (PJ) invited us to swim at the Tudor Arms again. I got in the pool and swam only a few strokes before discovering the water was too cold to remain very long. After swimming, we went to Settlers' Tavern for dinner and came home to play Parcheesi. We also showed some home movies.*

Edith made me so angry today because she insisted I bring Mike to her apartment to see him before leaving for New York. I had to leave and pick him up as she was too lazy to come to our apartment.

January 7, 1961: *I couldn't get enough sleep today and didn't go out all day. I did some of Ed's mending, but Mike wouldn't let me. Today, Ed went to look at some houses, and he saw one he liked but felt that it was too expensive.*

January 8, 1961: *As usual, another lazy Sunday. I typed for four hours on some work Bunny sent home from the office. Ed, Mike, and I took the crib to Ed's Aunt Henrietta's house for storage.*

Dr. Bloomfield had suggested we let Mike cry at his door because it took an hour every night to put him to bed. After 45 minutes of his crying, I convinced Ed that the only thing left to do was to let him cry. He cried for about five more minutes, climbed into bed, and went to sleep.

January 10, 1961: *I took Mike to the doctor today. He weighs 26 pounds, 10 ounces and measures 33 inches. He received a Schick and TB. I went to Maxine's house to play Mahjong and lost 30 cents.*

January 12, 1961: *We stayed home all day except when I took Mike out to play. Tonight, I went to Shirley's to play bridge. We played with two other doctors' wives, Louise and June, and I was the big winner for the night.*

January 13, 1961: *Today, I took Mike out to play. Tonight, I was drained and fell asleep watching TV.*

January 14, 1961: *We drove around today looking at houses in various neighborhoods. And we stopped by the house Ed saw last week, so I could see the inside. I am crazy about the house. We went to Big Mike's apartment tonight for dinner, and Mike and PJ cooked. It was terrific, and* *they had the most enormous steaks I've ever seen. After dinner, we played Clue and came home.*

January 15, 1961: *Mike and I walked around the apartment today with the wagon. I can't seem to do anything with him when Ed is home, and Ed gives in to him too quickly and spoils him. I must have a talk with Ed.*

Ed went to talk to Uncle Joe about financing the house. We had a Settler's Tavern dinner. It has been four months since the baby I'm carrying was conceived and that long since Ed and I made love. I suggested it tonight, but nothing doing. I feel as if our marriage is indeed failing.

January 16, 1961: *I went to my doctor today and weighed 134 pounds. I must stop eating, and I'm coming down with a cold. Marv heard a heartbeat today.*

January 17, 1961: *I had the women here today for Mahjong, and I was the big winner by about 90 cents, and I spilled coffee.*

January 20, 1961: *This was indeed an eventful day. Shirley and I left at 12:20 to attend the ORT luncheon at the Summerset. We saw a black pillar of smoke rising toward Shaker Square, and we drove over to investigate and discovered an apartment house on fire. At the luncheon, we played Bingo. Shirley won a pair of roller-skating tickets, and I won a lovely pair of sunglasses.*

I started to hem my black wool coat when Ed came to take me to Mike B's, where we met Jerry and Norma, plus Ed and Peggy from Virginia, and had a martini. From there, we journeyed to Settlers' for dinner. I felt great for the first time in a long time. We showed home movies at home. Ed, Peg, Big Mike, and PJ played Clue, while Ed, Jerry, Norma, and I played bridge. We broke up around 2:30 in the morning."

January 21, 1961: *I was worn out today from being up so late last night and drinking, so I didn't accomplish much. Mike came down with a cold.*

January 22, 1961: *Mike's cold kept us busy all day.*

January 23, 1961: *Mike seemed to demand a lot of attention today with his cold, so I didn't accomplish much. I was up almost every half hour all night with him and was tired.*

January 24, 1961: *I tended to Mike all day but needed and welcomed a change. Shirley invited me to play bridge with Elayne and Mim at Mim's house. It turned out to be quite an enjoyable evening. Edith returned to Cleveland today and spent about an hour at our home.*

January 25, 1961: *Mike complained about an earache, so I called the doctor, who came over at 10:00 p.m. to see. He has no ear infection, but he has viral bronchitis. I was tired from the long week of tending to Mike under pressure. Edith was over for about an hour before supper, and she brought a pretty little pin for me.*

January 26, 1961: *Edith came over again today and stayed around an hour or more. As usual, she announced she was going home, and Mike would say, "no." She would stay and end up sneaking out so Mike wouldn't cry. Shirley and I went to Ellen's to play Mahjong and played five with a betting game, and I ended up $2.00 ahead.*

January 27, 1961: Because *Edith "missed Mike so much while away," she requested to keep Mike all weekend. When she came to pick him up, she wouldn't listen to my schedule for Mike and was insulted when I repeated myself. Then, she had to call back to find out when to give him his medicine. When I told Ed, he excused her because she probably was excited about getting Mike and told me I should have written it out. She never follows it anyway when I do write it. We had dinner with Big Mike, PJ, Norma, Jerry, and Marty at the Chinese Peacock and went to Norma's after. I wanted to have a discussion, but it seemed the wrong time.*

January 28, 1961: *I went to lunch alone, shopped, and came home. We met Shirley and Mort outside at 7:30 and went to the Blue Grass for dinner, where I had Lobster Tails. We went to the Fairmount Theater to see <u>Inherit the Wind</u>, but it was crowded, so we ended up at <u>Butterfield 8</u> with Elizabeth Taylor and Laurence Harvey at the Vogue Theater.*

January 29, 1961 (Sunday): *I spent the day at home while I finished hemming my black coat. We went to pick up Mike at six, and I almost got into it with Edith. I feel so much antagonism toward her; it is hard to hold back.*

February 3, 1961 (Friday): *I stayed home all day and worked on the black velvet coat. It snowed like crazy and was quite slippery. We met our friends at Settlers for dinner, and they came over to the apartment after we put Mike's puzzle together backward and forward for entertainment.*

February 5, 1961: *We went house hunting today, and Mrs. Gleck showed us two nice ones, but as usual, Ed is against* *them because he wants everything. We were going to take Mike with us, but suddenly Ed decided we'd take Edie's car; then Ed suggested we leave Mike there, and I told him that he should ask her first. We walked in, and he didn't even ask her; it looked prearranged.*

February 6, 1961: *Ida couldn't come today, so I cleaned the house myself. I went through my drawers, and Edith stopped in.*

February 7, 1961: *I took Mike shopping today and cleaned my front and linen closets. Mike fell in the bedroom while daddy was playing. He hit his head, and as usual, Ed jumped on me. "What did you have on the floor, etc.?" He is always trying to blame someone. Then he wouldn't even let me give Mike any sympathy. If it was anyone's fault, it was his because we didn't have room for Mike to run around.*

Edith came again tonight. I told Ed and began to cry. We had a small discussion where we both agreed to try to do better. Then, I went to Ellen Glass's home for Mahjong, and I lost 73 cents.

February 8, 1961: *I attended the ORT meeting today at Renee Swelling's house. I was elected to serve on the nominating committee to elect officers for next year. Jean Spira and I decided to get together for lunch soon. Rena Newman gave a book review of Jon De Hertog's* The Inspector.

Ed finally made love to me tonight. I have only four months to go. I bought a $17.95 Westinghouse iron at Uncle Bill's for $8.25."

February 9, 1961 (Thursday): *I worked hard all day. I chose today to clean the kitchen walls and ceiling. I couldn't stand the sight of the caked-on grease any longer, even though Ed said not to do it because we were going to move. I did a lot of pushing that I suppose I shouldn't have done. I would like to do the carpet now. I went to an ORT card party at Carol S's and played bridge with Marge Young, Claire E., and Rita. There were about 24 women. I got to bed around two in the morning.*

February 10, 1961 (Friday): *Today was Ed's birthday, and I slept almost all morning. I was so worn out. Edith insisted, as usual, that we spend his birthday with her. At least Ed didn't give up our swimming night, but we went over after dinner and took Jack Feldman, PJ, and Big Mike for cake and coffee. Ed had asked Edith to keep Mike. Why? I don't know. I took him over around 4:30. Later, I gave Ed two hankies, a pipe, and books: <u>Decorating Ideas, How to Get Rich in the Stock Market</u>, and <u>Epigrams of Men, Women, and Love</u>. I went swimming.*

February 11, 1961 (Saturday): *Ed went house hunting for four hours and found nothing. I picked Mike up around 12:30. Ed and I went to Shirley and Mort's to play Canasta. We had a good time and left around 1:30.*

February 12, 1961 (Sunday): *I could not get going today. Too many late hours this week, in addition to cleaning the kitchen walls, left me exhausted. Edith called and wanted Mike to come over, so Bunny came to get him.*

February 14, 1961: *Today was Howard Miller's birthday party. He was three, and Mike had a good time at his party.*

I went to Rita H.'s, where we met to nominate officers for next year.

February 17, 1961 (Friday): *It rained all day. I went to the City of Hope luncheon at Sherwin's Party Center. It was nice. We played Bingo and saw a play. I rushed home and got ready to go swimming. Ruby came at six, and I left. Jack F., plus Don and Barbara J., joined us, and we went to Frankie and Johnnie's Restaurant for dinner and returned home to play Clue.*

February 20, 1961: *I went to Jean S's house today and had lunch with her at the Virginian. When I arrived home, there was mass confusion. The TV man was there, Ida was leaving, and Jean and Edith were there. Oh, for peace and quiet!*

February 21, 1961: *I played Mahjong tonight at Ellen's and came out $1.52 to the good. I had Mike outside today, and Bobbie Eckhart punched Mike in his mouth.*

February 23, 1961: *I finished my black velvet coat's lining and sorted pictures for the photo albums. Ed went to a steel distributor's meeting, so I took Mike to dinner at Clarks. I saw Rabbi Dan and his family and went over to their table to reintroduce myself. Ed was home at 10:30.*

February 24, 1961 (Friday): *Edith came at 5:00 and reportedly left after Mike was in bed. Ruby came to sit at 6:00 when I left to swim, and I didn't get to touch Mike. Bunny also came over, adding to Mike's confusion. After swimming, Jack Feldman, Chuck (Big Mike's cousin), Big Mike, P.J., Ed, and I had dinner at Settlers and then came home to play Clue.*

February 25, 1961: *It started as a rainy day, which turned into a freeze and snow in the evening. Ed and I looked at houses again, but as usual, nothing satisfied him. Edith called early in the evening for Ed to come over and hook up my portable TV because her set blew a tube. This is terrible! She won't let him live his own life and has to interfere with mine.*

February 26, 1961 (Sunday): *Today was a nothing day. Edie and Bunny showed up to take Mike as I was getting Mike ready to go outside this afternoon. I wanted him to get some fresh air, but they took him home soon after we got outside. They got him there no sooner than they called for me to pick him up. Ed was taking his second nap of the day. I worked on the photo album tonight.*

February 27, 1961: *I went to Dr. Marv's today and weighed in at 135 ¾ pounds, a gain of 13 lbs. Everything is fine. PJ called and invited us to dinner at Big Mikes (Spaghetti). First, Ed said yes, then later said no. When I reached Phil, she had already started dinner, so she had Big Mike call Ed and convince him he should come. We took Mike to Edie's to stay all night at Bunny's suggestion, even though he was invited. It was a lovely evening. Just what Ed needed to get his mind off his troubles at the office.*

February 28, 1961: *Picked Mike up at Edie's and brought him home for lunch, and then we took Ed to the rapid transit. My day was completely thrown off, so I took another nap, cleaned the house, and took Mike outside. I played Mahjong at Shirley's tonight and won $1.43.*

March 1, 1961: *I began the appetite suppressant pills Marv prescribed today, and Wow! What a lift! I didn't need a nap and accomplished more than I had in any two weeks. Ed and I discussed the house situation, and I hope to have convinced him we should buy on Beachwood Boulevard. We're going Sunday to look at them again.*

March 2, 1961: *Wow! Those pills make me nervous, and I smoke too much. I had many things to do tonight, but Bob and Connie came over, and I couldn't do anything as they stayed till almost eleven. My mother called today and asked me to come to Plymouth on the 13th to play bridge.*

March 3, 1961: *I really knocked myself out today. Ida and I cleaned the crystal, china, and silver and made pies and dinner for Mike, PJ, and Jack F. I didn't have a chance to sit down all day, and my legs were killing me.*

March 4, 1961: *I went with Shirley to the AKO Luncheon as Ellen Glass's guest. Maxine and Rochelle were there, too, at Higbee's. After the luncheon, we window-shopped through the store.*

March 5, 1961 (Sunday): *We took Mike to Edith's and went to Beachwood Boulevard to decide on a house. We ate lunch at Clark's. We spoke to Herman Brown about the split-level and a couple of his homes on Wendover. Then we checked Kahn-Miller homes and talked with them. We decided on 2448, a two-story colonial. Now to get the loan and papers and whatever else.*

March 6, 1961: *I went to the dentist this morning and went shopping.*

March 7, 1961: *Worked on the house design and went to the Square with Shirley Kress in the evening. After I got home, Mike and PJ stopped by and stayed until after 11. I took Edith out to look at the house.*

March 8, 1961: *It was a miserable rainy day today, but I went to the ORT meeting at Elayne Z's on Brentwood Drive. I also worked on the house design. I stayed home tonight, and Ed went to Kahn's to pick up the Land Title Contract.*

August 22, 1961: *Four years of marriage. We moved into our house, and Gary is three months old. In a letter to my mother, I wrote of the unhappiness prevailing in the household.*

Dear Mother,

I'm in bed at eleven every night and get up with Gary sometimes two or three times a night. I'm up at six or seven in the morning with 5 to 6 ½ hours of sleep. I have no time for a nap and am busy all day. All I ever hear is how tired Ed is. This morning I just about blew my top.

Mike has been coming into our room every night to sleep with Ed. Not me. He won't even come near me because I would put him back to sleep in his bed. I never hear him come in. This morning was different. Mike came in at four o'clock, and Ed decided to change his diapers in the bed next to me. But is he quiet about it? No. He has to talk like it is the middle of the afternoon. That woke me up totally, and I couldn't get back to sleep for an hour.

Then, Gary was up. I'm just staggering back to bed at 6:15, and Ed and Mike decide to get up. I asked Ed why he was letting Mike get up this early, and he said, "Well, you won't have to worry about Mike not taking a nap today." He didn't take one yesterday. Well, needless to say, I couldn't get back to sleep then because I was too angry. Ed also said he hasn't been getting any sleep because of Mike coming in, but this is Ed's fault. He could break Mike of the habit if he wanted to. Also, he does get sleep and doesn't have to stay up for a half-hour trying to hold his eyes open while feeding Gary. But I was so mad at him for his lack of consideration. I may end up with neurosis myself one of these days if I keep having all my problems.

Up to this point, I tried to point out how damaging it could be psychologically for Mike to sleep with either Ed or me or both of us. I want to add that this habit of Mike coming into sleep with Ed went on for two more years until I filed for divorce, and Ed finally saw this after two years.

My Mother's Letter Above Continued: *Mike, PJ, and a few other couples were planning to go to Chautauqua Lake in New York over Labor Day, and we had committed ourselves to go, although I knew Ed would back out. He gave our friends the excuse that it would be too much money. So, it would be beneficial to have a weekend away when I said we could give up going out for a few weekends and save the money we would have spent. Besides, it wouldn't cost us more than $30. Then he came up with the excuse that we couldn't leave our three-month-old baby. I said our maid could take good care of him. Then he asked me where my sense of responsibility lay. He said I have so much work* *to do around here that I should be home doing it. (Put contact paper on shelves, make drapes when we can't afford the material, rearrange shelves, drawers, etc.) I haven't done all this thus far. One more weekend won't hurt. He gave me the last excuse when I said we could afford to go to Plymouth for Labor Day.*

He seems to be getting old and stodgy or something I cannot figure out. I just don't understand him anymore, but I know that I am becoming heartbroken. I guess he wants to keep me barefoot in the winter, and pregnant in the summer, or in other words, to enslave me.

My pediatrician recommended reading Their Mother's Sons by E. A. Strecker, MD. I read the book. It is about Momism and was remarkably interesting. As Dr. Bloomfield told me, I would understand my mother-in-law better and Ed more. My mother-in-law is a mom, and so is Ed, as he is a victim of a mom and is a mom himself. Thank goodness you are a mother and not a mom.

When I took Gary in for his checkup last week, I talked with Bloomfield some more, and I feel that he is on my side and that I no longer feel so inadequate. Bloomfield told me that Ed is a mom, and this means immaturity. He told me that I was the strong party in this marriage and that I had no chance of changing Ed or his mother. Maybe some other woman could change them, but Dr. Bloomfield doubts I can. But I must stand up for my rights and assert myself regardless of the consequences, and Ed will either make or break us. This is only in connection with the children. He doesn't want to be quoted. He also said that Moms never admit that they are wrong. Even if I told Ed or Edith that they were wrong and Bloomfield said so, they would still not admit it.

The problem we discussed was that Ed told me the day before to give up breastfeeding because it made Mike jealous. So, I told Bloomfield this and added that I thought it was Ed who was jealous. Bloomfield said that Mike would not be that jealous or even jealous at all, so it should not make me give it up, and if I did, I would only be doing it to appease Ed. If I gave up breastfeeding for that, then I would go on being stepped on. If I am unhappy about being stepped on, could it be any worse if I stood up for what I feel is right? No. I would just bring things to a head where they should have been long ago.

So, this last week, the baby seemed to not be getting enough at the breast, and I called Bloomfield. Even if I have made up my conscious mind, he said my subconscious is still at work, causing my milk supply to suffer.

I needed someone with authority to say that I am strong and do what I believe is right regardless of the consequences. The "regardless of the consequences" has made me timid and submissive all these years. Every time I've had a discussion with Ed or his mother, I always ended up being the person who was wrong and unhappy because I feel the discussion gained nothing for my side. So, bit by bit, I will try to creep to the helm, and if it doesn't work, then I must suffer the consequences, which, I am sure, can make me no more unhappy than I am now.

Dr. Bloomfield told me to read <u>Their Mother's Sons</u> when I was in the hospital after delivering Gary. I was concerned because my mother-in-law planned to toilet-train Mike while I was there, and I knew this wouldn't be good for him psychologically. Dr. Bloomfield told me that she was only trying to show her son, Ed, that she was a better mother than I. He also told me to have Ed put a stop to it. But as I told Dr. Bloomfield, Ed would never listen to me, so he suggested I read that book to better understand.

November 5, 1961: *I am still up two to five times a night with Gary. In my letter to my mother about visiting the child-parent guidance clinic, I told her that I didn't believe it was doing me any good because I still didn't have any nerve to speak up. I'm squelched every time I do.*

Around August, I applied at the Jewish Family Service to attend the Parent Guidance Clinic because I could see Mike developing problems. I couldn't convince Ed that Mike needed help or that we needed help in better handling Mike's problems. So I went by myself.

I continued through to December, when Mrs. Brody, my counselor, wanted to talk to Ed to hear his side of the story and see if, by talking to him, he might understand and be more helpful in handling Mike's problems. After coming home from that session, Ed blew up at me for having him go to a third person to find out that we also had marital difficulties. After all, I had been telling him right along but not making much of an impression. He didn't want me to continue any longer, and after he had calmed down, we talked things over. And he convinced me that I was wrong again and talked me out of continuing the counseling with him.

CHAPTER 12

1962

While we try to teach our children all about life,
our children teach us what life is all about.

—ANGELA SCHWINDT

Three Months Later

February 11, 1962: *Things have not been well here for a long time, and they continue to worsen. Ed seemed decent today, but tonight, he blew up like he usually does. Mike was standing in the corner; I was in the bathroom, and Gary, evidently, got hold of an ashtray. Ed came in yelling at me to get one of the kids upstairs. He yelled that it seemed there never could be any peace and quiet around the house. Then he proceeded to scare poor Gary by leaning him over the sink and splashing cold water on his face and mouth.*

I told him to relax before he frightened poor Gary to death. I would do it. I said, "If you want peace and quiet, you never should have married." Like a child, Ed stormed up to his bedroom. He wouldn't let Mike in, frightened to death by this time. Ed got mad because Mike needed reassurance and said he was going out for a while. Then Mike was extremely frightened and told Ed not to go and that Mike loved Ed. Finally, Ed calmed down enough to know he better not leave. Mike was quite upset tonight as it took him a long time to fall asleep.

I never wanted to live with this much tension in my marriage or family life. There is never any love or praise, and I am always anxious about what will be wrong next. I desperately need someone to talk to.

March 10, 1962: *The years are passing swiftly, and nothing has changed except that things are worse. I believe we have no more marriage; at least, it seems as if Ed feels that way because of what just happened.*

We were discussing what had happened to Marty and Harry's wedding gift. Ed said, "I decided not to give them one." I said, "I feel we should because of all Marty has done for us." He still didn't feel it necessary and remarked, "You used to be frugal, and that certainly has changed." I asked him, "What do you mean by that? Indeed, I haven't spent money on anything that wasn't needed, and even then, I feel guilty."

Then he said, "Do I have to go downstairs to watch this, or are you going to be quiet?" I said, "You never seem to want to discuss anything anymore." He picked up his things and started downstairs. I said, "If that's what you think of our marriage, go downstairs and watch your TV."

There was no answer, and he watched it for about a half-hour and returned.

He said, "We'll discuss things when we both feel like it."

I said, "That isn't always good because, by the time we get around to it, there is a big resentment built up over however small a matter." Because this is what has happened to me.

Yesterday was a horrible day. Ed was home, sick. By the time I was ready to go shopping, it was 3:00 in the afternoon. I went out to start the car, and nothing happened as usual. We had to call AAA. The AAA man told me, "I don't mind coming out, but you've had me come several times to start this car. This has been happening for at least three months, but the Auto Club might cancel your membership if you don't get the car fixed." By the time he left, it was almost 4:30, and time to take Mike to the doctor to determine if he had another ear infection. Then, Ed accused me of not knowing how to start the car properly.

It was 6:30 p.m. when Mike and I were ready to leave the doctor's, and need I say, the car wouldn't start. I was afraid to call AAA or Ed because he might jump on me again for no reason, and I began to cry. Then, poor Mike was tired, hungry, and sick, and he began to cry when I did, so I decided to go back to the doctor's office. A couple of men were waiting for their wives, and I explained my predicament. They came out to push me, but couldn't, so one of the men went to a gas station, brought back a jumper, and started the car. I had to get a prescription for Mike but decided I had better get him home before anything else happened. I got him home at 7:00 and went to the drugstore.

When I came out again, the car wouldn't start, and it coasted down the hill where I sat until a mother with two young girls came along and helped me manually push the car back into a parking space. They asked me, "What are you going to do next?" I told them, "I will probably sit down and bawl."

Then I spied the Sohio station on the corner and walked over to summon help. Three men came over and pushed me to the station. They checked the battery, and each cell was dead. They recommended that I get a new battery, which I had already decided to do because I was so embarrassed having to ask for help every time I drove the car. I said, "Okay, after I check with my husband."

I called Ed and said, "I'm going to get a new battery, okay?" He answered, "What for?" I nearly exploded at that point. Then I told him how often I had asked for help that night. He very reluctantly told me to go ahead.

It makes me so angry because when anything goes wrong with his mother's or sister's car, it is in the garage immediately, with Ed taking over. Needless to say, I've had no difficulty starting the car since I got the battery. We've had the car for three-and-three-quarters years, which is pretty good for one battery.

Thursday was a nightmare, too. My mother and Miles were in town for the Home and Flower Show. We were all supposed to meet at the Statler Hotel for dinner, but Ed was sick and should have said so before meeting us. We ordered dinner, and he ordered none, then excused himself to go to the men's room. After dinner, Miles looked for him *and returned, saying Ed was heaving his cookies. So Ed came back and wanted to leave immediately. I wanted to get Mike a toy. After all, I promised him an animal with a hump because I never got to buy him any treat.*

Ed yelled across the lobby, "You're not going to buy him that!" I did, but I was somewhat embarrassed about it, though. On the way home, I tried to find out what was wrong with Ed, and he wouldn't tell me. I didn't find out until morning what had happened (It was food poisoning.). My mother-in-law was there when we arrived home at 8:00 (I had told the maid I would be there then). Mike was coming down with another ear infection. I was upset, though, because Edith appears whenever we go out. She makes life hell for the maids. What a night! My attitude showed disapproval, so she didn't speak to me for about two weeks.

April 19, 1962: *Never have I been so confused and mixed up. I think I know what is bothering and upsetting me, but then Ed turns around and dispels all my ideas. He is either correct, or he has a way of saying things that make me feel like the worst individual ever to walk this earth. I don't know whether to believe him or what I feel is wrong. If I believe him, then I'm in great need of help. If I believe in myself, I am also in need of help.*

Last night, the first night of Passover, my campaign to assert myself began. We were to go to Ed's Aunt Henrietta and Uncle Joe's for dinner. I was almost ready, wearing a simple basic wool jersey dress, which I felt comfortable in and thought would befit the occasion. Then Ed started on me. "Don't you have something dressier?"

"No, I've got all my clothes with the hems halfway done."

"You knew about this occasion long enough that you should have been prepared!"

True enough, but I felt what I was wearing was proper enough. I wore my dressiest outfit and felt utterly out of place and uncomfortable.

We were late getting started because I had to change and because I couldn't locate Mike's shirt, which he had taken from his drawer and packed in a suitcase, which our sitter Barbara found.

Most of the evening progressed smoothly until time for my mother-in-law and sister-in-law to leave. They wanted to take Mike, and I told them Friday would be all right. Then they told Mike they had a surprise for him when he came Friday. (Ed and I, at least, agree that Mike has too many surprises and presents and is spoiled). I waited for Ed to speak, and he didn't.

I said, "No, surprises, please. We've discussed that. (We had.)

Edith argued, "The surprise is an old toy we've put away."

I said, "That's all right, but tell him that - no surprise, and it's the idea of the surprise that spoils."

Ed tried to say this was not the time to discuss this, and I felt it was. Mike is having problems, and every present moment is essential.

I went to get my coat, and Ed told me, "You are acting like a bitch." I told him, "That's right, I am."

He retorted, "This is not the place." I said, "I will any place I need to do it." I knew that we would discuss this later, and we did.

Again, he said, "You're selfish; you've made my mother and sister not feel welcome in our house; you're lazy about the house; you're cold as a stone wall; you haven't been trying." He didn't like anything I did, but on the other hand, in the past, he had said I'm doing a good job.

He wanted to know how I felt and what I suggested: "I feel nothing. I'm depressed and unhappy. We are incompatible as we enjoy nothing together." The following came after Ed said he was willing to do anything to make me happy. I suggested separation (He won't hear of it); going back to modeling (Ed won't let me model); doing little theater work (four nights a week away from home. Ed will never see me. He doesn't now); if I stay home, there's nothing to share anyway; a vacation (someday). He says he loves me, but I don't feel it. It is not a healthy, overpowering love; now that I analyze it, it never has been.

He told me, "Never mouth off to me as you did last night, or we will never go out in company again." It may have been wrong, but I felt it was so right. I know I can't be all wrong, and neither can Ed. But where are we both right?

I'm struggling to be me because I don't think I've been me for five years, and I believe I've been a phony. Now I want to say what I think, feel what I feel, do what I want to do, and enjoy life as I believe it can be enjoyed, but I can't find a solution.

April 20, 1962: *I wonder if Ed does respect me. Tonight, I brought up what he said about he'd do anything to make me happy. I suggested we join the Executive Club and Shaker Swim to meet other people and have a place to go together and a day camp for Mike. First, he said, "No. There is nothing but the worst people as members." I said, "Maybe, but everyone can't be that bad."*

He said, "And we can't afford it." Then I suggested using membership as a goal if I returned to work part-time.

He said, "Modeling is out of the question because people think models are whores nowadays." I asked, "If that is so, why did you marry me?" I don't recall his answer, but I felt a lack of respect.

Then I said, "Maybe I can find something else that would give me satisfaction, boost my ego, and earn money." He replied, "It can't be full-time or nights, or I won't hear of it. If it makes me grouchy, I will not work my tail off for these things." His suggestions for things to do in the evening are drawing and reading a book on sex positions. (Good: He complimented me on how I looked and because I was ready.)

April 21, 1962 (Saturday): *I'm really lost. I had feelings of absolute hate tonight, and I just wanted to walk out.*

This morning Ed confronted me with an old letter of my mother's he discovered when he couldn't sleep. It pertained to the Home and Flower Show evening when Ed became ill and was miserable company. She simply stated, "All I could think of was how you must have been raked over the coals on your way home."

Ed was then agitated that I might be listening to my mother's advice or ideas, which must be thwarting my own. He is insane because I do my own feeling, leading to my thinking!

Tonight, the discussion of Easter and Christmas came up. Mainly the Easter Bunny and Santa Claus. Not religion. I told Ed before I married him that if I married him, I must still have Christmas with a tree and Santa Claus and the Easter Bunny and eggs because it was a good part of my life that I couldn't give up even if I did my religion. Ed said, "Don't forget these boys are Jew boys, and don't you make a big thing of all this." He keeps wanting to drop all my holidays. It is hard for him to understand how difficult it is to give up someone's past. If he had wanted a complete Jewish life for his children, he should never have married a gentile. He got upset because I told him I wanted to shop for Easter candy for Mike's basket, which brought on the discussion, and he went downstairs saying, "Now we have a new issue to discuss."

Then I had trouble getting Mike to bed (which usually occurs after spending time with Edie, and this time against my wishes. He spent all day Friday to Saturday night). He had one tantrum after another, kicking and screaming. He didn't want his bath, etc. Then, I couldn't get him into bed. So I gave up because this is halfway a result of Edith's over-spoiling, our tempers, and his association with Mark next door. I called downstairs to Ed that he could finish putting Mike to bed as I couldn't handle him anymore.

Ed was mad, and I was mad. So another discussion. He asked me to define love, which I did by saying it's respect, wanting to do for the other person, and accepting the person as they are. It looked as if I didn't love Ed when I had finished because I didn't have that feeling for any of those three qualities anymore.

So, Ed said, "I will never give up the children."

I said, "Neither will I."

Then he said, "We'll have to live as friendly strangers."

I told him, "I won't agree to that. How do you think we can raise happy, healthy children that way?"

"Well," he said, "You can leave any time you want."

Although he declared his love, I don't feel he does or feels what I mentioned. It ended up with what can we do? If I have no feelings, what is the sense of trying? I said I was willing to try to see if my feelings would return.

So we agreed, again, to try (I believe that it is still on his terms because I didn't have an understanding that my wishes had been accepted in any way other than he would show me more affection and make love to me more than once every month or two). We ended up making love; this time, I had some feelings return.

April 25, 1962: *Edith took Mike today. I thought it was too soon. But I'm trying to be nice to her, which is going against my wishes. But no matter how tactfully, I wouldn't be considered nice if I refused. This is also true for making her uncomfortable and not welcome in our home.*

Ed made love to me tonight following Millie and Harvey Mandel's departure after visiting for a couple of hours. My feeling has again disappeared.

This week has been relatively pleasant. Ed hasn't been grouchy, and we have done a couple things together. But I still have a feeling something is lacking.

May 1, 1962: *Well, as I say, things go smoothly for about a week after one of our talks, then everything slips back into its old patterns.*

Ed came home with a grouch on again tonight.

I asked him if he wanted to help me give a party on May 11 to celebrate our first year in the house. He was not eager. I asked him for a yes-or-no answer and received, "If that's what you want," with no enthusiasm. I told him I wanted to give it with his interest and help. Then, he wanted to know who I would invite, and he didn't want Bert. Suddenly, Bert's not a friend of ours anymore.

Since I had been told that exchanging summer and winter coats in the coat closet was my job, I went through the closet to prepare the coats for storage. I noticed a couple of things Ed never wore and mentioned that I'd like him to give them away so they wouldn't take up room in the closet and so someone else could get some use who needs them. Also, I referred to his shoes, which he hadn't worn for years. I mentioned it to him, and he said this wasn't my business and to forget it because even if he was teasing me, he was getting angry.

This evening, he said we would do no more Twisting because three Fridays in a row are too much. It hadn't been three in a row, and I believe it was because he didn't like to see me drinking, and I am sure it was because of the money involved.

May 2, 1962: *Tonight, dinner was horrible. As I carved the roast in the kitchen before dinner, I told Barbara that I would hear about how tough it was and that I had better start shopping elsewhere for it.*

Mike started crying before we sat down because he wanted Ed's Coke and didn't want his milk. Gary cried for his bottle after we sat down. As Ed cut into his meat, he said, "Why didn't you set steak knives on the table for this?" I didn't say anything, just sat there. I hadn't even touched my food when he told Mike that was enough and carried him up to his room, where Mike screamed. Ed put Gary in his room, where Gary also screamed, and finally, Ed ended up in our room, closing us all out.

I got Gary; gave him his bottle. Mike came down. We ate together. Ed fell asleep and didn't kiss Mike good night, and I knew Mike wanted his kiss because he was looking for extra comfort and security when I put him to bed. I knew how he felt because that was precisely how I felt.

I didn't even want to talk to Ed and felt very tired (emotionally). I fell asleep on the couch and woke up there at 3:00 a.m., and went to bed.

May 3, 1962: *This morning, Ed said to put water at his place at the table, Gary's high chair in the dining room, and buy my meat elsewhere. He told me yesterday to get an* *exterminator to eliminate the spiders. So, I called the exterminator. Tonight, I fed Mike early with Gary, but Ed ended up at the table with us anyway. So why should I bother making two meals? It seems impossible to accomplish anything without cooperation.*

Ed and I disagreed again on why Mike was so unmanageable. Ed said, "It is Mark's influence." I said, "Mike is susceptible to Mark's influence because of us."

Last night Ed lost control, and Mike was more disturbed today and harder to handle. I must watch for the results of more of these outbursts.

Again, he had to bring up no more Twisting Friday nights and staying up until 4:00 in the morning.

I washed shirts today and found lipstick on Ed's collar and shoulder. I kidded him about it at dinner that his girlfriend should wear lipstick that didn't come off, and he looked a bit too guilty. I wonder if he does have a girl.

May 4, 1962 (Friday): *I told Ed that the exterminator would be out either this morning or later today. He asked if I had called only one, and I said, "Yes." He said, "That's the trouble with you; you're a pigeon for these guys. I want you to call more than one and get an estimate."*

I told him, "I'm sorry, but this is how I am. Accept me so. If you want it done to your satisfaction, do it yourself."

He said, "I'm tired of doing it myself." I don't know what he meant because he hasn't done many of these things at all. Also, he is a penny saver and a dollar spender. He seems to believe that he'll save one or two dollars by calling many pest controllers, but I haven't seen him call many landscapers about quotes regarding the lawn or shrubs. That runs into hundreds and should be given plenty of thought.

Here I go again – afraid I'll do or say the wrong thing. Ed keeps trying to place me in the mid-Victorian era. Speak when spoken to; don't think; do as I say. He is acting like a Father who is a total and complete authoritarian. I cannot live like this because it is breaking me apart.

So, I have to be nice and try again to please Ed, his mother, and his sister, and I should have no thoughts, feelings, or ideas of my own.

Monday, I tried as nicely as possible in every way I could to keep Edith from taking Mike. But she took him for late afternoon, all night, and all day Tuesday. I was punishing Mike for getting wet, but Mike's going with Edith turned into a reward.

Mike had to stay in at least until Noon. Again, at Noon, she called, "Can Mike go to lunch?" I felt that the morning punishment wouldn't be effective if he saw her, so I told her his lunch was ready and that he was tired. "Then I'll take him to the office to see his Daddy after his nap," she said. She cannot take a polite hint that I don't want her to have him that day. Most people, by this time, would give up. And if I tried to have my way, I would have to become quite blunt and tell her no, at which point, she would feel unwelcome.

So, I gave up and said okay. When Mike came downstairs from his nap, he told me he didn't want to go, so I put him on the phone so Edith would believe it. She tried to entice him with lies. Her usual way. "We'll go see the donkey at Halle's that blinks its eyes at us." Mike inquired if it was a real donkey, and she said yes. I don't like lying. Mike will soon believe that lying is all right if Edith does it.

I suggested (so she wouldn't feel bad) that she come over and play with Mike. She agreed but with her thought that Mike would go with her. When she came, poor Mike had to choose either Edie or his new companion, Johnny. I could really see the strain he was going through. Mike ends up going with Edie because she makes him feel guilty. She kept backing out of the drive until he decided. He also was dirty from head to toe, which constituted a thorough cleaning up. Poor child! His mommy is weak, but she isn't allowed to bark and is tied hand and foot. What can I do?!

May 11, 1962: *It finally dawned on me tonight why I feel Ed is doing the mothering, and I feel that that has been taken from me. Mike rolled off the bed, and I reached to pick him up. I held him for a minute because, as usual, it was a race to see who would get there first. Ed was taking him from my arms to comfort him. This is what he always does. No wonder I have this ache inside, this yearning that can't be filled. I'm not allowed to really mother my children. No wonder Ed tells me I don't give my children enough affection. I never had the chance. Ed always jumps first when someone is hurt or cries. Till he is the one always there when a parent is needed. Therefore, he is the first one Mike yells for when he is hurt. No wonder I feel lonely and unfulfilled. I have no way to release my true affections bubbling away inside me.*

Joe Battle is alone this week, so Ed asked me to call and invite him to join us for dinner and a movie tonight.

When Ed arrived home, I couldn't even get a civil answer from him about the consummation of our plans. I guess Ed had a brutal day at the office. I finally called Joe to say that Ed didn't particularly care to go to the movie because he wanted to be home at 11:30. Joe invited us to his house to have coffee or drinks, and we could just sit around and talk. Ed said he didn't want to sit around and talk. Then Ed said, "Why don't you and Joe go Twisting? I'll stay home and sleep." I said, "there'll be no such thing." So, I had Joe talk to Ed.

We ended up having dinner at Mawby's Restaurant, going to Joe's for coffee, to the movie, to Budin's for more coffee, and home at 1:00 a.m.

I am beginning to have feelings and emotions I don't understand because they also frighten me. I had stated that I was not the person I was before I was married, and I didn't like the person I had become because I was nothing. Now I feel that I might become someone I don't like, and somehow, I need help because I want to become this person. I've got to call Dr. Wiant because I need help, and maybe he can guide me to the right help. With my emotions running rampant, I'm all torn up inside.

May 12, 1962: *I stopped at Dr. Wiant's office today. I didn't call because I was afraid to let Ed know I was going. He is complaining about the doctor's bills. Dr. Wiant took me in.*

He told me I was experiencing a kind of emotional hysteria, some of which is quite normal under my circumstances.

Like a child, I reach in all directions for as little or as much love, affection, and understanding as possible because I don't receive it where I should. I'm trying to prove to myself that someone loves and needs me.

From what he sees, we have nothing left on which to work; he hopes he is wrong but gave me three alternatives from which to choose: (1) See a psychiatrist. This helps me corroborate or confirm what he said or see if something else is wrong, (2) See a lawyer. Set about to do something about my situation, either separation or divorce, but I've got to try something. Also, to see where I stand legally, (3) See both. I think he wants me to do this, but the decision should be entirely on my own. He gave me an appointment for next Saturday and told me he wanted me to do something before coming in next week.

May 13, 1962: *Today began to be half the best Mother's Day I've experienced since being a mother. Ed let me sleep late, but due to the commotion downstairs, I almost got up early.*

Ed was tired and, therefore, short of patience. As stated, Ed is never guilty of raising his voice. But he did with poor Mike. On this occasion, poor Mike was the recipient of it. Mike sounded like he was demonstrating excellent behavior. But when Mike didn't do precisely as Ed told him, Ed warned him that he would be spanked or receive whatever punishment came into Ed's mind.

When I got up, Ed suggested we all go to lunch with Edie (MIL). He helped Mike get dressed, and Mike behaved beautifully, but when he didn't put his arm where it should go at the right time, Ed would explode.

Needless to say, after we had tried three restaurants and found long lines with quite some time to wait, we decided to go to Edith's to eat; then, we came home. I felt it was a waste of everything, especially with Ed's picking on Mike, which continued all day. Tonight, I made a light supper for Edith and came outside on the patio when everything was quiet. Ed did apologize for his behavior today because he said, "I didn't feel well."

May 14, 1962: *Gary cried this morning because he had just completed his breakfast and was very impatient for his bottle. I was buttering Mike's toast, and Ed came flying down the stairs in a rage, "Why is that baby crying? A person can't sleep around here with all that racket." What can I do? I can't live with the tension he creates in these episodes. My stomach is tied up in knots as a result. It makes my decision more apparent when I think this can continue for the rest of our lives. I can't believe the situation will be any better when business improves.*

Tonight, another discussion about my getting too friendly with the maids. I haven't been able to tell Ed that Barbara's reason for leaving at the end of the month is because of him. He believes it's because he is dissatisfied or because I can't handle maids as he has been brought up to do. If I told him, he would have her leave now. I live in fear of him, of what I should or should not do; I can't be myself.

He also brought up again my not being as frugal as I used to be about money and why I can't manage as I should. Once, he told me to spend money when I needed something, but I never did. Now, I feel guilty about buying anything I need. I have $60 a week to manage and find it impossible to get *all my bills paid without asking for extra: groceries are $35 to $40 a week, gas $30 to $40 a month, electric is $20 a month, milk is $20 a month, cleaning is $5 a month, soft drinks are $5 a month, water averages about $5 a month, and medications are $5 a month. This equals about $260 a month. This leaves me with little, so I splurge on something for the kids or a magazine. He tells me never to buy the cheapest or check the papers for specials. So again, I am up a tree.*

Ed told me again that he didn't want Mike to play with Mark. He came into the house with Mike and said, "Now Mark is teaching Mike to take his socks off and wear just his shoes." I see nothing wrong with it. I do the same thing when it is hot, and Ed is too meticulous to allow that. Then he told Mark to go home, and Mark said a bad word; therefore, Mike couldn't play with him for a week. It is impossible to keep the two apart, with Mark living next door, particularly without starting a neighborhood feud. I believe in teaching a child what is right and what is allowed, knowing if he is loved enough, and if he loves enough back, he'll try to please. Besides, when Mike goes to school, I'm sure he'll meet a lot worse, and when I think about it, this is where the seed of prejudice begins.

May 15, 1962: *As I was dressing Mike this morning, Ed called from outside for the tape. I asked, "What tape?" He replied, "The measuring tape!" He yelled, "I never seem to find it when I need it." I replied, "You were the last person to have it, but I know where the folding measure is."*

"Get it," he said. That means immediately. I left Mike to get it and returned, and I couldn't find Ed. Then, when he

came back, he didn't even use it. He surprised me with the tone of voice he used outside the house. Usually, everything is hush-hush when we have our discussions.

I asked Ed about the car tonight. Yesterday was the third time he had taken it to the garage, and it returned in the same condition. He told me he's not going to have it fixed right now. The carburetor needs cleaning out. I asked how he could risk my life and those of our children. His reply was that I would get used to driving it. When I get in traffic, the car stalls. I can't trust it when pulling into traffic or making turns, and it frightens me, but he said, "No, we can't do it now." Maybe he secretly hopes something will happen to me.

Ed said that he thought the "Twist" was sensuous, and there he was, pushing me into the arms of another man to Twist.

May 17, 1962 (Thursday): *Ed didn't come home for dinner, so I took the maid and kids on a picnic because it was so hot. I took advantage of the opportunity because Ed detests picnics.*

Later, when we got home, Ed told Barbara to throw out the potato salad that had been in the refrigerator for a couple days. I had already discussed this with Barbara earlier, and she came to me with this comment, "Who is the lady of this house?" Even the maid is puzzled.

May 18, 1962 (Friday): *I cleaned the garage tonight, took everything out, and was ready to hose it down when Ed offered to do it. I told him, "Nothing doing." He only wanted to do the enjoyable part. It took me nearly five hours to* *complete, but I had no looks or words of gratitude. Rhoda A. walked down and looked at it and said it looked terrific. She told me that I should get a medal.*

When Ed came out to look, he said, "It still looks cluttered." Here was our opportunity for togetherness, and he muffed it.

May 20, 1962 (Sunday): *Ed told me tonight, as the ketchup and salad dressing were about to be put away, "I don't want to tell you your business, but make sure the maid wipes the tops of these bottles before putting them away. See, I'm not telling you your business."*

I retorted, "This is my business; you just told me what to do."

I took Mike to Kiddieland today. His eyes were as big as saucers, and it was all I could do to bring him home. He had such fun.

Things were reasonably smooth this weekend, but I still have no feeling.

May 22, 1962: *Last night, Mike started coughing until it kept him awake. Ed started on me, "That does it. Tomorrow, you take him to see Dr. Bloomfield."*

I replied, "Yes, I will call the doctor." Ed said, "I said you would take him." I replied, "That's enough." (Always picking even in the middle of the night.) I agree that Mike should see the doctor, but I won't be told to do every little thing as if I am his servant.

Last night, Ed began losing his patience with the children and immediately yelled for me to put them to bed.

(Mike only seems to cough in the morning or middle of the night.)

June 4, 1962: *A week has passed, and things are deteriorating to a point where we have started raising our voices. I thought, with adjustment, I would try to make a go of this marriage. But I cannot live like this. Everything is smooth when Ed is gone, except I worry that what is or is not done will upset him when he returns. The minute he steps into the house, I'm exhausted, my stomach immediately ties up in knots, and I begin to shake and fidget.*

Tonight, Mike began crying because he buttered a hole in his bread and didn't want a piece of broken bread. I gave him another slice, but Ed gave him some "broken" butter, making him cry more. Then Ed directed me to move him into the kitchen, making Mike feel rejected and cry even further. Ed threatened Mike to stop crying, or he would go to his room. Mike came to me for comfort, and I put my arm around him but told him to do what his father said.

Then, Gary began to cry. Ed inquired, "Do they wait till I come home to get into trouble?" I answered, "No. They are into things all day." He said, "Then it is your fault. You don't discipline the kids; I must come home and do the job for you. You have to stay with them all day." I said, "I'm sorry, but I don't want a home where I have to say 'no' every two minutes. I do discipline them. You can ask Junetto or Barbara if I don't. Besides, half of Mike's trouble is that he's spoiled." Ed said, "Oh, don't start that with me! From now on, I will be home at 7:00 p.m. I want Mike fed and Gary in bed. I don't like coming home to a madhouse."

I retorted, "If that's how you feel, why did you ever have children? Every family has active children."

A few more comments were tossed, and he said, "I'll eat my dinner downtown and come home when they are both in bed." He got up from the table, went upstairs, and slammed his door on us.

That's what he has done, all right. He is slamming his door at us right out of his miserable life. I cannot live like this and don't want to subjugate my children to it!

Yesterday, Sunday, was just as bad. He was spanking or punishing Mike or threatening him every five minutes. No wonder the poor child doesn't respond to authority. He has so much of it he probably figures, "What's the sense in trying? No matter what I do, I get yelled at."

The Kuzmas came over at 5:00 p.m. Mike was already in his room for the night (being punished for running into the street). I finally convinced Ed to let him come down while our company was there. Ed kept yelling at Mike as he played with the Kuzma's three kids, plus our two. Ed was never a caring host to them either. (I supposed that because Ben is undereducated, and they have no money.) They are my friends. So, he wasn't much better. He was ordering me about. Then he came up with the comment, "I think I'm beginning to hate kids."

Because of all this, I know I must find a better way of life. It may not be easy for me, but happiness is more essential than many material things.

On **June 6, 1962:** *Monday evening after my Ort meeting, I couldn't sleep when I returned home and went to bed. So I finally got up. It must have been 4:00 a.m. when I finally succumbed. Last evening, I was up late when my cousin, Joyanne, whom I hadn't seen in four years, unexpectedly called to say she was in town. She and a mutual friend came over and stayed until around 2:30 a.m. Again, I couldn't fall asleep and must have succumbed around 5:00 a.m.*

Today, I tried napping but couldn't fall asleep as tired as I was. I thought of retiring early but couldn't, and here I am at midnight, still unable to sleep. I don't know what has come over me as I go from one extreme to another. First, all I want to do is sleep; then, I'm incapable of it. I've also noticed heart palpitations in the last two weeks, excessive daily gas, and hiccups. I hope I don't lose my physical strength because it's all I can do to exist now.

Life has become, for me, a living hell. (I used to love waking to greet the challenge of each new day with a warm heart and a smile.) I cannot exist much longer in an atmosphere like this. It has become an acknowledged, silent cold war, and Ed told me the one alternative was to live as friendly strangers. It seems that this is what is taking place without a word to begin it.

Last night, Mike was sent to his room for the evening at 6:00 p.m. by Ed for (1) running from him when he called; and (2) playing with Mark, which he declared at the dinner table. I had been telling him all day.

I told him that Mike had stayed away all day but that at 6:00 p.m., while I was trying to get dinner and feed Gary his bottle, I had little time to watch Mike.

Then silence prevailed, and no word was spoken for the entire meal. Food mouthfuls entered my stomach like rocks sliding down a steep incline, landing at the bottom with a thud. This silence has extended through tonight, with only polite courtesies extended when necessary. This morning Ed walked out of the house, said goodbye, and looked me square in the eye as if to say, "No more kisses for you." This evening no "good night" or kiss. Last night, he didn't even extend the courtesy of saying "hello" to my cousin. What kind of man is this? He must be sick inside!

Also, I'm apprehensive about Mike. I believe Ed, as well as our tenseness, is adversely affecting the child. He is emotionally upset, I know. He is continually being sent home for hitting other children. He is defying orders and has taken to spitting. He uses "I hate you" and other bad words. He has no desire to do right because he loves us. Instead, he must feel very insecure. I will call Jewish Family Services and find out if they agree with me.

Ed, of course, even with the silence, continues his nagging.

I have never felt so lost. My whole concept of life and love has been blown into millions of pieces. I'm beginning to feel that I will never trust another man. I don't want to stand by and see my children's lives ruined, Mike and possibly Gary becoming delinquent as they grow, becoming the same kind of men, and making their wives and families as miserable as ours. I can't let it happen!

June 9, 1962: *Gary's birthday, and what a long day! It is now 1:15 a.m., and I have finished ironing eight shirts and sewing many buttons on several articles. Now we'll see if Ed complains again about his shirts.*

Speaking of complaining, I think he must look for things to complain about. He told me tonight that I open the living room windows too wide because they are too hard for him to close.

I saw Dr. Wiant today, hemmed a dress, had lunch with Phyllis, came home, and made dinner. I had scheduled dinner for 5:00 p.m. We sat down at 6:00, and Bunny still wasn't there. She arrived just when I was bringing out the cake. Ed must have said something terrible to her, which I didn't hear because Edith went outside to calm her, and when I looked, Bunny was hysterical and recklessly backing out of the drive. Then Edith had to yell at Ed for being a terrible host. Believe me, they are all sick!

Dr. Wiant did help me to straighten out my ideas a little today. He suggested, too, that it would be a good idea for me to take a few modeling jobs to help rehabilitate me, so to speak. But he has given me the strength I couldn't get by myself.

June 14, 1962: *I told Ed I had seen an attorney this morning. He wanted to know on what grounds, and I told him to see the attorney. Then I told him why and that it was because of how miserable he had made me.*

He retaliated, of course, that I've made him miserable and that it is all due to the business, that the children and I are his whole life, and that without us, he has nothing. I said,

"Is it worth it to be so aggravated about your business that it breaks up your whole life?"

He said that I hadn't been any help. I asked, "How can I be when you make me feel like nothing?" He said, "That's not true. You're the greatest." I told him that he sure didn't let me know it. [He was out of touch with reality.]

He wanted to know what I would do, and I said a third person was the only one who could help us.

June 26, 1962: *A couple of weeks have passed, since the fourteenth, since I told Ed I intended to get a divorce. We talked things over, but as usual, we came to no conclusions. I had made up my mind and had lost all feelings for him. How can I regain the feeling? Not overnight, undoubtedly, if ever. The huge irritants from day to day make it nigh impossible. He agreed to see a marriage counselor, and we each have had one consultation at the Jewish Family Service. Thursday, we are due for one together.*

Ed seems to be trying, but his personality is the same, and he needs help with that. I am not putting in an all-out effort because now, I don't have the feeling to help me do it, and also, I'm afraid, and I don't trust Ed anymore. We have both individually talked with Dr. Whitman, my OB-GYN.

I need help just to become a stronger person and to calm down my nerves. I have been continuously trembling since the Fifteenth. Dr. Wiant checked me Saturday and said that it was nerves. Another tranquilizer, which so far hasn't made it cease.

I was sick again on Saturday with a fever, which broke into a cold. Last weekend I was sick also, and I couldn't seem to move. What is the answer?

July 18, 1962 (Wednesday): *I felt low and depressed tonight. Ed sent me out for a ride. When I returned, he asked me if I cared if he went out with another woman to make love to. I was stunned and told him I was there for that purpose. He told me to think it over.*

July 20, 1962 (Friday): *Ed wanted my answer tonight. I told him, "No." He said he asked me only to discover my reaction but had entertained the thought.*

July 21, 1962 (Saturday): *It is 6:00 p.m., and Mike B. just called. Ed went upstairs to talk to him. When he came down, I inquired about what Mike wanted. Ed said Mike wanted to fix him up with a girl and that Mike's customer's wife's friend or someone wanted a good "schtup" (sex with). Mike wanted Ed to go out on Tuesday with her, Mike, and someone else. It will be a double "schtup" and an all-day "schtup."*

I asked him if he was kidding. He said, "You know that I never kid." I asked, "Does PJ know, or is she going?" "No," he replied.

I asked, "Are you really going to do this for Mike?"

He replied, "Sure, he would do it for me. Anything for a customer."

(Other Notes for this day) I believe Ed is seeing someone. He left the house this morning to go to work, which he doesn't do on Saturday. Accidentally, near 10:15 a.m., I called the

office, and there was no answer. I continued all morning at half-hour intervals, and there was no answer. On his return, I questioned whether he had finished his work. He answered no. I asked if he had brought any work home. He said he couldn't because he needed the calculator. He is lying. Where was he?

CHAPTER 13

1963

He who has a why to live can bear almost any how.

—FRIEDRICH NIETZSCHE, 1844-1900,
GERMAN PHILOSOPHER

Filing for Divorce After the Fall

This diary contains entries from the year 1963. It began at the beginning of the week when I told Ed I was going for a divorce. I had not planned to file for divorce at this time, even though it was constantly on my mind. Circumstances opened my mouth, and the words came out.

We had spent Christmas with my parents, who gave the children a railroad set consisting of a track nailed to a large plyboard with an electric locomotive, plus some cars to attach. It was New Year's Day. There were football games on television, and I was polishing Ed's silver in the kitchen. The boys were after their father to help them get the train going on the track, and they kept pestering him to help them until he lost his temper again. He picked up the track and train set, opened the basement door, and threw it all down the stairs. I heard what was going on and thought, "I will not allow him to treat my kids this way!" I marched into the den and said, "Ed, I want a divorce!"

January 1, 1963: *This was a solemn way to begin a new year for everyone concerned. Mike was pushing and hitting Gary and regressed on his toilet training. Gary was whining and wanted to be cuddled. Ed pounded away at my heartstrings, but I thought, "I know I'm right. I don't want a sick father for my children. I can't live without love, even when I can't give it. It's too difficult to be a good mother when I'm unhappy. I'm sure I will find happiness." I told my mother and Miles tonight when they called, and they were shocked and not ready to accept it.*

January 2, 1963 (Wednesday): *I called Mr. Marsh (an attorney) for an appointment tomorrow at 2:30. I had lunch with Edie today. She told me she left Ed's father and has lived to regret it. I told her she might have regretted it if she had stayed. Everyone has different ideas and personalities and is raised differently, thus formulating different opinions. It has taken a long time to reach this decision, and I believe I am doing the best for my children.*

Edie told me she knows my therapist, Mrs. Page, and that she is a bitter woman. (I doubt it.) She said that we needed a psychiatrist, and I had seen one, and he told me I didn't need a psychiatrist.

January 3, 1963 (My Birthday): *I didn't delay today. I saw Mr. Marsh and filed my petition; it looks in my favor.*

I talked to Dr. Bloomfield about it during a consultation. He assured me I had made a wise decision. He knows Ed to be my third child and says I have matured where he hasn't, which is part of the reason for the conflict. He told me what to expect from Ed and told me I had handled Mike correctly, and he was with me.

Went to Announcer's school tonight. [At some point, I registered for this school with Ed's agreement.] *When I came home, Ed told me never to tell Mike again that he was leaving or that we might move. He was so angry, he frightened me, and I was afraid he would hit me if I said anything, so I remained quiet. I know I'm right.*

January 4, 1963: *Today, I went to see Mrs. Page. She thought it would be better if Ed and I lived separately, and she didn't see how I could put up with him. I told her it wasn't easy.*

Mr. Marsh and I talked, and he advised me to stay here. I believe my petition was filed today.

I made the final migration to the guest room today by emptying the closet and chest of drawers and taking everything I needed.

Ed came in tonight, and when he saw all my clothes were moved, he told me we are on an austerity program - no more counseling, no maid, and no more school because he had to cut down. He didn't file taxes last year because he said he didn't make any money. And the year before, he had turned in all his money that he would draw on. Thus, it must be gone. So how have we been living? I will never understand.

My nerves have started on me again with the tension created here. I itch and can't seem to stop scratching. I have welts all over me. And I am afraid to sleep as I don't know what Ed might do.

January 5, 1963: *Ed left the house at 9:30 and returned at noon. I left at around 1:00 and returned at 2:00. Ed left again and returned around 4:30. I found out later that he saw Dr. Bloomfield.*

This itching almost drove me crazy today. My body is a mass of marks where I have scratched. I called Dr. Wiant, who prescribed another pill and told me to stop all other pills. I picked it up after the kids were in bed. When I came home, I took it, and it made me very dizzy and sleepy. Maybe it's because I'm worn out from not sleeping. I can't seem to stop itching when Ed is in the room.

January 6, 1963 (Sunday): *I could hardly move out of bed this morning and felt really exhausted, but I managed to get dressed, make lunch, and clean up the dishes. Gus Stoer stopped by for his stationery book.*

Ed has been quiet today. Mike wanted to go out to play, but we couldn't find anyone for him to play with. So, at 4:00, I put the boys in the car and started for a drive, ending up at the Frails. Shortly before the kids and I left, Ed commented, "Suddenly, I realize just how sick I am." Maybe this separation will help him more than hurt him if he seeks help. We ate dinner at the Frails and returned home at 8:00. Ed said he had worried about where we were, and I told him to get used to it because we no longer had to tell him.

January 7, 1963: *Ed informed me that I must cut out the bakery and dry cleaners because he can't afford bread weekly or the cleaning monthly. He also told me to give him a receipt for the groceries. He will fix it so that I won't have a penny left for a sitter or anything.*

I did the laundry today, and that's about all I could accomplish. Ed arrived home at 7:00 p.m., and even though my itching subsided while he was gone, it began driving me wild the minute Ed walked in. Last night, Mike had a slight temperature, none today, but Mike seemed to be full of energy until this evening when he fell asleep on the couch. Mike's nose sounds plugged, and Mike also complained his neck hurt him. I'll see tomorrow how he is, and then I will call Dr. Bloomfield.

I am about to go crazy with Ed. I took his gun out of his closet for two reasons. I didn't want Mike to get it, and I was afraid Ed would use it on himself or me. He wanted to know tonight what I did with it, and I explained I didn't want Mike to get it. He kept after me until I gave it to him. Why was Ed so upset? Why did he want it?

January 8, 1963: *I'm exhausted. It's all I can do to keep going. Mike has a cold and no fever, but he tires quickly and sometimes seems somehow closer. He shunned Ed completely tonight. Gary had a 102.6 degrees fever and was up a couple times tonight. My itching almost goes away when Ed is gone, but I can't stop scratching when he's home. I went to school tonight, leaving at 7:45 but arriving 45 minutes late. Johnny McKinney, our teacher from now on, asked me to stay after class to help me catch the point I missed. He lectured me that you can't let the world* *know you're having problems in the announcing business. I couldn't concentrate too well on the lecture tonight.*

I cleaned the cupboards in all the bathrooms, washed a load of clothes, lined drawers, and rearranged a few things today.

January 9, 1963: *I have really dragged today. I think I'm coming down with something again, as my throat hurts. Mike seemed okay until he woke up coughing and sick to his stomach tonight. Gary is still under the weather, but Dr. Bloomfield told me to look for other symptoms, and I haven't found anything.*

I learned from Mr. Marsh that Ed was served Monday, the 7th. I had called to ask him about the guns, and he told me to disregard them. After talking with her director, Mrs. Page told me that I should leave the house because Ed might do something to harm me in his sickness. I'm perplexed. Ed also called the JFS to cancel all our future appointments, and I told her that it was without my knowledge or consent.

I ironed five of Ed's shirts, cleaned Mike's room, and put some things away.

January 10, 1963: *I sent Mike to school this morning, and he came home very tired. He ate and went right to bed. Ed called this morning to inform me he had canceled our appointments with JFS and won't let me go to school, and I told him I intended to go. I took Gary with me to see Mrs. Page. He also was tired this noon. I felt sick today as I have come down with nasal congestion, cough, and chest discomfort.*

I rearranged the family room, moved the boy's toy boxes in there, and cleaned up the mess they made. I have difficulty getting my work done because there isn't enough time. Mrs. Page believes I should get out of here because of the possible danger to my life and keeping my sanity. If only I had money to get started, I'd go, and I only want the kids to get a good start. He complained about me going to school tonight, but I went anyway.

January 11, 1963: *I finally had to take a pill to pep up today. Then, I accomplished a lot. Mike was still under the weather and took a long nap. Gary didn't sleep too well. I ironed, cleaned the kitchen, laundry, hall, back closet, and floors, straightened the family room, washed three loads of clothes, and hand-washed quite a few things. Ed was quiet tonight. Edie picked Mike up to stay all night because Mike wanted to go.*

January 12, 1963: *I did my housework this morning. Ed supposedly went to work and returned late, so I arrived late for my doctor's appointment. I seem to have the same condition as before, my third cold or allergy, and I think I'm allergic to Ed. Ed called the doctor's office to tell me to be home by 3:00 p.m., so he could go to the trucking company by 4:00. So, I left my doctor's and hurriedly did my shopping to be home in time. Ed left and returned by 4:30 when I departed to go to the drugstore to fill my prescriptions. I returned, prepared supper, did dishes, put Gary to bed, and retired to my room. Mike wanted to stay at Edie's. The house is too quiet without him, and I miss him.*

January 13, 1963 (Sunday): *I didn't sleep well all night as I was too congested. I dragged around all morning and* *accomplished nothing. Gary's glands were quite swollen today. I put him down at 11:00 a.m. for a nap, and I took one, too. Ed didn't return with Mike until 3:00 p.m., and he didn't say where he had been.*

This afternoon I washed six of Ed's shirts and a load of lingerie. I ironed the shirts, sweaters, and other items, made supper, and cleaned the kitchen. After getting the children to bed, I picked up the family room and dusted the floor and the hall. I cleaned the bathroom and kitchen, soaked stove parts, and cleaned and ironed a few things. Ed doesn't lift one finger to help. He is the laziest person I've ever seen. He must think he is a king.

January 14, 1963: *I sent Mike to school this morning. I took Gary's temperature, and it was 101 degrees. His glands were terribly swollen. I called Dr. Bloomfield but didn't reach him until 5:30, when Gary's temp was 102. So, I took Mike and Gary to Bloomfield's office, where Gary received a shot. Both kids wouldn't go to bed till almost 10:00 p.m. I was exhausted tonight. I laundered three loads of clothes, completed cleaning the range and oven, and started to clean the scum off Ed's shower. I couldn't get much else accomplished as Gary wanted to be held. I am very depressed tonight and don't know why. I guess I feel somewhat lonely.*

January 15, 1963: *Today, I was really exhausted. Just as I was about to fall asleep at 1:00 a.m. last night, Gary woke up and was completely uncontrollable, and he wouldn't go back to sleep. At 2:30, Ed woke and took over for a while, as Gary called him. I finally got to sleep around 3:00.*

Aunt Henrietta stopped this morning all the way from Florida. She told me Ed had called Joe and told him. Joe has loaned Ed a considerable amount of money and wants to take it back before it gets entangled in the divorce. First, she told me that I had been very level-headed about it. Then she told me or asked if I knew Ed had no money. I told her I'd been told that, but I'd never been in on the company's financials.

January 16, 1963: *Today was relatively uneventful. I seem to be having a hard time concentrating on my studies. Edith dropped by and told me that Bunny was married. Thank God! I retired early with another sleeping pill.*

January 17, 1963: *Rush, rush, rush. This morning dress the kids, send Mike to school, get dressed, leave Gary at Pat's, go to my counseling appointment (I felt I was getting somewhere into my past today), go back to school for Mike and Sally, leave Sally off, back to Pat's for Gary. She invited us for lunch. Then we came home and took naps. Afterward, I straightened the house, made supper, ate, got Gary ready for bed, and got ready for my school. Ed didn't get home till 7:45. But I went anyway. When I got home, I cleaned the kitchen, and Ed came to tell me his lawyer told him to cancel all charge accounts. Where do we go from here? He hasn't answered Domestic Relations Court and doesn't intend to talk with Mr. Marsh.*

January 18, 1963: *Again, another rushed day, and I guess I'll never get caught up. I washed sheets today, remade beds, picked up Mike, and cleaned the kitchen after lunch, including the oven. The kids napped, but I woke them to take them to the dentist at 1:30. We didn't get home until*

4:00. I cleaned all the bathrooms, made dinner, and when Ed arrived home, he didn't like what we had, so he made his own. I cleaned the kitchen, put the kids to bed, and retired to my room. I wrote my mother a letter. Mr. Marsh called today to say that Ed's attorneys want to know precisely what I'm charging him. So, they want a fight. I told him to do whatever he needed to get my divorce. It doesn't look to me that Ed really wants me. He just doesn't want to lose any money.

January 19, 1963 (Saturday): *I washed towels and went shopping. It took me nearly all day to shop, put away groceries, clean vegetables, etc. Tonight, I joined Nina Wayne and Carol Battle to see <u>Whatever Happened to Baby Jane?</u> with Bette Davis and Joan Crawford. It was a tense, morbid drama that was very well done. Afterward, we went to Manner's Coffee Shop at Fairmount Circle, and I stayed for about an hour talking with Carol at her house. I arrived home at about 1:30 a.m. It was a race to get to the movie on time while getting the kids in bed before leaving.*

January 20, 1963: *Today, I washed and ironed seven shirts, tee shirts, and one white load. That was all I accomplished, it seems, and just picking up. Tonight, I washed my hair and ironed all the laundered clothes.*

January 21, 1963: *Last night, Mike came down with another ear infection. Gary was up for an hour, and when I got him settled and just about dropped off to sleep, Mike came to me. After many trips back and forth, I decided to stay all night in his room. No sleep. He was up every 15 minutes complaining of pain in his right ear. This morning*

I took him to Dr. Bloomfield. Gary cried when he saw him. Mike had a blister and got a shot.

I let the house go today to stay with Mike. Gary came in, too. I sure was exhausted. Later in the afternoon, Mike began to rally and felt better by evening. Then, Mike was tricky to get to bed.

January 22, 1963: *I began cleaning the bedrooms today. I accomplished only Gary's and mine. Mr. Spence from the Domestic Relations Court came to interview me. The house was a mess because I let the downstairs go to do the upstairs first. I finished straightening the downstairs. The legs on the TV broke in my room, which delayed and upset me. I talked with Mr. Marsh this afternoon and made an appointment to see him at 2:00 p.m. on Thursday to discuss details. I also received a letter from the Domestic Relations Court to appear on February 4 to solve problems (conciliation). Ed helped me fix the TV tonight. Mike behaved well today, but it was difficult again to get him to sleep.*

January 23, 1963: *I cleaned Ed's and Mike's rooms today. I washed six loads of clothes and straightened the downstairs. I typed 15 pages of my diary and didn't retire until 1:30 a.m. That is when Gary woke up from what seemed like a nightmare. He kept crying and screaming with Ed. Ed kept doing things to scare him and thought Gary was having a convulsion. I told him he wasn't and to give Gary to me. I walked into a softly lit room with him, and Gary calmed down and clung to me. Finally, he was calm enough at about 2:30 a.m. to be put in bed. Gee, this life is driving me more insane. It seems challenging to control my temper.*

I'm always nervous. This is terrible for the children. It was terrible before, but worse now.

January 24, 1963: *Today wasn't my day. Ed answered a call this morning that I assumed was Jenny calling to say she couldn't come. Everything else went smoothly, though. I got dressed, shoveled the drive, started the car, and Jenny didn't come. I called Mrs. Page, and we talked for a while. She agrees I should move out because of the harmful effect on the children, especially Mike. I talked for about an hour and a half to Mr. Marsh about how much we had spent on living expenses and asked him if I could make it. He said we'd have to sit tight for a while and see what happens with the temporary alimony. The weather is way below zero, the coldest winter in 100 years. I had a splitting headache and no time to rest.*

January 25, 1963: *It seemed to take all day to straighten the house. I stripped the beds, washed the sheets and towels, and cleaned the dining room. At suppertime, Bunny came to take Mike. I smelled liquor, and she acted drunk. I was afraid to let Mike go. I think I'll set my foot down if it happens again. There was snow and more snow. I paid a man $5 to shovel the drive. Tonight, I was up until almost 2:30 a.m. working. Cleaned all the cabinets, drawers, and books in the family room and lined the drawers. It was quite a job as it has been a long time since they've been done. Our mortgage reminder came, and I talked with Mr. Marsh.*

January 26, 1963 (Saturday): *This was another full day. I was up with Gary and working until 2:30 a.m. last night. He misses his pacifier. I straightened the house, cleaned the living room, went shopping, came home, and put things* *away. Then, I finished the living room. Then Mike came home. We had supper, and I put the kids to bed. I waxed cabinets in the family room and cleaned living room lamps. I finished around Midnight. I could hardly stand up my body ached so. Then Gary got up. I gave myself a pedicure. I've got to leave Ed and this house before I have a physical and mental breakdown. There's too much to do.*

January 27, 1963: *I could hardly move this morning. My body just won't go anymore. I have so much pain, and it makes me frightened. Ed let me sleep late this morning, as I was up with Gary until 2:30. After I finished working last night, I cleaned the kitchen and floor, washed Ed's shirts, and did all the ironing for the last week.*

Gary had tantrums all day because he threw away his pacifier. I had another headache today and was a little grouchy. I sure do need some help. Ed paid $7.50 to have a man plow our drive. Here it is, Midnight, the earliest, I think, that I've gone to bed this week.

January 28, 1963: *Ed asked me for the money from shopping; I had $7 left and gave him $2. He blew up and said he wanted the grocery receipts from now on. I cleaned the bathrooms today, washed the whites, and took Mike to the doctor.*

Tonight, Ed took all my credit cards, including my gas card. I told him, "I don't know why you're contesting because you're doing everything to lose me." He said, "I do love you, but I must protect myself because you keep hurting me." He still thinks I'm at fault but should blame his mother. I hope he gets help and can be helped.

He kept interfering with my putting Mike to bed, but I kept trying to establish the rule that he should go to bed when it was time. Ed keeps giving me trouble even with my firmness and his solicitude. Mike said, "Daddy's making me sick." (I have to get away from Ed. I am terrified.)

January 29, 1963: *Today went much smoother and more tolerable. I cleaned every bedroom, Gary's closet, and the upstairs hall and straightened things downstairs. I'm beginning to see a cleaner house and get above it. The kids were in a better mood, and I got a better start this morning. Mike was better tonight.*

I talked with Central National Bank and learned that I didn't sign the financial statement. I called Mr. Marsh, and he told me he had sent the letter to Ed's attorney stating we had spent approximately $255 a week. Ann Cohn called tonight to say she was shocked when she heard from the court. She told them she hadn't seen us in a long time but knew I had problems and tried to solve them.

January 30, 1963: *Another late night, and it is almost 1:00. I will have to stop this as I'm afraid I'm sick. I lost nine pounds since the first of January and am now 118 pounds. Today, I cleaned the family room, hall, and hall closet and washed two laundry loads. This doesn't sound like much, but it keeps me busy and is a thorough cleaning. I also waxed, polished, and buffed floors and washed woodwork and doors. Now I must do the kitchen, back hall, and laundry and be pretty well caught up. Then the basement. I am so tired.*

I wish I could get out of here. More damage is probably being done now than when the kids and I leave. I wish I didn't have to do it to them, but life with Ed is unbearable.

January 31, 1963: *Today, I accomplished nothing with the house other than straightening it up. I felt I deserved a rest. I took Gary to Pat's while I went for my counseling. Mrs. Page said again that I was too passive about staying here and that my passivity was abnormal. But Mr. Marsh told me to sit tight. I guess I'd better push him a little more. This passivity seems to be my biggest problem in every direction.*

I went to school tonight and stayed after class with other students to practice sounding more convincing in our presentations. I signed out around 10:30 and arrived home at 11:00. Pat and I had lunch today. Then the kids and I came home and took naps. I couldn't sleep as tired as I was and couldn't get going today. It was good to be out among people again. This tension sure has been getting me down.

February 1, 1963: *I think I will drop. Today I began to realize again that I need help. This whole business is getting me down. I think I'm reaching the breaking point and am very depressed. I just don't have enough time to do everything. The kids need so much extra love, and I don't even have time for that. I've got to get us out of here. I called Dr. Wiant for an appointment because I didn't feel well. This morning, I went for my driver's license, picked up Mike, laundered sheets and towels, and cleaned and waxed the built-ins in the laundry room tonight. It doesn't seem that it would take longer, but it does. I also waxed the doors around the family room. It is 2:30 a.m., but I'm too tired to sleep.*

February 2, 1963 (Saturday): *The groundhog saw his shadow today. Anyway, six more weeks of this weather are predicted. Tonight, my body gave out. It just couldn't seem to move anymore. I saw Dr. Wiant today, and he took a throat culture as I have pustules on my tonsils again. He gave me something hot, which is hurting in addition to everything else. He believes my other pains are due to tension. He gave me capsules for my cough and told me to call Monday. I shopped, came home, thoroughly cleaned bathrooms, and straightened the kitchen before my body died. Finally, I was rested enough to get the kids into bed.*

February 3, 1963: *Today, Ed acted like an upset child when Mike called him names. I felt as if I had been run over. All I wanted to do was sleep. My body felt frail. Either it is giving up, or it is because of the shot Dr. Wiant gave me.*

I did manage to wash two loads of clothes, get meals and clean up, and mend some of Gary's things, but I couldn't accomplish much else.

February 4, 1963: *Jenny came to sit today. Ed and I met with Mr. Johnson of the Conciliation Department at 1:30 at the Court House. We left around 3:00 p.m. There is no chance of reconciliation, and it was a grueling session that left me tense, tired, and with a headache. Ed lied about his sister's age and wouldn't admit his mother and father were separated. Ed told me he was seeing a psychiatrist but wasn't sick. Ed also stated that he is going through a rough period and is not getting any better. Ed said many things against Mrs. Page, and I didn't mention the other people who believed he was sick.*

Afterward, I saw Mr. Marsh and gave him my diaries, a letter, and a D&B report. I told him to get me out of the house and tell Ed's attorneys.

I called Dr. Wiant, who said my fatigue was due to increased activity and mental tension. He also said to let my cough go and stop sleeping pills. He agreed I would be better physically if I moved away from Ed.

February 5, 1963: *This morning, Ed came down and asked if I would do his shirts, and I told him I would send them to the laundry. Then he said he would take them. Also, he growled, "From now on, give me a grocery list, and I'll do the shopping since you haven't enough time and because the food you put on the table isn't fit for the kids or me." Ed said this in front of the children, and I said, "You make me laugh when you say let's be civil for the kids' sake."*

I cleaned Ed's and my closet today. I didn't feel too well and began to feel nauseous when I was getting ready for school. When I arrived at school, I was chilled and left early. When I came home, I was very chilled. I had a 99.8-degree fever and ached all over. I see now that I've overdone everything. During the night, I was up three times to vomit. Each time, my knees ached like they would fall off. I thought I'd never get through the night.

February 6, 1963: *Today, I was spent, weak, and dizzy. It was all I could do to get Mike dressed and off to school, and Millie offered him lunch. Then he came home. Both boys took naps, so I slept as well. Dr. Wiant came and told me it was probably due to my congestion as my fever was gone.*

I didn't do anything all day as I couldn't navigate. I just managed the kids.

Ed only took the dishes to the dishwasher and helped put the kids to bed. Toys, of course, were strewn all over. When I went to bed, my fever was 100 degrees.

February 7, 1963 (Thursday): *Today, nausea and dizziness left me. I felt unbelievably weak. I called Mrs. Page for my session today, and Millie picked Mike up. We all napped this afternoon. Dr. Wiant called, and I told him how I was. He then diagnosed me as having a virus and sent some medicine over. Edith took Mike to supper but brought him back, and I found getting him to bed tricky. I did manage to straighten the house tonight and do some mending."*

February 8, 1963: *I took a diet pill to get through the day because I wasn't well enough yet. I experienced a violent reaction. I kept biting my tongue and clenching my teeth all day.*

I changed the sheets today and decided to mend all of them. This took me longer than I expected. I then washed the sheets and towels, too. I had to quit earlier to get the kids dressed for Edie's party for Ed's birthday. They looked just darling. When we arrived at 6:00, Edie's apartment was dark, and she was dressed for bed. I asked about what was going on. She said it was for Saturday night. I even asked her yesterday. She said Friday because I asked if she would be home from the office. She is getting senile or something [It turns out she was developing it]. *I was irate. I told the boys I'd take them to dinner, and she offered to feed them.*

223

I had to get out of there because of anger and never being her friend. Why should I be a hypocrite? So, I told her I had an appointment and went to get my dinner. Then I came back to get them, and she had called Ed. They got things more mixed up. Ed said the party was Sunday. Who knows?

Ed was more human tonight and offered to make drinks. He offered me sex, and I told him, "No chance."

Later, he came in wanting to talk, and for the first time since I've known him, he let his barriers down and let something out of his mind that had troubled him. This is a good step for him. I cannot break his trust in me because this is the first time he has trusted anyone. Got to sleep at 3:45 a.m.

February 9, 1963 (Saturday): *Today, I was tired. I took the boys to Manners Restaurant and also got them haircuts. Then, we came home and took naps. I made spaghetti for dinner, after which we discovered Peter Pan was on TV. So I sat down with Mike to watch and explain. He really enjoyed it because he sat still the whole time watching it. Then we played Peter Pan into bed. There was no problem tonight. We had fun. I did dishes and came upstairs to do some more sewing. Bedtime was at 1:00 again.*

February 11, 1963: *Still draggy today, but I managed to get the laundry done. I went to bed at 11:00, but Gary was having trouble sleeping. I wish I could devote more time to Mike and Gary. I'm sure they need more attention than I can give them, but I find it so difficult now because of all the work.*

February 12, 1963: *I took a pep pill today and went shopping with Gary this morning. We picked up Sally and Mike to bring them home. This afternoon, I cleaned the bedrooms, came downstairs, and finished the kitchen. I rushed around to get ready for dinner and school. The school was out at 10:00. I stopped at the drugstore to get a Valentine for Mike. I cleaned the kitchen, showered, and mended one of Gary's sheets when I got home. Ed brought up my diaphragm again. He must be trying to make something of it. I showed him where it was and enquired why he looked in my cosmetic drawer.*

February 13, 1963: *I cleaned the family room, living room, hall, and yellow bath. Tonight, I baked a Valentine's Day cake for the kids. I discovered a sizeable unsightly bruise at the bend of my left leg on the outside. I don't know how I got it, but it worries me. Mike was happy to help me with the cake, and I let him play in the icing. I went to bed at eleven. I'm still exhausted.*

February 14, 1963: *Mrs. Page believes I'm still too passive and tells me I should stop doing everything for Ed. Maybe it will make him realize that I mean business. I know I must do something. I took the kids to Pat's and brought her some cake. We were home by 3:00 when I cleaned the Pink bathroom. I did ironing tonight.*

February 15, 1963: *I stayed up until 3:00 a.m. I did more mending tonight and finished the doors and Ed's bathroom. I talked to Mr. Marsh today.*

February 16, 1963: *I took the kids to Lefton's for lunch, and I had a splitting headache but cleaned the linen closet.*

February 17, 1963: I cleaned the dishwasher, kitchen, and utensil drawer. I told Ed that I would do nothing for him anymore. I want the divorce and will move out when I can. He accused me of threatening him, but I'm not. I simply have to get away from him.

February 18, 1963: I asked for grocery money, and Ed told me to make a shopping list. He would do it. I enquired whether this meant he would give me no more money. He replied, "After the way you threatened me, what do you expect." Tonight, he said we've been broke for years, and I wanted to know why and how we managed to live as we have. He replied, "With my blood and guts." I said, "Then that is indeed crazy. I don't believe you when you say you have had no money. Why bother with a business that goes nowhere but down?"

Tonight, Mike spilled coke on Ed's bed, and Ed wanted to know what I would do about it. I told him where the sheets were and that he could take care of them himself. So, he stripped everything off, including the mattress cover. He asked, "Is this the way it's going to be?" I said, "Yes." I want him to know I don't want him anymore.

February 19, 1963 (Tuesday): Mr. Marsh called to tell me about a hearing on March 6 regarding the alimony. I cleaned the upstairs bedrooms and bathroom.

This afternoon, Mike, Gary, and I went to Mary A's for a while. We had dinner at Manners and came home, and Mike went to bed immediately.

Ed had grocery-shopped, so I had to put things away and clean the fruits and vegetables. I feel like I can't stand it here any longer. Ed doesn't love me and keeps making it harder for me. So, I have to retaliate. This is the main reason our marriage has failed. Neither of us loved the other. I had no cigarettes or coffee today as I was all out.

February 20, 1963: *It looks like we'll be stuck here again tomorrow. Snow is drifting. Gary has a cold. Will it never end? Mike was upset quite a bit today. He didn't want to go to school. I called after he was there for a while, and they reported he was doing all right. I cleaned the family room, living room, hall, and yellow bath but accomplished nothing else. Ed was late tonight, and Gary was in bed already.*

February 21, 1963: *We were snowed in, and Ed almost didn't get out. I called Mrs. Page but didn't talk much. Gary's gland is swollen, and maybe his ear is infected. I cleaned the Lazy Susan and the cupboard next to it. This was an absolutely nothing day.*

February 22, 1963: *I got Mike ready for school and remembered the holiday (Washington's Birthday). I worked on the kitchen cupboards today. Snowed in again. Gary's cold is terrible. I sewed tonight. I have nothing much to report except that I wish I could get out for a day. It is terribly depressing being in the house day in and day out. I have another cold.*

February 23, 1963: *Mike tripped and hurt his right foot above the big toe. It pains him, and he can't walk on it. Ed was gone almost all day. Thank goodness, as I can't bear to have him around. I worked on more kitchen cupboards.*

February 24, 1963: *I got up, accomplished things early, and had time to play with the boys. The snowplow even* *came early. Ed took Mike to the hospital for an X-ray of his foot. There was nothing wrong with it, and it was probably a sprain. I was sure of it. After supper, I went out for an hour and looked at one of the houses offered by Bates and Springer. Two bedrooms for $140. I must decide the best place for us to live, which is problematic.*

February 25, 1963: *Mike was really well-behaved today. So was Gary. Maybe it's because I was calmer. I'm trying my hardest to make the best of it because I hope to get out of here soon. I did the laundry and ironing today.*

February 26, 1963: *Today, I seemed kind of depressed. I don't really know why other than I want this to end. When I said divorce, I meant it, and now I want to get out.*

I cleaned the bedrooms and bathroom upstairs. Downstairs, I did the family and living rooms, plus the hall. Ed shopped again, and Mike went to school today. Another Gary and Sally came to play this afternoon. I've got to leave! Gary's glands are badly swollen, and I'll call the doctor if he isn't better tomorrow.

February 27, 1963: *I bought cookies for PTA and took them to school when we picked up Mike. My spirits were somewhat improved today. I worked in the kitchen today, cleaning and waxing the table and walls. Ed and I had a tiff. He started telling me something about my business. I knew what Ed was going to say, so I told him not to say it (It's always been this way, but I never dared to fight back) and to give me credit for having some brains. He seems to want to do the thinking for everyone around him. There is always trouble getting Mike to sleep at night, even when*

228

Mike is tired. He just can't seem to relax. I must find a way to help him.

February 28, 1963: *It snowed again last night, but I was confident I would get out of the drive. And I did and made it to my appointment at JFS. We talked about my fear of Ed and other times in my life. Pat and I had lunch. I saw Carol as I was leaving. I had to shovel the apron of the drive before I could get in because the street plow had pushed it relatively high. I wanted to go to PTA, but Ed didn't show up till after 9:00 p.m. I thought it very strange that he came home so late tonight. Hah! Mike and Gary were well-behaved today, and Gary's cold is better. Mr. Marsh called and read our petition to answer Ed's question on the grounds. He didn't add everything but said that Ed had persecuted me until it affected my mental and physical health, which it has.*

March 1, 1963 (Friday): *Snow and more snow. I went to pick up Mike and couldn't get back up the drive. The juice man came by and helped us by pushing. We made it! Gary and Sally came for lunch and stayed all day until 5:00. They all played together reasonably well today. Mike was exhausted and fell asleep immediately after he ate. I cleaned the kitchen floor, utility, and back hall. We were plowed out at 7:00 p.m.*

I didn't get much sewing accomplished tonight. Mike wouldn't settle down until 11:00 because he was awakened when Ed arrived home. So, I sat with him, trying to calm him. It was 2:30 a.m. when I retired. I called Dr. Wiant about my cold. He prescribed a new capsule, which already seems to have helped me.

March 2, 1963: *I finished reading* Positive Thinking *tonight. I typed copies of all my letters to my mother that she had returned to me. Ed left around 9:00 this morning and didn't return until after 5:00. I wonder if he's seeing a girl now, but then he wouldn't contest the divorce unless it's for the money.*

As usual, I felt very agitated with Ed tonight at the children's bedtime. He keeps postponing the time, then offers them Coke and any number of things. I can't get any routine established with him around. He will ruin their teeth with all the Coke and gumdrops every night. I can't wait until I'm free of him and start building a happier atmosphere and life for the children. Mike was upset tonight. It seems the kids go berserk when Ed's home. But lately, Ed has exercised a great deal of patience.

March 3, 1963 (Sunday): *Tonight was terrible. Ed insisted he wanted to eat with the kids and fixed himself a steak while I had planned bacon and eggs for them and myself. Mike saw Ed's steak and wanted it, too. Then he burst into tears as he did last night at supper. This is just too much for him to take. This is the time that hurts the children more if only Ed would realize it. Then tonight, I set my foot down and said no more Coke, and Ed, as usual, pleaded with me in front of Mike. I told him I was tired of daily gumdrops, Coke, and cookies for the youngsters. They will have no teeth if this keeps up. I can't get the children to bed until late. I always have trouble with them when Ed is here. Things are normal, happy, and quiet until he's around. Ed upsets us all. He was angry because he thought the music was playing too loud.*

March 4, 1963: *I cleaned the bedrooms and upstairs bath and washed whites and colors. Then, I worked on putting a budget together. Tonight, Ed came home and demanded the keys to Edie's apartment and to the Chevrolet. I had opened the doctor and dentist bills addressed to him but referencing my visits, and he told me not to open his mail anymore. I saw George Lindsey (married to my cousin, Joyanne) on "Rifleman." He did a good job.*

March 5, 1963: *I cleaned downstairs and worked on the budget. Mike went to Sally's for lunch; they all came here later.*

March 6, 1963: *Court hearing at 9:00 a.m. It was a tense situation this morning, and nothing was settled. The attorneys will get together Tuesday to talk it over. I said that I wouldn't live with Ed anymore. Tonight, things were quiet.*

March 7, 1963: *I'm all excited tonight because, at last, I found the apartment for the kids and me. It has three bedrooms, a garage and private utility, a kitchen with eating space, air conditioning, carpeting, a bath-and-a-half, and a swimming pool and playground for $160. It is just off Green Road, 10 minutes from here. Mike can still go to Nursery School. This is what I have prayed for. I had my counseling this morning, and we went back to my high school days to see if I was passive then. I had lunch at Pat's, and Carol came over. It was relaxing.*

March 8, 1963: *I talked to Mr. Marsh today about the apartment. Allegedly, Ed has to support us if we move, but who knows? He told me to wait until Tuesday and see what happens. I blew up at Ed tonight because of trouble with*

Mike, and I told him that it resulted from our still living together. Poor Mike doesn't know what's happening.

March 9, 1963: *I was fatigued today, so I took a nap this afternoon but couldn't move tonight. I changed the linens today. The kids and I went out for a while and stopped at Grace's. I talked to my mother, and she said she would send some money.*

March 10, 1963 (Sunday): *I'm fatigued again today. I don't know what's wrong, but I'm dragging again. I did some work in the basement and put books away from the bookcase tonight. I also ran three loads of clothes today, but I was too tired to do much else. Ed took Mike and Gary to Edie's tonight for a short while.*

March 11, 1963: *Cleaned the whole house and did two loads of laundry. Very tired tonight.*

March 12, 1963: *I worked in the basement today and picked up most of the toys. When Mike awoke from his nap, he had a 103-degree fever and tummy ache. He vomited a couple times during the night. Dr. Bloomfield and I expected mumps because he had been exposed. I was up with him all night, so I brought in my blankets to sleep on the floor when I had a chance. It began to thunder, and he was pretty frightened. My mother called me today, and Ed gave me $20.*

March 13, 1963: *I was drained today, and I didn't do anything until tonight when the kids were in bed, and I only straightened up a bit. I discovered Mike had a rash, headache, labored breathing, and cough tonight. Gary seems to* *have diarrhea. Dr. Bloomfield and I thought of chickenpox, and he will stop by in the morning.*

Mr. Marsh told me I must stay here, resume cooking for Ed, and do things for him until we all talk. Then I may be forced to give up Mrs. Page, go to a psychiatrist, and lose all the time I've invested in therapy. This makes me so depressed that I want to leave and start a new life. Why do people have to be so cruel as to take a person's life and bat it around like a ping-pong ball? They may just mess me all up. I am feeling very desperate tonight, and I cannot and will not take this much longer.

March 14, 1963: *I feel terribly angry and upset about this divorce. I can't understand a man (I never could, with Ed, anyway) wanting a woman who practically hates him. Mike is still sick, and I am up with him again, and I can't get enough sleep. He has broken into a rash tonight, and Bloomfield said he would stop tomorrow morning to see if it is chickenpox. Poor little guy.*

March 15, 1963 (Friday): *I felt like I was on the brink of insanity today. I had no control over myself or my emotions. I wanted to scream, throw things, smash things. I was after the kids all day over every little thing they did. I feel so much anger inside, plus a desperate need to hurt Ed, but he's not here, so I yell at the kids. That makes me frustrated and even angrier. This all adds up to deep depression. All because I want to get the kids and myself out of here. I'm so worried about their emotional health. I tried to reach Mrs. Page (out of town), Mr. Marsh (at a meeting), and Dr. Wiant (tied up until nearly 7:00). He just gave me words. When Ed came home, I left. I went to Carol Battles.*

We went to see <u>Gypsy</u> and then to the Red Rooster. I got home around 2:00 a.m., but I did feel better.

Dr. Bloomfield stopped by this morning, and it is not chickenpox but an earache again with a shot for it.

March 16, 1963: *I was somewhat calmer today but still very depressed. I can't seem to shake it off. I am also so exhausted. Mike was much improved today, but he is all keyed up, and Gary didn't sleep well for his nap today. I couldn't accomplish anything. I did change the beds. I tried to take extra time with Mike to let him know I loved him and for him to forgive me for my disposition.*

March 17, 1963: *My period came three days early this month and two days early last month. This worries me because of my regularity, and I hope it's only because of tension. This may somewhat explain my depression over the last couple of days.*

March 18, 1963: *I cleaned the whole house today, minus the bathrooms. I slept all night as I was exhausted. Tonight, I lay down on the bed fully clothed, watched <u>Boy on a Dolphin</u>, and fell asleep as I watched. I talked to Mr. Marsh, who didn't have anything set up yet, as Mr. Wallick is too busy.*

March 19, 1963: *I had a hard time accomplishing anything today because of many interruptions. I cleaned the bathrooms, washed Ed's clothes, and ironed. Ten o'clock again when Mike fell asleep. He says he's afraid.*

March 20, 1963: *Snow. Will it ever be warm? I told Mr. Marsh today to set up the meeting for this week; if Ed* *couldn't do it, there wouldn't be any meeting. I had Sally come for lunch today, and the kids played nice until Mark came. Then Sally left, and they played well. Mike fell asleep on the couch after dinner.*

March 21, 1963: *I was busy all day. I went to Pat Lamont's house this morning and brought her and Rene back when I picked up Mike. They had lunch with us. We left around 4:00 for Pat's house to pick up her two other kids and went to dinner at Manners. Then I took them home, went in for a while, and returned to my home. It was nice being out all day and away from routine. I started discarding magazines tonight. I talked with Mr. Marsh, who told me that Mr. Wallick has not returned and that I should say something to Ed. Ed was out tonight and got home a little after 11:00 p.m. I called my mother.*

March 22, 1963 (Friday): *I went to the bank to cash my mother's check. I spent the day going through magazines but still haven't finished. I went to the drugstore tonight to buy cosmetics, and it seemed I had run out of everything. Mike was tired and went right to sleep, even having a nap. I was calm today, and he seemed calmer, too.*

March 23, 1963: *Ed came home early today because Edie and Aunt Jean were coming. They came after 5:00 p.m. Ed and I talked after the kids were in bed. I told him, "I hate you, and you are tied to your mother's apron strings. You're not facing reality, which drives me crazy living like this. Also, it is terrible for the children." Ed said, "I realize I will never get you back, but I won't make any move. And you are right, I am not facing reality, but I am not tied to my* *mother's apron strings. I do know what it is doing to the kids and you."*

Then he asked if I would consider giving up the children. I told him, "No, because I want to be free of you to raise the children as they should be." He said, "I will subsidize a career and give you anything." I said, "I want to have the children." He said, "I can pay an excellent nurse to do what you do." I said, "They need me. They need both of us but can't have us together, so they need to be with me, and a nurse can't be their mother." Then he said as if he had someone lined up, "But I might remarry. My wife could do it." I said, "She wouldn't be their natural mother, and you're not emotionally able to."

I went to see the movie Freud, *stopped at Mawby's for coffee, and got home around 1:00. Gary had vomited twice while I was gone. I took Mike for his checkup and talked to Bloomfield. Bloomfield reminded me of the conflict Ed is going through. I'm cutting the apron strings his mother should have done. He reminded me that I must do what I consider suitable for the children.*

March 24, 1963 (Sunday): *I was fatigued because of little sleep last night. I took Mike to the lake to see ducks today. He said he was happy and having fun with me. Then we stopped at Carol's. What a beautiful day, over 70! Mike vomited tonight.*

March 25, 1963: *Exhausted, I fell asleep last night with my clothes on. Today I cleaned everything except the kitchen. Finally, I finished going through magazines. The day wasn't too bad.*

March 26, 1963: *There is one day every week when I have trouble accomplishing everything I set out to do. I did the laundry and ironing today and tonight but didn't clean the kitchen. I took the kids to the dime store and picked dinner up from Kenny Kings. Edie came over for 10 minutes late this afternoon.*

March 27, 1963: *While sorting laundry today, I noticed makeup on Ed's shirts on both sides of the front in the chest region. Now, I'm sure he has a girl.*

I took the boys for their haircuts, and John did them. They looked so cute. I talked to Mr. Marsh, who told me he had heard from Mr. Wallick but couldn't say when we would get together.

March 28, 1963: *I had my counseling appointment this morning. We discussed impulsiveness, loneliness, and what isn't happening with the divorce and moving. We spent almost all day at Pat's and came home around 4:00. Then, I joined Pat, Carol, and Carol's friend, Martha from Akron, tonight. We went to the Commodore Bar for a Hootenanny, and Carol got up to play and sing. We, save Martha, went to Red Rooster to eat after we left. I got home around 2:00 a.m.*

March 29, 1963 (Friday): *I was tired today, so I had to take a pill to keep going. I didn't accomplish much around the house this morning or afternoon. I took the kids for shoes, and Gary got his first low-cut shoes, size 5 ½, blue and white, but Mike didn't need them. Then we went to Zayre's and bought Mike two jackets, a pair of Levi's, and a gift for Johnny's party. When we got home, I took Mike's* *temperature, which was 101 degrees. Mike felt miserable and complained that he had an upset stomach. Gary has been in pain, apparently from his second-year molar.*

Ed went out tonight. He showered and dressed except for a tie, which he replaced with an ascot. When he was leaving, he went to the liquor cabinet and took a couple bottles. They appeared to be Courvoisier and vermouth. It looks like there is another woman. Ed didn't return home until after 2:00 a.m.

March 30, 1963: *I was home all day until nearly 5:00 when I left to look at a duplex for rent by Mr. And Mrs. Asnien on Idlewood. It rents for $140 with three bedrooms, two rooms on the third floor, and 2½ baths. There is the possibility of renting out the rooms to pay half the rent, but I have become accustomed to living in pleasant surroundings and would find it difficult to live in a house badly needing decorating. It would take all my time to decorate the place. Mike went to Johnny's birthday party this morning and had a good time. He was pooped tonight.*

March 31, 1963: *I did the wash today and more mending. I'll never catch up, although the pile gets smaller. I kept Mike in because he had a slight fever.*

CHAPTER 14

THE FINAL MONTHS OF 1963 WITH CHANGE AT LAST

The worst problems for children stem from parental conflict before, during, and after divorce or within marriage.

—Stephanie Coontz

But It Is Not Easier; Only Different

April 1, 1963: *I threw my schedule away today. I just had to do it or go mad. I invited Sally to lunch and washed the car this afternoon. Mike and Gary were fatigued because of the fresh air and play, although I was worried about Mike. He's always tired, even though I can't get him to rest.*

April 2, 1963: *I had to hurry this morning and tried to reach Mr. Marsh's office by 9:30 but to no avail. I arrived at 10:00 after leaving Gary at Pat's and arranging for Mike to go to Mandel's. Mr. Marsh and I walked to the Society for Savings Bank on the Square to Mr. Wallick's office. We sat* *till 12:30 p.m. discussing what was wrong with our marriage, but we didn't finish, so we made another appointment for Friday.*

When we got home, I put Gary to bed for a nap, and I had to lie down. When I got up, I began sneezing as if I had just come down with a cold, but it stopped later. It could be tension. And Mike now has hives.

April 3, 1963: *I took a diet pill today, which I shouldn't have done. I was really on edge from yesterday. It took me just about all day to clean the refrigerator. Gary went to bed with a temperature of 102, and Mike went to bed without any trouble.*

Ed inquired about what faith I intended to raise the children, and I told him I hadn't decided. It would depend on several factors. He told me he had his insurance set up so that their money would go to charity if the children weren't raised Jewish.

April 4, 1963: *Gary is sick with swollen glands and a fever of 102.4 degrees. So, no counseling today except by phone. I took Gary to Dr. Bloomfield and talked to Dr. Bloomfield about (1) A psychiatrist. He said, "You don't need one, but if you get psychoanalyzed, you will become stronger. The stronger you become, the more Ed will dislike it." (2) Mike's Fear. He agreed with me about staying with Mike for his security. (3) Would he sign a note saying it was terrible for the children to live in these circumstances? He answered, "No because you can use it as a weapon." Then I asked, "Would you agree it harms the children emotionally and* *physically to live in the house with Ed, as we are? He said, "Yes." That was all I needed to boost my confidence.*

I talked with Mr. Anthony from Radio School. He offered an advance in money to get me out of here to do modeling as he also owns La Continental Model Agency.

April 5, 1963 (Friday): *At Mr. Marsh's meeting with Ed and his attorney this morning, I told them not to go over what we all did on Tuesday. I stated simply, "Regardless of Ed's finances, I am moving out. And living the way we are is detrimental to the children." I had lunch at Howard Johnson's and saw three women from Plymouth. I recognized only Sherry Ensel. Mrs. Dempsey, who babysat, worked wonders with Mike. He liked her.*

Ed called to say he wouldn't be home for dinner. Then he called to say his plans had been changed and he would be home, and I couldn't accomplish anything today either.

April 6, 1963: *Again, I couldn't accomplish anything today. Ed was gone all day and was not in the office again. Bob Colin called from the office and asked where he was. His mother called for him late in the day, saying she couldn't locate him. I'm sure he has a girlfriend. He didn't get home until 6:30.*

April 7, 1963: *Today went reasonably smoothly. I did the wash, cleaned all the bathrooms, and cooked a good dinner. Gary is still sick, and Ed left tonight for a short while, saying he had to see someone.*

April 8, 1963: *Tension is creeping in again. Gary has been sick since Thursday, and I haven't been out for a break. I* *felt myself getting angry with Ed again today. I also tried doing too much in one day and cleaned everything but the kitchen. I finished at 9:30 p.m. when Ed and Mike came home from the Seder. Gary couldn't go because he had a fever again today. Gary has been so cranky. He is still up tonight at 11:30. Gary has a sick need for Ed. Like Mike, he wants Ed to do everything. My mother called.*

April 9, 1963: *Mr. Marsh called and said he received a letter from Mr. Wallick stating that Ed has no funds. He said, "We can examine his books; he can't move home with his mother and cannot maintain two households." So, I go to work. My tension is increasing, and I'm becoming more nervous. Gary is still sick and was beginning a slight ear infection. Ed insisted I take Gary to the doctor, where Gary received a shot.*

April 10, 1963: *Mike wanted to go downtown today and began limping again (from a fall Monday). Ed called Bloomfield and then called me to make an appointment. Dr. Bloomfield didn't find anything wrong with Mike other than a slight sprain, and he got the measles vaccine shot. We drove along Euclid Avenue, looking at apartments that are too far away.*

Tonight, I was served with an answer to my petition for divorce. It states that Ed thinks he is the proper guardian for the children and is asking for a restraining order forbidding me from taking them and the furniture. I can't sleep tonight as I'm too keyed up. I am trying to think of how I can get out of here now.

April 11, 1963: *I picked up Mrs. Davis, the babysitter, and went to see Mrs. Page. She was surprised that we hadn't seen this happening and assured me something could be done. I then looked at an apartment and went to see Dr. Wiant for something for my nerves. He told me I should at least go to work and start building a fund, but also, there must be a way out. When I got home, I called Mr. Marsh, who checked the "answer." Because it read "without bond," Mr. Marsh thought it would be okay for me to leave. I decided to go immediately before he could post bond. Mr. Marsh was sure they had gone through improper channels.* [I hurriedly packed a bag for the three of us after arranging with my friends, the Kuzmas, to stay with them temporarily in Avon Lake, far on the other side of Cleveland.]

April 12, 1963 (Good Friday): *Mr. Marsh hasn't heard anything today, but he is sure I am all right to make this move. I talked to Pat today, and I don't think she knew I left. The children are having some difficulty adjusting. They don't have their toys and miss Ed, but they are busy playing, which helps somewhat.*

April 13, 1963: *This morning, my throat was very sore. I called Dr. Wiant and made an appointment for 12:30. Mike came with me, and it took us an hour to drive there. He took two throat cultures and gave me a penicillin shot. Then he prescribed penicillin pills, cough medicine, and eye medicine for my conjunctivitis.*

We had lunch and stopped at Heights Pharmacy, where I bought the children's Easter basket presents and a skincare item. I got up and got breakfast for all the kids, and I could barely see as I didn't sleep well and went to bed at 3:30. I talked to my mother today, and she hasn't heard from Ed, which seems strange that he hasn't called her.

April 14, 1963 (Easter Sunday): *I went to church today with the Kuzma family because their friend included me when he brought flowers for everyone. Gary fell this morning and bit his tongue, and Mike fell, bruising his thumb. They are both alright, though. They were difficult getting them to bed tonight, and I figured they must be unhappy about this arrangement. We must move.*

April 15, 1963: *I came into town today for counseling to find the office closed because of the holiday. I searched for new quarters for us and decided to temporarily settle at the Commodore Hotel in University Circle for $43.26 a week. So I returned to Bobbie's, packed up, and moved in. The kids were already happier by this move and went to bed without trouble.*

April 16, 1963: *I took Pat to the Mental Development Center today, the kids included. That is about all I accomplished. Gary was up a little tonight.*

April 17, 1963: *Pat kept the kids for me today while I returned to the house for clothes and other items. We stayed for supper.*

I took Gary for a recheck of his ear and his measles vaccine. Bloomfield told me he had heard from Ed and that, more than likely, Ed missed me more than the kids, but he would reassure him if he called that the kids were okay.

April 18, 1963: *Ruth Ressler came to sit today and was good with the children. I went for what was supposed to be* *an interview for modeling with Mr. Anthony and instead worked for the new Corporation of American Announcer's Academy. They all seem to think I've got great potential. My salary, to begin with, is $50 a week. It is an amiable atmosphere, and I know I'll enjoy working there. Mike came down with a reaction to the measles shot with a 104-degree fever.*

April 19, 1963 (Friday): *I began work today. I was alone for the morning, but there was a hodgepodge of people coming and going all afternoon. They finally settled that my position is to work in the sales force, with a $50 plus commission salary. I hope I can prove myself as a saleswoman.*

When I arrived home, I called Mr. Marsh, who was gone for the day. His secretary informed me that Ed had filed a motion for me to return the children and that there would be a hearing on May 6 at 2:30. This upset me somewhat. The kids and I then went to pick up the TV set. It was nice having it tonight. I accomplished some work and became a little more organized.

April 20, 1963: *I was going to work today, but Ruth couldn't make it. This did give me an excuse to do the laundry. So the kids and I took the laundry to Morge Dry Cleaning and Laundry Village. Keeping track of them was tricky, but they eventually calmed down. Saturday, of course, is a bad day to go.*

I called Mr. Marsh, who assured me they wouldn't make me return home. We might get some support for the children this time, and I'm sure things will work out. Frank Myers called and offered to bring us the doughnuts left at the office. He must have made the trip just to bring them, and the Bellboy brought them up.

April 21, 1963: *Today, the kids and I walked before lunch. After their naps, we drove to Strongsville to see Susan Peters* [from work] *and her sons, Kevin and Kile. We arrived home late and retired.*

April 22, 1963: *I worked three-quarters of a day today. I went to see Mrs. Page and then back to the office. I didn't feel well when returning to work and could hardly move tonight. My fever was 100 degrees. I called Dr. Wiant, who called Wade Drugs to send some medicine.*

April 23, 1963: *Today, I was forced to stay in bed with a fever of around 100. It was difficult getting complete rest.*

April 24, 1963: *I attended a career day at Strongsville High School with Susan, Len Anthony, and Al Diamond. I had to drive Al home first so he could change clothes, and then we went out to Strongsville and home again. I arrived home at 5:30, weary and sick. This morning I received a shot at Dr. Wiant's.*

April 25, 1963: *Mr. Marsh called and told me to call Ed and tell him we were all right. At work, we spoke about my position, to be a sort of Gal Friday and help Susan and the sales staff. The salary would be $50 plus commission, $75.*

When I got home, we called Ed. Mike cried, "Daddy, I want to come home. Have Mommy tell you where we are." Mike was distraught.

Ed said that he had a change of heart. He realizes that we can't or never will live together again, but he will continue to contest and that we are only hurting the children, but let's try to remember only the good things. He's ready to sell the house, help as much as possible, and set us up in an apartment.

April 26, 1963: *I came to work around 1:30 and left around 9:30. There was a sales meeting tonight, which was exciting. Getting the children settled tonight was difficult, as these sleeping arrangements are terrible.*

April 27, 1963 (Saturday): *I went to work today and opened the office at 9:00. I couldn't get into the other office until we thought of the Master Key. Then I began typing the notes from the meeting last night.*

Mr. Marsh called and told me Ed had called him. Ed wanted me to call. Mr. Marsh wants me to play along with Ed; maybe he is ready to bargain. So I called Ed. He said he would get an apartment so we could move back into the house until it is sold. He believes I am the right one to have the children, and I must quit my job right now. Again, he told me he is broke and has liquidated all his assets, which means we'll have to live on a bare minimum. The kids and I drove to the drugstore to get something for my throat and cough. They were challenging to get settled tonight.

April 28, 1963: *I finally achieved what I set out to accomplish last week. The kids and I left the apartment around 2:30 for Susan's. We arrived around 3:30. Kevin and Kyle gave Mike a set of marbles, a harmonica, and a ball for his birthday. Susan baked a chocolate cake. The children played for a while, then we had dinner. Some of Kevin and Kyle's friends came, and they all had cake in the basement.*

Mr. Anthony dropped by. Mike was very tired and had to cry. Then he felt and behaved better. When we returned to the hotel at 8:30, I called Mr. Evans to see if the boys could see his dog before bed. I took them over and discovered he is Michael Evans, the actor from New York. Mike had a good time with Boo.

April 29, 1963: *My hours were 9:00 to 5:00. I had to leave to see Mrs. Page. We discussed visitation, and she said the children shouldn't be gone away from me or home overnight, and once a week was enough.*

I talked to Dr. Bloomfield tonight, and he said the same thing, but we should work out whatever is agreeable without problems.

They both seemed to agree about my job considering finances, the children, and me. I believe I should continue to work.

I ran into Ed downtown on my way to see Mrs. Page. He gave me the birthday cake and came to Mike's birthday party tonight. The kids (after not seeing him for 2.5 weeks) behaved beautifully and were not upset. Mike called Ed later and talked for a half-hour.

April 30, 1963: *This morning, Janice came to interview for babysitting at ten o'clock. The kids and I drove out to the house, exchanged dirty diapers for clean ones, and picked up some food to carry us through the week.*

I went to work at 2:30, and when I came home, it was snowing with snow already on the ground.

Ed called today and asked about visitation and my job, and I told him I had talked to Dr. Bloomfield about it. He then said we would leave it up to our attorneys. Ed wanted to forget the animosity, but it began all over again after this conversation. I talked with Mr. Levenson, and he reassured me that I was okay.

Mike has some matter in his eye.

May 1, 1963: *I tried to get a job on the Queen for A Day Show, but the slate was already filled, and I was too old. Mr. Anthony and I drove to WEWS to see Mr. Spiro, producer of One O'clock Club.*

May 2, 1963: *I went to see Dr. Whitman today for a pap smear and discovered I have vaginal yeast, giving me the irritation I've been experiencing. Then Mike and I went to see Dr. Bloomfield and found two ear infections, and he received a shot. Then I went to work.*

May 3, 1963: *I walked the kids down to the Art Museum to watch the fish and ducks, and they had a good time. I went to work, took minutes at the sales meeting, and received my paycheck.*

May 4, 1963: *Janice, my sitter, didn't show or call this morning, and I was supposed to open the office. Mr. Anthony called (he was hot under the collar) and said he might as well get someone who didn't have sitter problems, and I agreed with him because he needs someone he can rely on. I went to the office and picked my things up, but I didn't see Mr. Anthony.*

Miss Cooper from the sitter's agency came. When I got back, I went shopping but didn't get the kids settled until after eleven.

I talked to Mr. Marsh, and we decided to get us back into the house, car title in my name, visitation every Saturday or alternate Saturday and Sunday every other week, and two nights, written as three by consent.

May 5, 1963: *This morning (after being up intermittently through the night with Gary), I awoke to Gary shaking. He was having a convulsion. I immediately put his head down with his stomach over my knee and my finger, then a spoon, in his mouth. I called Dr. Bloomfield. As I talked to him, Gary quieted down, vomited, and went to sleep. I put Gary in a lukewarm tub and held him up because he kept falling asleep. I took him to the doctor, and we found the start of an ear infection in his left ear. He received a shot and was immediately better. He slept almost all afternoon, and Mike went with Ed today.*

May 6, 1963 (Monday): *Janice came to sit while I had my session. When I returned, I took the kids to the house while I did the laundry. We left around seven, and Ed wasn't home yet. We had dinner at Lefton's Deli.*

May 7, 1963: *I went to the house to leave the diapers off this morning. This noon, my mother came and stayed all afternoon while Miles was at the Clinic. We all had dinner together at Howard Johnson's at University Circle, where Mother and Miles stayed.*

May 8, 1963: *Ed came tonight. I was fed up with him because he kept changing his mind about things, although he contends things are still the same. We ended up going to Manners Drive-In with him for dinner.*

May 10, 1963: *We drove to Plymouth with Miles today. He is apparently okay, just his neck from whiplash. Ed called and said he had paid the rent until the twelfth, but he didn't know what would happen after that.*

May 11, 1963: *Mike has been having a wonderful time fishing and helping Miles plant flowers. He was outside almost all day. This afternoon we drove near Greenwich to see Jay and Polly* [cousin and wife] *and their three dogs. My mother bought Mike and me a new pair of sneakers, and I didn't do much.*

May 12, 1963: *This was my nicest Mother's Day ever. I gave Mother only a hug and a kiss. Aunty Jo and Uncle Joy came by before going to Jay's. We flew back to Cleveland from Mansfield. At the airport in Mansfield, Mike approached a Marine and told him, "When I grow up, I'm going to be an Air Force gallant man like you." The Marine said, "If you were 10 years older, I'd resent that." Mike and Gary were very excited toward the end of the flight, and Mike became nauseated but didn't flip his cookies. We took the limousine from the Statler and a taxi to the hotel.*

May 13, 1963: *We negotiated today with Mr. Marsh, Ed, and Mr. Wallick, although I only conversed with Ed and Mr. Marsh. I think soon we will have an agreement. Then, we'll get back into the house. Meanwhile, we'll have to wait it out here. Mr. Marsh is disgusted with Ed. I'm confused and didn't go to my counseling session today. Ed came tonight to play with the kids.*

May 14, 1963: *Today, Astronaut Cooper was supposed to orbit the earth but didn't because of radar difficulty. Before* *that, they had diesel trouble. The kids and I went to the house today, and I did the laundry and some ironing while they played. We went to see Dr. Bloomfield this afternoon for their six-month checkup. Mike is 39 inches and 36 pounds, and Gary is 33 inches and 24 pounds. They are OK. They each received a TB test: Mike on his right arm and Gary on both arms. Dr. Bloomfield believes Mike to be the greatest: He's alert and does not miss anything.*

May 15, 1963: *Astronaut Cooper went up this morning, and we watched. I took the kids to the house to play.*

May 16, 1963: *I took the kids to the house to play again today.*

May 17, 1963: *Again, I took the kids to play.*

May 18, 1963: *I took the kids to a drive-in movie tonight. They enjoyed it, and Mike had fun on the slides before the movie began.*

I received the agreement in the mail today and called Mr. Marsh to discuss it. There's nothing I can do but sign it. I can't pay the hotel bill or go back to living with him because he changes his mind every time I speak up. Now I understand why I became weak in my marriage with him. I never could get my way, so I knew trying was useless.

May 19, 1963 (Sunday): *Ed took the kids today, and I drove around looking at houses because I thought I'd like to buy a house after this mess was over so the kids would have a home.*

May 20, 1963: *Helene watched the kids while I saw Mrs. Page today, and I made a trip downtown to sign the agreement.*

May 21, 1963: *I took the kids to the house to play today.*

May 22, 1963: *At 10:30 this morning, Ed called and said he was out of the house and please move back in so he wouldn't have any more hotel rent to pay. So I called Pat to watch the kids while I moved. She offered her aid and station wagon as it could have taken me three or four carloads of mine to get the things home, and it took us all day as it was.*

We arrived at the house at 5:00 p.m., and I discovered Ed had made off with everything of any value. He took both beds, the dining room table with six chairs, the breakfront, all the best silver pieces, silverware, china, crystal, and many other varied and sundry items. I spoke with Mr. Marsh about it or complained to him. We unloaded the car and went back to Pat's house. I took them all out to dinner for having helped me. We got back at 7:00, and Ed wasn't there. He called later, and I told him he could see the kids tomorrow. We had to eat.

May 23, 1963: *Today, I attempted to straighten the house and put things in their proper location. Ed saw the kids tonight, and Mike started school today at Ed's insistence.*

May 24, 1963: *I asked Ed for money for shopping, and he gave me just $25. I already spent money today to get some needed items. He had the nerve to ask if I minded if he took a 40-watt bulb from the basement. He also told me not to charge anything besides prescriptions at the drugstore.*

I worked until 3:00 a.m. this morning, cleaning the house. The kids found three wild bunny rabbits and brought them to me to care for.

May 25, 1963: *I went shopping today, and it took me all day to clean the kitchen. I was exhausted tonight as I tried to work late but gave up and retired at 1:00 a.m. I spent $35 on groceries.*

May 26, 1963: *Ed took the kids today, and I worked like a demon to clean the house. I was just relaxing after four when Ed drove up with the kids, and I tried to figure out what he was trying to pull. He left around 5:30 and returned the kids at 7:00 but left immediately. Ed told me to stay within my $25 budget from now on. He gave me $14, but I needed $1.90 more to come out even. I needed $4 for the boy's haircuts. I gave the rabbits back today.*

May 27, 1963: *I couldn't get a sitter, so I couldn't see Mrs. Page today. Ed called to tell me to use the three green-stamp books and green stamps around the house to buy the kids some clothes at the May Company, but I can't buy much for only $12.*

May 29, 1963: *Today, I took the kids to the Cleveland City Kennels and bought our first dog, a mixed breed, for $5. We had trouble with the car and got stalled in the middle of an intersection. I was almost out of gas, and I inched the car along the road until I finally made it into a gas station a block away by pulling the starter repeatedly. Even when I had a full tank, it kept stalling out. We'll all be killed if I don't get some money to repair it soon.*

Miles was in town tonight, so I had dinner to fill him in on recent events. He gave me the money for the sitter and for some extra besides.

May 30, 1963: *We stayed home today, but I gave the boys a picnic anyway. I roasted a chicken, made potato salad, and deviled eggs, and we ate on the patio. These are things I never could get Ed interested in.*

May 31, 1963 (Friday): *I took the kids with me to the dentist today. Mike went in by himself and acted like a very big boy, but I was nervous because both boys kept climbing all over me when I finished. Mike has a cavity.*

Ed gave me $25 tonight and told me to stay within my budget. I asked for more money for my haircut and $3 for gas, and he wouldn't give it to me. He gave me a worthless book of coupons and told me to use them for dry cleaning, but they were no good after March 1963. I took the dog to the vet for his shots. I am even afraid to ask Ed for what is rightfully mine, money for essentials.

June 1, 1963: *I took the kids with me to the store this morning. This afternoon, I cleaned the vegetables and kitchen. I had difficulty getting Mike settled tonight, and I was so exhausted that I fell asleep on the couch and stayed there.*

June 2, 1963: *I worked around the house this morning. Ed picked up the kids at 10:15. Mike told me they went to the aquarium. Evidently, Gary's bottom was red from not having his diaper changed. Both boys seemed to be very defiant to the world tonight. I spent the day driving. I came home and then went out to Lefton's for dinner.*

June 3, 1963: *I kept my appointment with Mrs. Page, and Helene Kasamov watched the kids. I did my wash today, and the realtor showed our house to a buyer.*

June 4, 1963: *I ironed today and finished everything. The kids and I drove to Pat's house for a while, and the realtor showed the house again.*

June 5, 1963: *I cleaned the bedrooms today. Ed picked the boys up early this afternoon, so I went for dinner.*

June 6, 1963: *Today, a stray cat seemed to adopt us. Me with my big heart. I had to give it some milk because it looked half-starved. Then I opened the garage so it could sleep there if it didn't go home. I let the kids play in the sprinkler while I tried to mop all the floors. I think I try too hard.*

I went to Dr. Wiant today for my cough. He listened, said it sounded like allergic bronchitis, and prescribed some new medicine. I took the kids with me. We stopped at Campus Drug at the circle for an ice cream cone and then traveled home.

June 7, 1963: *Today, I cleaned the laundry room, back closet, and hall. The kids played in the pool. I also straightened closets and packed all the old clothes we'd never wear again. Ed brought only $25 again, and he seemed to disregard our argument of Wednesday.*

I decided tonight to keep the cat and call it Cha Cha. I tried to find the owner, but no one around here had one. Wormed the dog today.

June 8, 1963 (Saturday): *I am weary and exhausted. My legs and feet won't hold out. It was 11:30 when I finished my bath. It is hot, 78 degrees, and my legs ache very much. My disposition hasn't seemed to improve much. I guess it's because I can't slow down. It's more than a full-time job keeping this house up in case someone stops to see it. The kids are mischievous all day and short of temper. I bought Mike a new pair of shoes today and Gary's first pair of red sneakers. Shopping today, $24. I then didn't get everything I needed. I cleaned the oven today.*

June 9, 1963: *Today was Gary's Birthday. I went to Edith's apartment for the cake so he would know I wished him well. I was glad to leave, and Bunny was there, but they were the same miserable people.*

June 10, 1963: *I washed today.*

June 11, 1963: *Today, I ironed.*

June 12, 1963: *Ed took the kids early today. I drove Pat Lamont to Baby and Children's Hospital and took Mike and Gary downtown. Ed surprised me by giving me $10 extra, the first, but it has to cover gas and shoes. Pat, her kids, and I had dinner at Howard Johnson's.*

June 13, 1963: *I attended Carol Nursery School's program today. Mike and his group sang three songs on the stage in the auditorium. Mike was not shy as he yelled out after the first song, "Did you clap, mommy?" and kept yelling, "Hi, mommy." I sure had a choked-up feeling with him up there.*

June 14, 1963: *Ed gave me $25 today, and I spent $6.50 on shots for the animals. Today was the last day of Mike's school.*

June 15, 1963 (Saturday): *Big Mike and P.J. came over tonight. They had to bring beer and popcorn because I had nothing to give them. I washed and waxed all the floors today.*

June 16, 1963: *I was nervous and upset today. I looked forward to a day of rest, and Ed brought the kids back to the house. This drove me out of the house. When I came back, Ed was still there. Mike wanted to be with me and seemed to be upset or sick. I didn't get much rest, needless to say. Ed left at 4:30 and was back at 6:30.*

June 17, 1963: *I completed washing and ironing today and was tired tonight, but it was good tired. Wormed the dog again.*

June 18, 1963: *I took the kids on a picnic at Shaker Lakes. We fed the ducks and walked along the stream. We had a good time, but I was jumpy again when I returned to the house. I feel depressed and want to yell, swear, and hurt whoever crosses my path. I have to get control of myself. Today I reached Mr. Epps, a comptroller at Lucas Machine Company, who cannot audit Ed's records. He suggested Mr. Cougill.*

June 19, 1963: *This was another rotten day with my nerves. I can't seem to control them even with taking tranquilizers. Mother called tonight to tell me about Mr. Cougill.*

June 20, 1963: *I saw Mrs. Page today, and I think it helped me talk because I believe I rid myself of most of the tensions I've felt this week. I spoke with Mr. Cougill tonight, and he sounds like the man I need to audit Ed's books. He has worked for Internal Revenue for 20 years and said something sounds fishy. Here is hoping I can prove it now. I went shopping this morning and spent $31.*

June 21, 1963: *The longest day of the year was cold. I took the cat for its shot tonight and couldn't pay for it. The Doctor also gave him medicine for ear mites. I asked Ed for money for the Frigidaire service man tomorrow, and he wouldn't give it to me. He said to forget it, but the range top burner and refrigerator need fixing for just $25.*

I finally got through all the toys today and had to sweep and hose down the drive tonight. I am so angry with Ed; at least I was calmer today. I set up an appointment with Mr. Marsh and Mr. Cougill for next Wednesday at 10:00 a.m.

June 23, 1963 (Sunday): *I stayed home all day. I took it easy and took a nap.*

June 24, 1963: *I did the wash today. Then I took the kids on a picnic at Metropolitan Park, and we ate, walked by the creek, and went swinging.*

June 25, 1963: *I went to bed quite dizzy tonight. The heat got to me, and I couldn't see straight. At 3:00, I was awakened by the phone and some mysterious caller who didn't speak. He called back and again, no answer. Then the phone kept ringing. I was pretty frightened for fear someone might try to break in.*

June 26, 1963: *I went downtown this morning to see Mr. Cougill and Mr. Marsh. We set up the audit, and I felt reassured that he could find it if anything could be found. The phone calls today were from 11:30 p.m. to 12:30 a.m.*

June 27, 1963: *Ed called and wanted to know if I'd believe an auditor, and I said, "Yes." He reiterated I was confused because I didn't know what he meant. Does he, or doesn't he? He said he would set up an appointment. I had phone calls again from 11:30 p.m. to after 2:30 a.m.*

I took the kids swimming for the first time this year at Wiley pool. At first, Gary clung to me, and then I got him to sit on my legs and dangle his feet. Afterward, we walked across the pool, and he was ready to swim and play around. Mike took to the water beautifully.

June 28, 1963: *We took the dog for his shots and went to Kenny Kings for a sandwich.*

June 29, 1963: *We went shopping this morning for over $25. I can't win. This afternoon I took Mike to Lesher's Shoes and tried to charge $4.07 for his sneakers, but they informed me the account was closed. I only had $4.00, but they let me go anyway. We stopped at Carol Battle's and then Pat Lamont's, where both kids walked in the wading pool wearing their clothes and shoes.*

As I was getting the kids ready, I said something sharp to them, and Mike, being hot and tired, began to cry. He said he wanted to go live with daddy. So, I told him if he wanted to spend the night with his dad, he could. I called Ed, who came over. Mike told me the dog would protect me, that

Gary would keep me company, and that he would be back in the morning.

June 30, 1963: *Today was Open House at our house, so I left to go swimming. Ed took the kids to Mentor for the day. He was trying to make a big issue out of Mike's wanting to go with him. I tried to reassure him Mike's behavior was expected, but I knew I could never convince him. I heard the downstairs door open tonight just as I had Mike settled, and I thought I had locked it. I went to look, and Ed was standing there with Mike's pillow. Mike saw him and wanted to go with him. I had trouble trying to get Ed out, and Mike resettled.*

July 1, 1963: *Today was terrifically hot. The kids and I joined Helene and her kids to go to Wiley Pool, but the baby pool was closed, so we journeyed to Thornton pool in Shaker, where we learned you must be a subscriber. The girl at the gate took heart and admitted us to the baby pool as her guest. The beautiful pool is like a country club. We had a wonderful time. Mike was going underwater and certainly losing all fear of the water. We had dinner at Helene's, then went to Franklin's for ice cream.*

July 2, 1963: *We took the cat in today for the second dose of ear mite medicine, and she hasn't come home tonight. I can't afford her, especially if she gets lost. So far, the vet has charged $7.00 for two shots and $13.00 for two doses of medicine.*

I ironed today and, after supper, took the kids to the Wiley pool. Mike is doing very well with the water, and he can go under now and keep his head under for several seconds. Emotions are better today for all of us.

July 4, 1963: *The kids and I had a good time today. Beachwood celebrated with a parade, booths, entertainment, and fireworks. We attended, and the kids were good and had a good time. We won some prizes and sat on the ground during the entertainment. They got their biggest thrill with the fireworks, though. I had to carry Gary on my shoulders, but it all made me feel glad to be an American and enjoy a day like this.*

July 5, 1963: *I was outraged tonight because Ed drove up in a new Pontiac convertible. Poverty-stricken, pooh! This will be his plea for life. When it suits him, he seems to find the money he needs.*

July 6, 1963: *Today, I cleaned the house, rearranged the living room, and tore down the drapes. Everything looked better, but I worked on the carpet to clean it up.*

July 7, 1963: *The Realtor didn't show the house today because they didn't have anyone show up for the Open House last week. So, I cleaned the laundry room and started straightening the basement.*

July 8, 1963: *I did the wash today. I tried to make fudge tonight, and it took about an hour to reach the softball stage. Then I waited too long before I added the nuts and marshmallows. The result was unattractive and hard. But it tasted delicious.*

July 9, 1963: *Mr. Marsh called to inform me that an offer of $40,000 had been made on the house. At first, he seemed to* *think I should accept. I said that I had no offer of security. How do I know how much Ed will pay me after I leave? I had signed the agent contract for $47,500 and will settle for no less than $43,500 and let them assume the assessment. We left it that Mr. Marsh would ask for a written amount of security before saying yes and that I'll need a few days to make up my mind. Mr. Cougill will start the audit on Thursday. A lot can be found out then for my decision. Ed said he had to buy a new car because he would need $500 to repair his old one. I'll not let him get away with anything now if I can help it. He even wanted to include the refrigerator.*

July 11, 1963: *Rosenblatt called to tell me Mr. Marsh was out of town, and we had a deadline of 12:30 on the house's offer. He worked at my heartstrings (better to be settled, not have to keep up the house, the first offer is usually best, etc.).*

July 12, 1963: *All morning, I was tied in knots. I called my mother and Mr. Nicola, but I didn't know what to do. Rosenblatt called me several times, and I was convinced we could get a couple thousand more and asked him to reduce his fee. He said he had done that for our buyers to buy our house and couldn't do it for us, too. So I told him I couldn't do it.*

July 13, 1963: *We went shopping today.*

July 14, 1963: *I stayed home all day and hardly accomplished anything.*

July 15, 1963: *They win again! Mr. Marsh called to read a letter from Wallick stating that Rosenblatt was embarrassed over the house sale and that I had asked him to split* *his fee. Ed will withdraw the house from the market and not make mortgage payments if I don't sign the papers. I could do nothing else. The bank would take it over, and I would lose everything. I thought about it all day and called Mr. Marsh. I hoped we could go to court, but no. So, under duress, I told Rosenblatt, "Okay."*

Tonight, Rosenblatt came over for me to sign the papers. I had to call Mr. Marsh to get his okay. Rosenblatt tried to get me to smile, and it made me angrier. I told him off about my bitterness. I felt good about doing that because it was the first time I'd ever been able to do so.

July 16, 1963: *I did my ironing today. That's about all.*

July 17, 1963: *Today, Mike went to the zoo with his camp, and I went to pick up my car.*

July 18, 1963: *I had to take Gary with me today to see Mrs. Page, but he was so good. I didn't even know he was there. Mrs. Page seems upset because I'm being pushed around so much. She wanted me to find out if I couldn't get a better deal.*

I talked with Mr. Marsh for a long time today and found out that I must be getting the best deal I will get. I asked him about Plymouth and Reno, also.

I also talked to Mr. Cougill, who wasn't too hopeful about finding any money with Ed's finances. The kids and I had dinner at MacDonald's after looking at a house we didn't like as it was too small. Then we went to the Gateway Apartments, but pets were not allowed there.

July 19, 1963: *Tonight, I called my mother to determine if I could go for a visit. She was very enthusiastic. I also put $10.00 down on a two-bedroom apartment at Colonial Park Estates. During the day, the boys and I looked at three apartments. If nothing else, I'm eliminating a lot.*

July 20, 1963 (Saturday): *It took a long time to get organized today, and Ed was late picking up the kids. I got underway to Plymouth at 1:15. My parents and I were going to go swimming, but the sky clouded when we were ready, and it was too cold in addition to the eclipse. We had dinner at the Paradise and returned to Plymouth to the Sidewalk Sale for the drawing. We ran into Jay and Polly (my cousin and his wife) and then came home to watch the Miss Universe contest. Then we went to the Ox Roast. We began talking with the Paddocks. Mr. Paddock told me about a position with a friend working for a suburban paper.*

July 21, 1963: *I returned from Plymouth tonight refreshed and relaxed. It was a wonderful weekend. When I'm in Plymouth, it seems like I'm in another world, and all my troubles seem to be a million miles away. It was delightful to wake and look out at their lake and eat breakfast on their sun deck. Diana Bachrach, Jay, and Polly came out to swim. My whole family went in. I even took So-So (our dog), and she swam.*

I was so glad to see my kids when I returned. They were tired and went to bed without any trouble. Now my muffler is really gone. Such a lot of noise!

July 22, 1963: *Today, the kids and I drove around and looked at four apartments, and I finally decided on the one at Euclid and Richmond.*

July 23, 1963: *I did the wash today, which seemed to take forever.*

July 24, 1963: *The kids and I drove to the apartment today to sign the lease, and we had to hurry back because Ed was picking them up early.*

I received a letter from Mr. Cougill stating that Ed doesn't show any income. Then I received a note from Mr. Marsh with a letter from Wallich stating I had intended to sell the furnishings Ed thinks are his. Ed was upset because he thought I planned to do away with the children's furnishings and toys, but I planned only to buy them a double-decker bed. Ed had said I wouldn't have a problem with the toys if I encouraged the boys to pick them up, which isn't accurate. How does he know whether or not the kids pick up their toys? When I called Mr. Marsh, he read another received letter citing me for $7.00 worth of long-distance calls to my mother. This was too much of a financial burden for Ed.

I ironed today and tonight.

July 25, 1963: *I saw Mrs. Page today and gave her my diary and letters to my mother. This afternoon the kids and I drove out to Golden Gate to see Mike's teacher, Mrs. Friedman, but she wasn't home. We went away and came back later, and she hadn't returned. So we came home and went swimming.*

July 26, 1963: *Ed picked the kids up early tonight, so I drove to the new apartment to select my room colors. We went shopping today and took the dog for her distemper shot.*

July 27, 1963: *I did some housework today to catch up. The house was so dirty. We went to Ann and Larry Cohn's tonight for a short while. Donald and Gary got along really well. I took the car in this morning to have a new muffler put on. Now it all totals around $73.00 for repairs to the car.* [Of note, Ed and I married six years ago on this day, and we were still a long way from our divorce.]

July 28, 1963: *I cannot bear having Ed around me. Every time I see him, I begin to churn inside. He returned to the house around 2:30 today, and I told him, "Can't you stay away from here for one day?" Shortly after, he left. I tried to get the house finished up today and did. Tonight, Mike was all keyed up and had difficulty falling asleep.*

July 29, 1963: *I'm back in the running today and did the washing and ironing. It was a rainy day, and Evan was here, so I invited him to stay for lunch.*

July 30, 1963: *It's a good thing I did everything yesterday because Mike became ill last night. He had a fever of 103.2 with a sore throat, stomach ache, and vomiting. I became worried at six o'clock tonight because he seemed in constant pain, so I took him to Dr. Saunders, but the doctor couldn't find anything. It must be a virus. I was up all night last night and tonight with him.*

July 31, 1963: *Mike was better today, but I kept him inside because he still had a fever, and I also got him to nap.*

August 1, 1963: *Today, Mike was well again, but I suspected Gary was ill, and I was correct because Gary had a mild convulsion while we were having dinner at MacDonald's. I took him home and kept him doped with phenobarbital and aspirin. He slept pretty well after midnight.*

August 2, 1963: *Tonight, I was embarrassed when I went to Heights Pharmacy and charged mascara, eyebrow pencil lead, and baby aspirin. Before I walked out, someone stopped and told me I could only charge prescriptions, and I had no money, so I asked him to charge it in my name. He said he would, but I can't pay for it, so I don't know what to do. Gary still had a fever today but was much better.*

August 3, 1963: *Gary's fever was gone today, but he was grouchy. I took the paint stripping off the cupboard today and pushed it upstairs to work on in the garage.*

August 4, 1963: *I worked almost all day soaking and chiseling the top of the cupboard and was finally successful. The top is a bit warped and nicked, but it's off.*

August 5, 1963: *I did the wash today, and a man from Shore Moving and Storage came to give an estimate. I decided to use him, so he left some boxes for me to use. I was going to check with Ed, but he wasn't in.*

August 6, 1963: *Today, I was upset again. Ed called this morning to check on the mover and said he wanted Andrews, and of course, I had already selected Shore. Before I had a chance to say anything, he was angry and said goodbye. Later, I checked Andrew's rates, $16.50 against the $14.50 from Shore, and called Ed. He consented. I called Mr. Marsh and told him about Heights Pharmacy and asked* *if I could keep Ed out of the apartment, and he felt that we could. I did my ironing today and packed some books.*

August 10, 1963: *We went shopping today. I painted the bookcase with a coat of Deft and the shelves while they were still in the garage.*

August 11, 1963: *I worked like a house afire today. I put the first coat of paint on the outside of the bookcase, a coat of enamel on the cabinet, and sprayed the bookcase, chair, desk, and file cabinet.*

August 12, 1963 (Monday): *Today, I put a second coat of paint on the shelves in the garage, another Deft coat on the bookcase, and a coat of paint on the cabinet. I also did the laundry. We ate at MacDonald's and drove to Zayre's and Uncle Bill's.*

August 13, 1963: *Today, I gave the third coat of paint to the shelves in the garage and one coat of shellac to the bookcase after sanding it down, and I sprayed clear enamel on the chair, bookcase, desk, and file cabinet.*

We drove to Blonder's for denatured alcohol. Tonight, Gary woke up with nose stuffiness, so I had the vaporizers running in both rooms. I also did the ironing today.

August 14, 1963: *Today, I gave the bookcase a second coat of shellac and spray-painted the table again. I didn't accomplish much today because Mark pulled the paint down in the garage, and Mike helped spread it around. Thank goodness the mailman came along, told me how to get it up, and helped me.*

They were into a few other things, so I had to clean up after them all the time. I seemed to be very nervous today. I got some more paint at Zayre's and stopped at Mawby's for coffee while Ed was with the kids.

August 18, 1963 (Sunday): *Today, I set out to prove Ed is a liar. I drove to Susan Peters and chatted with her, and then the two of us drove out on the turnpike to the service station that sold me the tires. I got the name of the man who served me and will give him a call tomorrow.*

August 19, 1963: *I asked Denny Yurick tonight to write a letter confirming that I bought the tires because one tire was ready to blow, the real reason. He said he would write the letter so I could use it to prove Ed is a liar.*

August 20, 1963: *What a day! We started to go to the dentist at 10:00 this morning and ran out of gas on Shaker just above Lee. We walked to the gas station from the dentist's office, where we got a lift and a ride back to our car. Then I took Mike to Nursery School.*

I decided to treat myself to a movie to get out for a change tonight. I drove over to Pat and Carol's. We went to the Colony and afterward to Clarks. From there we went to Pat's house and talked for a while. I arrived home at 2:00 a.m. Ed called to speak to the kids earlier in the evening, and Mike told him he would have a babysitter. Ed then called at 8:30 before I left to talk to them again. When I arrived home, Mrs. Rein told me the phone rang at 1:00, but no one answered, and then when I got into bed around 2:30, the phone rang, and when I answered, the party hung up. Who else could have done that? One guess.

The kids and I moved to our new apartment on Sidney Drive in Euclid, Ohio, with the help of my mother, who came to Cleveland for that event. We moved to the townhouse apartment on August 25, 1963. Soon after the move, I caught a cold, and shortly after that, I tinted my hair red, reflecting the red highlights I had when younger. The apartment soon became more of a home for us than our house ever did (because Ed didn't dwell there).

With my share of the house sale money, $4,300, I bought a matching walnut dining room table with four chairs and a buffet to match the bookshelves I attempted to finish. At first, I sanded the shelves and then finished them with special oil. But while sanding, I ran a long splinter into the right index finger. I called on my new neighbors to see if they could extract it. We worked on it for a couple of hours, but they could not extract the splinter. So, I ended up at a hospital emergency room for the extraction, where they had to use Novocain because the area had become so enlarged and raw from all the work done.

After moving into the apartment, I witnessed in divorce court for my friend, Bobbie Kuzma, and I got Mike into Nursery School, all by September 19, 1963.

Then, I decided to change attorneys due to Mr. Marsh not working things out for me, and I met with Dan McCarthy, Esquire, for four hours, on September 23. He brought in his Jewish partner, Gil Savransky, and both knew Ed's attorney, Ed Wallach. They told me that Mr. Wallach appeared to have an ace up his sleeve and alerted me to begin lining up my witnesses.

September 25, 1963 (Wednesday): *Ed had the kids today.*

September 26, 1963: *I let Ed have the kids this extra day because of the holiday.*

September 27, 1963: *Ed had the kids again today.*

September 30, 1963: *Today, I asked Ed for permission to take the kids to Plymouth for the weekend. He told me he would think about it, and I told him he could have the kids Thursday and Monday to make up for it.*

I got a sitter today, but the gears jammed on my car just as I left the school lot after leaving Mike off. I had to call a taxi to get to my appointment and another taxi back. The tow truck man who came out charged me $5.

October 1, 1963: *Ed told me I couldn't take the kids this weekend because he was going out of town on Thursday and Monday, and it would be too long between seeing them. That's just an out-and-out lie, and I decided to go anyway. I'll leave Friday when Ed brings them back and return Sunday morning.*

I need to get away from our routine. It has been too long since I've been anywhere or done anything. The kids need it, too.

October 2, 1963 (Wednesday): *Ed had the kids tonight.*

October 3, 1963: *I checked today, and Ed didn't go out of town. I took the kids for haircuts, and they looked so cute.*

October 4, 1963: *I asked Ed for the title to my car tonight, and he said I wouldn't get it. He told me to call my attorney. I told him Mr. Marsh told me that Mr. Wallick said I could have it. I told him that he'd have to buy new seat* *covers, fix the rust, and paint it, and by next year, it won't be worth much, and he didn't say anything. I wanted the title to sell my car and buy a used sedan for $500 to $700.*

When Ed left, I told him to have the kids back by 7:30. When he returned, he told me to stay in Cleveland tonight and leave in the morning, and I told him that solution wouldn't give me any time there. Then he said, "You know I don't approve of your driving there at night." I said, "Let's face it, you don't approve of my going." We left immediately, and it took two-and-a-half hours. The kids slept all the way, and it was a nice trip.

October 5, 1963 (Saturday): *We had a wonderful time today. First off, we drove to Greenwich to look at used cars. When we returned, Mike went with Miles, and Gary took a nap. When Gary got up, Miles and Mike were back and began to fish. I took Gary down to the pond and became interested in fishing myself. I never realized how much fun it was. Mike caught a couple of fish. Gary caught one, and I caught a couple. It is very relaxing. We then walked to my mother's neighbor's house, where Mike met Charlie, his own age. Mike brought Charlie back to play with. We went to dinner at The Brunswick. I felt very relaxed tonight, and the kids were happy and tired. Their behavior was the greatest yet. I wish we could have stayed longer.*

October 6, 1963 (Sunday): *Well, we were on our way this morning, and all I can say is that God was with us. Shortly before arriving at Route 21 on the turnpike, my battery indicator registered no charge, and my gas gauge began registering empty. We were about five miles away from a service plaza. When we drove up to the pumps, the* *serviceman told me my fan belt had caused that. It was hanging by a thread and had been drawing on my battery. The radiator was overheated. When he had finished fixing the fan belt, he asked me if I had far to go, and I told him about an hour's drive. He then showed me my left rear tire, where the tread was gone, cracked, and could blow any minute.*

God made the fan belt go so we would stop and find out about the tire. I didn't know what to do. The serviceman found out I'd have to take a larger tire because he didn't have my size, but then I'd have to take two so the car would not be unbalanced. This could have been avoided if Ed had given me the title. I could have traded it in. The time for all this made us an hour and a half late, and Ed had gone home, so I had to call him. I apologized to him for being late, but before I could explain, he cut me off and, as usual, sounded as if he disbelieved me. I again tried to tell him when he arrived to pick up the kids. I began by saying I had to buy two new tires. He said, "That's tough," as if I'll have to pay for them. He again cut me off. I won't stand for the disrespect. I try as hard as possible, but I won't have him around because he makes me sick.

So, I told him to get out, and I didn't want him here. He said, "Watch what you say in front of the kids." "I don't want you in this house; get out." Instead, he went upstairs and stayed, playing with the kids for a half-hour before leaving. I will not take such abuse as he gives me. It's no wonder the kids sometimes don't respect me when Ed doesn't show me respect or courtesy. I can't stand him.

Shortly after moving into our apartment, I wrote the following as it was a significant transitional time for me:

Taking Off My Rose-Colored Glasses

Like a thud on the head, it came to me. Life is not how the movies I attended while growing up portrayed it; it doesn't have a happy ending! There I was, alone at the dining room table with a cup of coffee in front of me. I had tucked my kids away in their beds upstairs a moment ago. Separation from my husband had occurred only a few weeks before.

But the movies had promised that the guy would get the girl, and they lived happily ever after. Life just isn't like that! I reflected. Why had I had such an idealistic and romanticized image of marriage and life? I guessed it was time to take off my rose-colored glasses and get on with the business of living. It sure would not be handed to me, and I would have to go after it. Mournfully, I got up to do the dishes.

CHAPTER 15

1964-1966

*Divorce isn't such a tragedy. A tragedy is staying in
an unhappy marriage, teaching your children the
wrong things about love. Nobody ever died of divorce.*

—JENNIFER WEINER, *FLY AWAY HOME*

1964: Not There Yet, But the End Is Coming

January 1, 1964: *Next to last year, this New Year was
probably the safest and sanest I've ever had. I didn't even
toast the New Year in. Our dog, So So, and I viewed TV as
the New Year rolled in amidst masses of cheers and noise-
makers. Then, I turned off the TV, retired to my room, and
read a few* Gone with the Wind *pages before turning the
light off. It began to snow at 9:00 this morning and snowed
steadily almost all day until there was quite an accumu-
lation. It stalled traffic and prevented many people from
reaching their destinations. Ed came around five, and I
went to Steve and Doris' house for a drink. Ed took us to*

Manner's tonight and dropped us at Tiny's, so we could say goodbye.

January 2, 1964: *It was clear but cloudy today. Marge and Paul had trouble getting the movers to their house to start their move. It was almost three before they started to move, and she had to come over several times to use the phone. We all felt sad to see Paul and Marge move because they had become terrific friends. Mike began school again today, and he sure needs it.*

January 3, 1964 (Friday): *It was beautiful today for my birthday, and things went smoothly. My mother sent a handbag and gloves, and Fate sent a gold billfold. My mother also sent a $30 check and an article on becoming 30. These should be my best years.*

January 4, 1964: *I didn't feel well today, so I didn't accomplish much. I certainly have been nervous and on edge.*

January 5, 1964: *Today, I attended Euclid Lutheran Church and signed a card showing interest in joining the congregation. I felt I couldn't hold off any longer and needed a close affiliation with God. It sure felt good, and I've been in a better mood all day. Leo Diamond, a former modeling employer, called tonight to ask if he could help me find work.*

January 6, 1964: *My sessions with Mrs. Page are becoming more and more fruitful. We seem to be touching on many things and are beginning to reach conclusions.*

January 7, 1964: *I won the booby prize tonight. The cards just didn't seem to be coming my way. Dia became ill at the* *end of the evening, choked, and vomited over everything. I rubbed her back and held her head, but no one else moved to do anything for her. I suppose it may have turned their stomachs. She is five months pregnant now.*

January 8, 1964: *I talked with Ed today regarding his letter from my mother. His superior **EGO** was hurt because she accused him of letting our children go poorly dressed, and he was outraged. He said he had told me to buy them what they needed (which he never did). So, he gave me the go-ahead to buy them what they needed.*

January 9, 1964: *I broke down and called Dr. Wiant today for diet pills. It seems like I can't get started alone. When I spoke to him, he informed me that he had conversed with Ed in November about the bill he owed, dating from the previous November. Ed had told him that he would not pay the bill and was considering suing Dr. Wiant for breaking up our marriage. I can see now that Ed has not been helped and doesn't know how or why our marriage broke up.*

February 3, 1964: *It was terrible tonight for the boys. Mike was keyed up after supper from telephone calls, and Gary whined. They saw Ed yesterday.*

I needed to find some income to help support the children and me, so I answered the World Book Encyclopedia ad, training included, to sell encyclopedias door to door. When prospects told me they couldn't afford the books, I understood since that was my situation, and I could not ask for the sale. Thus, that job was of short tenure.

I was 30, and in May of 1964, another nightly, part-time job during the business week practically fell into my lap. I heard about the opportunity and called for an interview. The position was for Assistant Producer for *Contact*, a radio talk show at the radio station belonging to the NBC affiliate television station, KYW-TV (now WKYC-TV), in downtown Cleveland.

> **May 1, 1964 (Friday):** *This was a busy day. I kept a job interview with Dave Babbitt, the Contact producer at KYW radio. I didn't know if I had the job when I left his office, but he called before I arrived home and left a message. I returned his call and discovered that I had been hired. I reported to my new job tonight.*

I was also lucky to find an evening babysitter down the street from where we lived who was affordable and whom the kids liked. So, I worked evenings in downtown Cleveland.

> **May 3, 1964:** *I hired Ginger M. to babysit for 50 cents an hour. So, I can make a little money from the job and get out of the house socially and legitimately.*

I worked this job from June to December 1964. My duties included meeting and greeting guests for the show, explaining the format, getting them something to drink, and screening phone calls from listeners who had questions to ask or comments about the show's guests and their remarks. We had a five-second delay if some cranks made crude comments so that their comments could not get through to the public. The job was fascinating.

The guests on Contact were exciting and mentally stimulating, and I wanted to respond to or ask them questions. Two of our guests were Dr. Sam Sheppard and his second wife, Ariane, whom he met while still in prison. I had read *The Sheppard Murder Case* during my latter days living with Ed after filing for divorce, and I must admit, at the time, it heightened my imagination. At night, when reading about Sam Shephard allegedly murdering his wife, I worried that Ed might murder me. That is when I hid his gun on a closet shelf in my room until he came seeking it. I felt forced to give it to him. Later, someone told me that perhaps Ed feared I would use it on him.

We also had Sonny and Cher as guests when they were coming into prominence. But we also had lesser-known guests, many of whom had written books that the host, Harv Morgan, had read.

A Job and My Introduction to Spiritual Development

The following narrative represents how the Universe, God, and my guardian angels worked to bring me the knowledge of Edgar Cayce (The Sleeping Prophet) and his enlightening psychic readings, which helped me grow spiritually and consciously improve my life for many years to come. His readings saved my life, so to speak.

For one show, we invited Ann Schreiner and some of the other Cleveland notables from the local chapter of the Association for Research and Enlightenment (A.R.E.). I listened with intense interest to what they were saying about Edgar Cayce. I heard them mention how he would lie down in a self-induced hypnotic trance to give psychic readings for people with medical problems that doctors could not cure. He provided remedies and found obscure medicines on pharmaceutical shelves in some remote drugstore in another town or city during his trances to help heal his followers. Additionally, he instructed those who consulted him as a last resort to create recipes for their treatments. I heard how those clients who followed his "physical readings" found health again.

Later, from his "readings" on metaphysics, I learned about reincarnation, how people had lived before, and how their former lives impacted their present life, mainly through karma but also for growth. I heard about a philosophy that answered the questions going around and around in my mind.

Did you ever wonder about the causes behind everything? I always wondered about the inequality between the rich and the poor, the disabled, maimed, and those whose bodies seemed perfect. There also are people who take unfair advantage of others. Why? And I couldn't help but wonder about what I had gone through. Why, why, and why?

There was even a philosophy about Creation and why we are on Earth in the first place. The group shared information about local study groups called *A Search for God* (ASFG), soul-growth groups, where people learned to grow spiritually and become better in this lifetime. Their study and subsequent action added to the growth of their souls. In time to come, I learned that prayer is my speaking to God, and meditation is listening to what God says to me. I discovered I am not a physical person with a soul but a soul living in a physical body.

At that time, I had a real hunger for the spiritual. I had grown up in the Lutheran Church but stopped attending church when I left home. I began to question everything and seek answers for which I had such a hunger and thirst. However, my mind held an image. From what our guests said, I imagined people sitting around trying to sleep like Edgar Cayce. Thinking like that put me off, and it sounded creepy. I thought they might be weird, even though those who sat before me in the sound booth did not appear so. Eventually, I discovered my anxious assessment of the ASFG groups was inaccurate.

However, I gave our guests my name and address for their mailing list. It wasn't long before they sent me information regarding an A.R.E. conference coming to Cleveland with a presenter from the A.R.E. in Virginia Beach, Colonel Frank Adams. I wanted to go but had no one I felt I could ask to go with me. I wrote my mother, a Spiritualist who knew of Edgar Cayce. For years, she tried to get me interested in spiritual matters, mostly her spiritualism. It was challenging for her to leave Plymouth to go anywhere. But, without restraint, my mother practically flew to Cleveland to go with me to the conference. My spiritual awakening was that important to her.

Attending that conference convinced me about everything Edgar Cayce, the A.R.E., and similar philosophies offered elsewhere. In October of 1967, I became a member of the A.R.E. and have been since, some 50-plus years later. I started reading his initial Readings, recorded by his faithful secretary, Gladys Davis Turner. I also read many books published on topics from the Readings, starting with his biography and the first book I read about Cayce, *There Is a River,* by Thomas Sugrue. As an aside, many of the readings require intense concentration for comprehension due to intricate phraseology. (*I discovered in due course that disciplining myself to take the time to understand his Readings helped me acquire the essential study skills I needed to return to college.*) The Universe is always in control, even when we aren't aware of it, which offers us more reasons to believe that our every challenge will work out eventually.

It was not long before I joined my first study group with some people who attended that conference. The group members became family, and I began praying and meditating. Eventually, I started my own group at home while attending my original group. Then, I had two spiritual families.

Although I was growing, my challenges did not cease, and they only facilitated my growth and transformation. By adopting a belief in reincarnation, I was satisfied that my children would not be condemned to Hell according to my Protestant religion. I love what Kahlil Gibran says in *The Prophet* about parents and children: *You are the bows from which your children as living arrows are sent forth.*

With knowledge about reincarnation, I discovered I have lived before and will again and that those bad or negative things that happen to us may result from karma or as an assignment. And they occur for our personal and spiritual growth. We pick our parents before incarnating based on their vibrations and the possible choices they will make, and then we select what challenges we wish to work on in this new life. We can improve our lives and those of others by meditating and offering ourselves to be of service in the name of God. I learned these and many other concepts when I became a follower of Edgar Cayce's many physical, life, and spiritual readings.

When I first heard of Cayce, I was in the middle of my three-and-a-half-year contested divorce after struggling to save my marriage of five-and-a-half years. Plus, I still had many challenges ahead from which to grow.

Repetition Compulsion (Sexual Harassment)

When it was clear that I did not have enough money for us to survive, I looked around for secretarial employment. (Thank you, Mother.) I picked up some PRN (Latin for *pro re nata,* meaning to work when needed) secretarial work in various departments at the television station.

Finally, in December 1964, I took a part-time job as a receptionist for Dr. Lych, a podiatrist, to gain much-needed income. His office was near home and the new babysitter I had selected for my sons. My duties consisted of receiving the patients and prepping them for service. There were administrative duties, and he taught me how to prepare bandages by cutting them in a specific way for various locations on a patient's foot. From time to time, his hand would brush my breasts or derrière, which I ignored because I couldn't speak up and needed the job. I was almost 31.

I don't recall the day-to-day activities, but I remember one fateful day. It was a chilly December morning with dark clouds hanging heavily overhead. As I let the kids off at the babysitter before going to work, I slammed the car door on my thumb in my lack of focus. I howled and jumped around in pain and agony. The nail on my thumb immediately filled with blood and started turning black. I wondered if I could get off work because I could not imagine working in that much pain.

I drove to Dr. Lych's office, and when I got there, I asked for the day off, showing him my nail. He said, "You're in the right place. I can relieve the pain and the blood by using one of my podiatry tools to drill into the nail base. Then you won't lose your nail."

I hated the thought of his drilling into my nail. It was almost as traumatic as the door closing on my thumb, but I agreed. He was right; it did relieve the pain. I again requested the day off. He did not have any patients scheduled. I didn't know the special occasion, but he had a tray of food and drinks he told me were for us. [*It was New Year's Eve Day.*]

He then took me to one of his treatment rooms and opened the door. On the floor, I saw a mat with sheets on it. I immediately flashed back to Toby and his closet floor. Again, there was that repetition compulsion that the Universe seemed to continue setting up for me (not that I knew it at the time). He said, "Well, that's a shame. Look at what I had planned for us today. What a disappointment."

"Ye-es," I responded sadly. My heart started pounding madly, and I began to look for a means of escape, a place of safety to which I could run. There was no bathroom with a flimsy lock. I recalled when he had touched me and thought, "*I should have known.*" No door with a lock, but I did have my injured thumb. I could not overlook this attempt as I did his other innuendos. He wanted to have sex with me. I didn't know where he got the idea that I would have wanted it, too. I had always been what I thought was kind, sweet, and compassionate, but I had not flirted with him or even flaunted my figure. How could he contemplate this for me?

I said, "I have to leave. I feel all shaky from my experience with my thumb, and I need to go home."

"Okay," he said. "I'll see you tomorrow if you're up to it."

Fat chance that I would be up to that or whatever else he had in mind. I made my escape, picked up the boys, and went home. I knew I would never return to collect my two-week paycheck. I didn't call him either to let him know. I needed to stay safe and secure at home. There were no rules with this employer against sexual harassment like there are today, not that that makes much difference for other harassed women. There was no supervisor higher up to go to about it. And it was another secret to repress. And now, I know that the Universe permitted me to close the car door on my thumb so that I would have an excuse to leave work that day and avoid another snare.

The kids and I struggled along as best we could without a steady income, but I again had to seek additional money to make ends meet. A couple of months later, the boys and I ate at a nearby diner when a man, Roy Ward, sitting close to us, struck up a conversation. He owned a small engineering firm named Regco, Inc., nearby in Euclid. I let him know I was looking for a job. He said, "I'm looking for a typist. Would you be interested?" He seemed trustworthy, but how could I know, actually? I was not very good at determining trustworthiness anyway. Having my children with me gave me a false sense of security. I said, "Yes." Subsequently, I worked for him on a PRN basis for about a year to around February 1966. I can also see now that the Universe had a hand in this arrangement. And he turned out to be trustworthy.

1965

January 1, 1965 (Friday): *Yesterday, I smashed my thumb in the car door, so I didn't feel well last night and fell asleep on the couch around ten. I awoke at a quarter to one this morning and didn't see the New Year in. Ed took the kids tonight. When they came back, they were good while I finished my paperwork.*

January 2, 1965: *Ed took the kids all night, so it was rather lonely without them. I did more paperwork as well as the laundry.*

January 3, 1965: *I attended church this morning and heard the sermon about* <u>What You Feel, You Are</u>. *In other words, think good or optimistically if you want good things to happen.*

There wasn't any <u>Open Circuit</u> *show today, Sunday.* ["Open Circuit" was another new job at KYW-TV, where I reported topics and conversations of interest from the show to the *Cleveland Plain Dealer*.] *Harv Morgan is in the hospital, and the guest canceled at the last minute. I wrote a story anyway. While working, Ted Wygant came into the office and put a bug in my ear. He suggested I apply for the Newsroom staff vacancy that Jack Bennett left. So next Sunday, I intend to go to the station and cut a tape for the News Director, Art Schrieber, to hear. This is an opportunity. Who knows? Maybe I can do it. I must try it!*

January 4, 1965: *I saw Mrs. Page this morning, and I came to a new conclusion about myself and reliving problems from childhood. The remainder of the day was relatively unproductive.*

January 5, 1965 (Tuesday): *This was a bad day. I kept bumping my thumb at home, and it was very sore. Tonight, as I sat with Mike while he was falling asleep, Mike told me that he is going to Venus when he grows up because it is loaded with pretty girls. I asked, "Do you like pretty girls?" He said, "Yes, but I will have to wait until I grow up to go." We watched* <u>McHale's Navy</u>, *and a parrot kept repeating, "Binghamton is a jerk." Mike said when he gets a parrot, he will teach it to say, "Mommy's a jerk."' He thought that was a cute joke, and it was funny.* [And sometimes, I felt like a jerk because of what had happened with Ed.]

January 6, 1965: *I picked up Mike after school and took him to Mrs. Wallace's. I had a headache. While the kids were with Ed, I put the train away.*

Ed and his attorney filed a motion that I was an "unfit" mother (their Ace up the sleeve) to move the case forward. I thought my witnesses, such as Mike's school principal, would prove otherwise. But it would not be until August before we would have our first hearing in court.

January 8, 1965 (Friday): *Today, the boys scattered all their toys in their room. I told them that if they didn't pick them up, I would gather them up in a big box and put them away and that they should learn to take care of their things. Mike said, "Daddy will buy us more toys." This simple solution indicates that they are overly spoiled by Ed's gifts. Sometime before lunch, Gary punched holes in his drum. The same answer, "Daddy will fix it or buy me a new one."*

Miles was in town tonight, and we went to the Top of the Town and talked about everything.

January 9, 1965: *I didn't feel too well this morning.*

January 10, 1965: *This was a busy day. I attended church this morning, did the laundry, and went to KYW. Ted Wygant helped me cut a trial tape for the News Broadcast. My voice level is correct, but I need to improve my reading. I ironed tonight as well as washed my hair.*

January 11, 1965: *I just can't get the energy these days to do what I should. Half of the problem is that I spend so much time with the kids after work that it is too late to begin anything.*

January 12, 1965: *Ed was at me tonight, and I've written an account elsewhere. I sure do feel immense fear when thinking about going through this divorce. For sure, Ed will start something else now. It'll be far from over even if I win the divorce and kids. Ed will always be after me. I fear even* *the point of his attempting to murder me. I might let him have the kids if he wasn't so sick, but he'll ruin them.*

January 13, 1965: *Another day – I called Dan McCarthy* [new attorney] *and told him about last night and that I intend not to let Ed talk to the kids if he calls, but I will let the kids call him if they choose. Tonight, when he came, he kept the back screen open, and I asked him to please close the door as it raised the heating bill. He said he would stay there till the kids were ready. I then closed the door in his face and locked it. Then he tried the door and looked as if he would break in but gained control of himself. When he returned, he jabbed my money at me and said sarcastically, "Thanks for being so gracious," and turned on his heel and walked away. Now there is more trouble. I broke down and had a good cry.*

January 14, 1965: *I didn't answer the phone all day. At 10:00 p.m., the Superintendent came to the door to inform me that Ed had called her to see if we were all right. Then I decided to talk to Ed and tell him I didn't want him to call anymore. He informed me he would take me to court if I followed through.*

January 15, 1965: *I changed my mind tonight and decided Ed could call if he limits his time. I stayed home all day except for taking Mike to and from school. I thoroughly cleaned the house and feel I have the right to take it easy tonight. There is so much I have to do; I feel guilty when I'm not busy.*

January 16, 1965: *After work today, I met with Roger Ailes to talk about the new teen show he's producing. He is* *considering me for a production assistant, part-time if the show is sold. After it is sold and runs for a couple months, it'll become full-time. Then if the station moves, so will the show, and so will I. I did the laundry tonight.*

January 17, 1965: *I went to church today, and the Sermon was about "A Thorn in Your Flesh." This afternoon I went to the station to work, and it began to snow badly on my way home, and it drifted, too.*

January 18, 1965: *I stayed home today except for taking Mike to school. My story was in the paper, and I had a cold.*

January 19, 1965: *A big nothing day.*

January 20, 1965: *I participated at Gary's school today and washed my hair tonight.*

January 21, 1965: *I went to work today. I chauffeured the kids to school this morning, went shopping, and went to the bank. I was exhausted tonight.*

January 22, 1965: *I stayed home today but took Mike to school. I cleaned the house and went to dinner at Howard Johnson's with Marilyn Baumann. I started exercising tonight and am really tired now.*

January 23, 1965 (Saturday): *I worked two hours tonight cutting my hair. Washed clothes today.*

January 24, 1965: *I went to church and worked this afternoon. Ted Wygant told me about another job of taking the feed from the network in the newsroom. It's a good thought if I can get it. Worked another hour on my hair tonight.*

January 26, 1965: *I had an appointment with Pastor B. this morning. He had a calming effect and advised me to remain composed, tell the truth, and accept God's will.*

January 28, 1965: *I drove for the nursery school carpool today.*

January 29, 1965: *One day is just like another. I only see the kids, and everything is the same. I'm so tired of it all.*

January 30, 1965 (Saturday): *This was another depressing day. I cleaned the house and did the laundry. I don't know what to do. I cried tonight and feel lost. I'm under a great deal of tension. I keep gritting my teeth and biting the inside of my cheek. I hardly smile or laugh anymore. I'm tired all the time.*

January 31, 1965: *This depressed mood sure is getting me down. I can't think clearly and can't decide what is right or wrong. I don't know what to do. I need a job as I fear I will have to give Ed the children because I can't afford to keep them. Suddenly everything seems overwhelming to me. I need a sign or an answer.*

I went to church this morning and took communion. The sermon was "Are You Seeking Security?" I went to work this afternoon at KYW.

February 2, 1965: *I talked with Ken Draper today, and he told me it would be another couple of weeks before he would know if he would hire anyone.*

February 3, 1965: *I went to PTA tonight, and Walter Harmon, the principal, talked, "Trick or Treat." The talk did me a lot of good.*

February 5, 1965: *Someday, I'll tell the world how stupid everything is and how hopeless and miserable. What chance do people have of finding happiness in this country and culture? How can certain people take something sweet and good, turn it around, twist it, and make it sordid and dirty? There is no tomorrow, and there is no happiness.*

I applied at Craftint today, but again, it is the waiting game until Tuesday to find out if I'm hired, and if I am, another wait until March before I can begin work.

February 6, 1965: *All I could accomplish today was the laundry. I went out to move the car, and the starter didn't work. All I can think of is more and more money going out the window.*

February 7, 1965 (Sunday): *Today was even worse, although I could clean the house. I seem to get increasingly depressed every day and am less able to rationalize. I have much conflict about whether I should give the children to Ed and try to start life all over again. He is wearing me down. But when I'm with the kids or look at their sweet innocent faces asleep on their pillows at night, I wonder how I can even entertain the thought. If only I could find a way to get through this without trying or knowing what's happening, then it won't hurt as much.*

February 8, 1965: *I had the car towed today to fix the starter switch. More money out and no money in.*

February 9, 1965: *Craftint called and told me they could only pay me $1.25 an hour (days) and $1.50 an hour on nights. It is not enough money.*

February 10, 1965: *Today, Ed picked the kids up early from Mrs. Wallace's. I applied downtown at Manpower and found their rate isn't much higher than Craftint. I also went to Patricia Stevens Modeling Agency, talked to Dave, and discovered it would take a couple of years to become a qualified teacher. Another hope is down the drain. I've got to find something I like and can do soon.*

February 11, 1965: *My attorneys informed me our court case had been accepted for advancement and would go on the active list. This could mean only one more month, and it will be all over. But I'm scared to death, and I don't know how I'll ever go through it.*

February 12, 1965: *Ed had to come in tonight because Gary was too sick to go out. Bless Gary's heart, though. When he is sick, he sleeps well at night.*

February 13, 1965: *Gary is better today, but Mike became ill and is pretty sick. I didn't accomplish much today.*

February 14, 1965 (Sunday): *I experienced more depression today. I've got to bring myself out of it. I went to church today and to work this afternoon at Open Circuit. There were no interruptions, but I finished at about the same time. Mike was pretty sick today, and I had no sleep last night.*

February 15, 1965: *Well, I was supposed to see Mrs. Page today, but Mike was still sick, and the muffler was dragging on the car, so I didn't go. Then I figured I'd better get the muffler fixed to get out of here tomorrow, so I took the boys to Mrs. Wallace's house and drove to Lloyd Motors. I had no sleep last night either because poor Mike is so sick.*

February 16, 1965: *Today, I went downtown and applied for a position as an interviewer at Superior Personnel. Then I met Gil Savransky, one of my attorneys, at Stouffer's to discuss my case. It aggravates me that Ed gets away with as much as he does, and I'm always on the defensive. I guess God will take His vengeance. I can't, but Ed will get his.*

February 17, 1965: *This was a reasonably busy day. Up early, I took Mike and went to my doctor. He had to clean out my ears. The left one was plugged, and a considerable chunk of wax came out. It felt good afterward, but then an all-day headache came out of nowhere, and I couldn't get rid of it.*

I saw Mrs. Page this afternoon, and when Ed took the kids tonight, I lay down on the couch and nearly passed out. I finally got rid of the headache and got some things accomplished. I didn't get the job at Superior.

February 18, 1965: *I drove to Nursery School and went shopping this morning. My headache reappeared this afternoon, and I felt terrible. Ted Wygant called around 2:30 p.m. to tell me about an audition for a woman's TV show at 3:30 p.m. He wondered if I could make it. I changed almost as quickly as Cinderella, with makeup, a suit, and everything else.*

February 19, 1965: *I took my car to the garage today to see why it was thumping, but they told me it was a tire. I cleaned the house this afternoon.*

February 20, 1965: *I did the laundry today and cleaned the kitchen, bath, laundry, and oven.*

February 21, 1965 (Sunday): *I went to church and worked after. I was a half-hour late getting home because the show ran late.*

February 22, 1965: *Gary had a sore throat, so I took him for a throat culture at 3:15. This morning, Edith dropped by unannounced, so I took advantage because Mr. Ward called and offered me some temporary typing work. I worked a couple hours. I called Jim Lowe at WEWS-TV and found out they haven't decided yet.*

February 23, 1965: *Well, I sure do have a lot of rushing around. I made calls and straightened the apartment this morning. At noon, I looked downtown for the retailer Ed purchased the tires from, but I couldn't find them. The tire worried me because, by this time, the car was shimmying. I went to Cleveland Employment and interviewed for a counselor position, and I picked up the boys after and drove to Dr. Bloomfield's. Fortunately, five minutes away, I got a flat tire in front of a gas station. After that was changed, the car drove fine. Gary got a shot for his strep throat. I came home, got supper, and played bridge with the girls. I talked to Savransky tonight.*

By **March 24, 1965,** I met with Savransky regarding my divorce situation and my request for help. We discussed Ed's broken promises after signing our separation decree. Also, our conversation concerned Ed bothering my babysitters by phone and his physical intrusion onto my premises.

Since I didn't feel listened to, I wrote the following letter to Savransky to put my state of affairs into writing on the same day I spoke to him:

Dear Mr. Savransky:

Misfortune, as well as my disastrous financial condition, necessitates writing this letter. I can no longer bear my circumstances, and I write to you hoping that you will be able to correct some of the injustices I have endured and hope that you might help me find a way to get back on my feet financially.

You were informed about the trouble I've had with my car, i.e., battery, flat tires, and other miscellaneous breakdowns that have depleted the funds I'm barely existing on. I am enclosing the children's pediatrician's bill in the amount of $90 that I have been unable to pay, that I cannot satisfy, and that I see no way in the future of making payment. Will you help me discharge this obligation? I also owe my personal physician $12 I'm unable to pay. I have a gum infection that requires dental treatment. If this isn't done, I shall probably lose my teeth. The children need their teeth cleaned and checked, but I don't have enough money.

Every day I am unhappy when I have to dress my children with their fast-growing bodies in trousers so short that they meet the top of their socks, full of holes inside shoes that are beginning to be too small for their fast-growing feet to wear.

It also grieves me that soon I must withdraw my youngest son, Gary, from the cooperative nursery school he attends three mornings a week. He needs it because of his opportunity to play with children his own age and the valuable instruction and supervision he receives, and I can no longer afford his $15-a-month tuition.

It disturbs me when I can't even feed my children an occasional steak or another expensive cut of meat because I cannot buy higher-priced meats.

When I signed the separation agreement, also signed by my husband, Edward H., on the 16th day of May 1963, I couldn't conceive that his intentions weren't anything but honorable. But he hasn't fulfilled his promise, obligation, or responsibility as outlined in the agreement. I believe that when an agreement is entered into, its provisions should be executed properly. It is beyond me why an agreement is drawn up and signed if there is no intention to do what is promised. Wouldn't it be better, to begin with, if there was no agreement? The agreement seems to have been only for Mr. H.'s benefit.

I was a good and dutiful wife while I resided with Mr. H.. Still, I found life with him intolerable because of his cruelty and neglect. Out of necessity for my health and the health of our children, I had to separate us from his overbearing contrariness and imperious manner. I have appropriately fulfilled every responsibility set forth for me in our agreement, but as is evidenced by my predicament, Mr. H. has not and has not for quite some time.

Item 5 of our separation agreement states that until "... no later than the date of the termination of the divorce proceedings in any way, Edward H. shall pay all bills for necessaries of Penelope H. and the children, and, in addition thereto shall give her such 'spending money' as ...." I never received any "spending money."

Also in your possession is a copy of a letter from Mr. H., which I gave you at our last meeting, addressed to my mother, stressing that regardless of his sacrifice, he would see that his children would have clothes if they needed them. This man doesn't know the meaning of keeping his word.

I'm not trying to be vindictive; it's only that I can't bear these problems alone any longer. Could you request that Mr. H. fulfill his responsibility? I would like him to take care of these matters to not deduct them from the $189.30 a month I'm receiving, and the remaining $24.30 is applied toward food for the children's growing bodies.

In a letter to Mr. Marsh from Mr. Wallach received July 9, 1964, although dated July 3, I was informed that Mr. H. would pay only $200 a month toward the children's and my support. My living expenses for the last year averaged about $500 a month. I would have to earn $300 a month to maintain this standard of living, but instead, I have used the money I received as my share from the sale of our house for living expenses. That money has now been depleted and has been for some time.

Mr. H.'s letter came at approximately the same time my apartment lease was automatically renewed. Mr. H. had agreed to pay $130 monthly rent when we first moved in. I didn't know he would reduce our living income, so by the time I figured it would be easier for me to help support the children if we moved to cheaper quarters, it was too late to cancel my lease. And as it becomes more difficult each month to make ends meet, I cannot afford to move even if I could break the lease. Also, I didn't feel another move would benefit the children's emotional welfare.

Also, it was suggested that I procure employment sufficient to pick up the slack (the amount of money he lacks the responsibility to pay). I have tried innumerable times to obtain employment only to discover that my lack of recent work experience prevents me from making enough money "sufficient to pick up the slack." Therefore, I've applied my energies to working part-time with various organizations, enabling me to equal what I might make if I worked full-time. This arrangement allows me to spend more time with the children.

Even if I could secure a full-time position today, it would be my obligation to tell the employer that I needed time off for court hearings and conferences with you. And an employer doesn't want to hire someone with problems, nor does he want his secretary unavailable when he needs her.

Also, if by subterfuge (if I don't explain my situation), I should gain a position and the time came for me to be absent from work, I probably wouldn't have my position when I returned. I am caught between and betwixt.

I would also like to mention a letter written by Mr. Marsh to Mr. Wallach, dated July 21, 1964, requesting Mr. H. to refrain from calling the children when they are in a babysitter's care and refrain from questioning the sitter about my whereabouts, etc. It seems like Mr. H. constantly takes it upon himself to break all rules and requests.

I find it challenging to keep sitters when they are put in the middle. My present sitter has been so bothered, and before Mr. H. started his phone calls, my sitter didn't know any of my business other than that I was separated. On one occasion, I reluctantly allowed him to pick up the children early from the sitter's house while I was at work, and he arrived 45 minutes early and stayed for an hour and a half. Gary was sleeping, so Ed plopped himself down, quizzed the sitter, tried to snoop throughout her house, and otherwise made her feel uneasy and uncomfortable. He calls the children on the phone, and if they don't talk to him, he asks the sitter what is bothering them, which makes her feel ill at ease and in the middle because they are only busy playing and have no desire to talk to him.

Since excellent sitters are challenging to find, and I will leave my children only with excellent sitters, I would like to request that Mr. H. refrain from bothering my sitter. He can call the children in the evening when we are at home.

I would like to add, what kind of man is this who says he loves his children and won't take steps to see that they are appropriately clothed, housed, and fed? How can he operate a business year after year without profit?

I beseech you to help me. I have no one and no other way to handle these problems.

Sincerely...Penelope H.

Then I wrote my mother the following letter on **March 25, 1965,** regarding Savransky's letter and stating my situation and need for intervention:

Dear Mother,

I am enclosing a copy of the letter I sent to Mr. Savransky detailing the impossibility of my situation. It is funny that you should say that I should go to my attorneys and ask them to get me some money even before you knew I had written or before you suggested it. I don't remember when I started that letter, but it was Sunday or Monday. I typed it three times before being satisfied and put it in the mail last night. Maybe our thought waves passed and received somewhere along the way because I strongly felt it was something I must do, almost as if God told me it would help. I had said it all and told the attorneys, but it never seemed to get any action. Then I guess I felt I might express myself on paper, where I might have the chance to see what I was saying and see if I was getting my point across.

I talked with Mr. Savransky, and he commented that I must have felt very low when I wrote the letter. I answered yes to that but continued that it was my general feeling most of the time and that everything I wrote was true. Mr. Savransky argued that I had told him all this before, and I said yes, but I felt I expressed myself better on paper. Then he commented that I should try to say it with fewer pages next time. I added that I wrote it this way so that he could show it to Ed's attorney if he wanted. He answered that he never showed the opponents anything his clients write but that he had dictated a letter this afternoon to Mr. Wallach asking for the doctor and dental bills (of which I'm supposed to go ahead and incur) to be paid. He told me to tell Ed about the children needing clothes, telling him that Savransky had urged me to do so and see if this doesn't bring some action. I might even go to the old lady herself. And I mean that just like it sounds.

Also, Savransky requests that Ed respect Mr. Marsh's letter in refraining from bothering the sitter. So it looks as if the letter did bring some action. I wrote it so he might feel sorry for me, as I had tried to do before but to no avail. It looks like I may have been successful because, at last, he is starting some action.

I finally found out why the attorneys were quizzing me so strenuously. Mr. Savransky said that he and McCarthy wanted to hear the other side's story first to see how the judge might view the situation, so they could help me better in court. They admitted that they didn't feel I had a chance and looked pretty bad. Then when they finally heard my story, they confessed that they did have compassion for me. But, they add that I don't have grounds for divorce (what Mr. Marsh had said) and that this might be even more difficult than proving my innocence in the accused affair.

As some people answer the question as to why they make it sound so tough, it is because if they make it look bleak, you can't be disappointed; if it doesn't come through as you would like it, they won't be dirty dogs, and if they win all you want and more, they become heroes. None of us can see the good in this situation, but "Thy will be done." God must have his reasons for the proceedings taking so long, and he must have his reasons why everything looks good for Ed while I keep being persecuted, and we cannot see them, but I am sure we will when this is all over.

You are worried that you have no way of helping me, but you are. First, you can't go through this for me; I must go through it myself, but you have helped me where I need it most. Thank you for your check, which will help me make it through this month and perhaps next. My car insurance came due a month earlier than expected and took all I hoped would see me through. I accept this money based on a loan as I otherwise could not. It makes me feel a little more independent and self-reliant. Someday, somehow I will pay it all back. But you see, you are helping me where I need it most. This frees my mind so that I am not so depressed about bills, etc. It helps me become more rational in my thinking. I really believe money is my biggest worry.

Next week, I may be back with the "Contact" show and my job with Regco. It will help me remain solvent and see me through the hearing when I have no other income source for sitters during the day. They have called me twice to come back. It's a nice feeling when your work and you are greatly appreciated. This is sure a boost to self-confidence as well as the purse. I will also have a full-time position available with Regco if I want it after this whole mess is over. So, I would have something steady lined up to work until I found something else I wanted more.

I've been praying to God for money or ways to feed the family, and he has come through with all of these avenues that are opening up. I feel God inspired them to do so, and I have to take advantage of every opportunity. I don't know the exact quotation from the Bible, but it goes something like this, "Give no thought to eat or drink; it shall be given you." With this quotation and a little faith, I have found it is true that God won't let his followers starve.

I am writing to you about everything that happened to me not to upset you but let you know what is happening and what I'm feeling. I get over my periods of depression and pop right back to take some more. So, try not to let me get you down. Somehow, "We shall overcome."

Love, Penny

While working on this section, it occurred to me that I knew nothing about the Welfare System then. I did not know if any financial assistance was available to me, and no one (such as my attorneys) told me I might get assistance from a welfare agency. I just continued trying to find full-time employment, working various part-time jobs until I found a full-time position and seeking alimony or child support from Ed to meet our financial needs.

June 2, 1965: *I just wanted to take some time to catch up on what I was doing and feeling. Feeling: Resignation and loneliness, and my hidden remedy is overeating. I have been gaining weight and can't seem to stop myself. I get more frustrated because of my weight, which leads me to eat more. Job: (Meldrum and Fewsmith Advertising Agency). I like it because it's a nest, a home. I have settled somewhere and am seeking to belong. I don't know if I belong yet. Health: Good, although I am exhausted after working all day. I'm up between 6 and 6:30, get dressed, get the kids up and dressed, drop Gary at Sandy Marsh's, let Mike off at school, pick up Marcie Komara and off to work, and home at 6:30, get supper, clean dishes, pick up the house, read to the kids and to bed, bathe and by this time it is 9:30 to 10:00. I'm too tired to do anything else.*

I am worried about Mike's behavior. I have one week where I wonder if he'll adjust and the following week when he's an angel. I know a certain amount of this is normal, but I see he's feeling insecure because Ed tells him the judge will decide where he'll live. Poor kids! Ed has even destroyed every bit of illusion and fantasy, which is part and parcel of every young child's life, by telling them there's no Santa Claus and that the Good Fairy putting the money under the pillow for the lost tooth is me. I wish the waiting for the divorce was over. I wish we could get this all over with now.

Divorce Court

Beginning with our first hearing on August 5, 1965, we appeared in court monthly for eight months before the Judge, The Honorable Victor Cohen. We each presented our causes for divorce by making the other marriage partner look like the most contemptible, despicable, and malevolent person. I could sue for only a limited number of causes. As I understood it and recall, the available causes were desertion of one year, adultery, extreme cruelty, fraudulent marriage contract, or gross neglect of duty.

My case was about Ed's mental and emotional cruelty (true). Ed countersued for custody of the children and tried to prove adultery and that I was an unfit mother who never cleaned the house (all false).

Even though I filed that time away somewhere in my brain and did not record the legal events in any journal then, I dimly recall that my witnesses may have included maids and friends, but I do not remember after all these years. I think I asked my concerned doctors, but I don't recall if they could be witnesses. Ed brought our best man from our wedding (Big Mike) and a private detective, and I don't remember who else he had either. I possibly could have used my diary entries over time to testify for me, but by the time we finally got to court, I had totally forgotten about them.

We summoned Ed's mother and sister for a deposition, and I felt ashamed afterward. His mother's mental faculties had declined, and his sister appeared worse than ever. They were an embarrassment to themselves. I wanted revenge, but I learned that getting it was never worth it when I saw them. I would not want anyone to lose their mental faculties or be in the condition in which I saw them.

Maybe a year or two later, Ed's mother ended up in an Alzheimer's unit of a nursing home after a maid who came to clean their apartment found that Edie had turned on all the stove burners and was wandering aimlessly around their apartment. Their maid also discovered Bunny dead, maybe from an overdose or suicide, and no one was overseeing either of them.

In one month of the eight, Ed's detective made his report. He accused me of riding with a man in a car and stopping at his house. When we left a short while later, the man wore different clothes. That was all he said, but it was with the implication that we may have had a sexual encounter there.

This was the first time I heard this actual accusation. Even though Ed's Attorney mentioned the man's name earlier in a question, I had not recognized it because it meant nothing to me. Then, when I heard their narrative, I knew it was Al Diamond, a very young man from the Announcer's School.

We (Len Anthony and my friend, Susan) were in separate cars. Al and I had to stop at Al's home, so he could change his clothes. It was his family home, and his mother was there. One crucial detail they left out was that the young man was also wearing a leg cast for an accident to his leg.

The other accusation was connected to the headliner of the program I worked on, Harv Morgan. We were known to occasionally stop for a drink or something to eat after his show to talk about the show and wind down. On this occasion, the detective reported following Harv from the station to a hotel room where I was supposed to have opened the door to him. This never happened! And I told them that, but could I prove it?

My attorneys could not and did not protect me. But I knew who the woman might have been and called her to appear as a witness for me. She declined. I asked my attorneys to bring up this new information, but they decided not to pursue either of these situations further. I had hoped they could subpoena either or both people in question as witnesses in my favor.

I don't recall which session of court continuance it was, but I think it was the final one somewhere around May of 1966 when Judge Cohen invited my mother and me into his chambers. Were my attorneys there? I don't recall, but they should have been because of the deal proffered by Judge Cohen. He said something like the following to us:

You and your husband have dragged witnesses into my court for several months. As it stands with the law, I should not grant either of you a divorce. But I am willing to offer you the following: I will grant you the divorce on the grounds of your husband's "Gross Neglect of Duty." I will grant joint custody to you both, but the children will reside with your husband during the regular school year, and he will be responsible for care and control, which he forfeits to you when they reside with you. You will have the right and privilege of visitation twice a week and having the children one day on the weekend. Any other times can be negotiated. Your husband shall pay child support of $25 per child when the children reside with you. Also, they will be raised in the Jewish tradition, and you cannot proselytize them. [Ed never paid me one cent whenever the children were with me, which prevented me from having them stay the length of time permitted. However, I exercised that right through the summer I lived in Virginia Beach with my third husband.]

I know this arrangement may not be satisfactory to you. I know your husband's attorney well, and if Mr. Wallach isn't satisfied with the results, he'll appeal and continue fighting until he gets what he wants. (I knew that to be true of Ed, and he would fight until he won. It looked like I could never win back the children and offer them the best care.)

Even though it appeared like I was winning the divorce, I would have to give in to these terms to keep Ed from appealing. I knew I could never return to living with him, and I did not have the money to appeal. I felt trapped and had to accept this compromise.

The Judge continued: *If your husband is as sick as you attempted to show him, by my granting you the divorce and Mr. H. the possession of the children, you can return to court and file for full custody after the debris has settled.*

My mother indicated we should try to get some time to discuss this before giving my final say. The judge allowed us something like an hour. We found a nice private spot to talk. My mother pointed out that I could not rely on Ed to pay support (or alimony) based on his pre-divorce behavior. And if I had the children, I couldn't expect him to make it easy. The other point was I only had a low income. How could I ever come back to court and file for custody? I would never be able to afford it.

But I could always be present for the kids during visitation and when the children were with me. The real problem was not that I would lose the children the majority of the year to Ed and not that

I lost them, but that Ed's sickness would harm them as they grew to adulthood. How could I protect them and fight against his sickness?

We decided that there really was not much I could do with this situation except to return someday to file for full custody, and that time never did present itself because of a lack of money.

Early on, Ed had offered me a substantial sum of money to drop the case and walk away when I filed for divorce, leaving him with the children. There was no way I could ever have done that. I was seeking sanctuary for them in addition to me, and I didn't want them to be raised by him because I knew he would psychologically and emotionally abuse them as he had done to me. And he did. (*Because of the outcome of the divorce, he won anyway, getting what he wanted.*)

I had the children with me for the remainder of the summer following the Judge's determination, but when they left to go to Ed's to live, I experienced the loneliest time I can ever recall. I am grateful for all my time with them during their formative years.

During the divorce process, I filled my "Hope for a Positive Outcome" container with small wins along the way, only to discover that I had missed seeing a hole in the bottom of the container.

And so, it was.

EPILOGUE

During those last months with my children, I decided that I needed to find a way to live with the Judge's decision. I knew I would need to fill my time with activity so I wouldn't notice the pain of losing my children ever again. Then, I set goals for myself. Since I was working full-time then as a Production Assistant in the Radio, TV, and Film Department of Meldrum and Fewsmith Advertising Agency, I registered for a Marketing Course offered by the Cleveland Advertising Club.

I had always wanted to play the violin but had none, so I intended to begin taking violin lessons in one year and have a violin by then. I soon discovered my mother had an old violin that she gave me, and I took private lessons at the Music School Settlement in Cleveland for about five years. Eventually, I took private lessons with Kurt Loebel, a member of the Cleveland Orchestra, for about eleven years. It was in an adult preparatory program at the Cleveland Institute of Music. Even though I missed having my children living with me, I kept all my visitations with them to influence their lives as much as possible in future years.

And many, many years later, with an insightful view of that marriage, I understood I should have turned my back on marrying

Ed before our wedding on the day my mother came to town. In only two days, my mother-in-law Edith had demonstrated what I would receive if I married into that family. If I had had experience or a greater understanding or had been more mature, I would also have pulled out of the marriage when Ed told me we had to be nice to his mother because of all she had done for him.

But you might say, "You loved him." Yes. But, perhaps, it was love addiction. Perhaps my mother could have warned me before I tied the knot, which might have helped.

But finally, considering my metaphysical underpinnings, which include my belief in reincarnation, there is also the concept of karma to explain the outcome. I believe that I was slated to meet and marry Ed, as I probably made a life contract with his soul/spirit before we reincarnated into this life that we would meet. I would have to face the abuse and pain I experienced to learn lessons of longsuffering, patience, tolerance, understanding, forgiveness, and unrequited love, among others. These consequences may not have been totally learned during that experience. But eventually, adding new life lessons, I reflected on all I had learned.

In my search for love, I failed to find it with Ed. Perhaps I failed because I really didn't know what love looked like. But neither did Ed know how to give it. So, I went forth again in search of it.

The narrative in this book covers basically the first third of my life, and you may want to discover how I proceeded with my life following the turnout of my marriage and divorce to Ed. There is much more to share in Books Two and Three, as I have more challenges ahead.

I will find myself amid the sexual revolution and women's liberation. Seeking my identity following my marriage, I try to find myself in the working world. Still, eventually, I discover emptiness or complications in every job, and I continue seeking love with its traps and snares.

In my third marriage, we move to Virginia Beach to be close to other Edgar Cayce followers and the Association for Research and Enlightenment (A.R.E.). Missing my children, though, we move back to Cleveland after a year.

Soon after, I became so depressed that I didn't care to live, even though I had no desire to harm myself. I had been counseling with my pastor, who referred me to a psychotherapist when I appeared suicidal. I continued with the therapist without revealing my sexual abuse issues which I had not yet recalled. These issues begin to emerge in Book Two, but I deal with them directly in Book Three. I learned to be stronger and bolder and started discovering my voice.

I continue developing my spirituality, discovering new adventures, and experiencing more challenges.

See you in Book Two?

ACKNOWLEDGEMENTS

I would like to thank those responsible for helping me write my story and those who helped me reach the final stage of publishing this memoir trilogy.

In the final days of my private practice as a psychotherapist, I elicited the help of Life Coach Laura Karasek from The Dawn of New Living. Thank you, Laura. Initially, we met weekly and then monthly virtually on Zoom. I found Laura to be highly knowledgeable about business and writing, among other things (she is multi-talented). Together we selected and accomplished goals for my retirement from private practice, and she assisted me in accomplishing the goals we set for completing Book One in my trilogy. [Laura's website is www. DawnOfNewLiving.com]

I would also like to thank my former English teachers, including Sister Michael Francis at Ursuline College, Nita Geilker from Cuyahoga Community College, and Mrs. Lanius and Guy Bishop from Plymouth High School. They all taught me different aspects of English grammar and writing, and I wrote throughout my life from that knowledge. Use it or lose it.

Likewise, I appreciate my discovery of Edgar Cayce and his 15,000-plus psychic readings (at edgarcayce.org) and other psychics, spiritual masters, or leaders and their information from which the rest of us can learn. And I want to thank my guardian angels and guides for supporting my efforts and providing for various discoveries while also helping me write this tome.

Teachers from the various people with whom I had relationships all my life came forth. They challenged and taught me valuable lessons, even though I was resistant then. But with my later growth, their life lessons sank in. I believe most of those challenges were to help me learn to be strong and stand up for myself, recognize when I was being abused, and learn how to remove myself from toxic situations and forgive. These teachers include my three husbands, my mother and stepfather and biological father, and my brother Toby, among many others. Thank you all for my lessons, difficult as they were.

And I express gratitude to my friends who supported my writing and always asked, "How is your writing going?"